The Twilight of the East India Company

THE EVOLUTION OF ANGLO-ASIAN COMMERCE AND POLITICS, 1790–1860

WORLDS OF THE EAST INDIA COMPANY

ISSN 1752–5667

This series offers high-quality studies of the East India Company, drawn from across a broad chronological, geographical and thematic range. The rich history of the Company has long been of interest to those who engage in the study of Britain's commercial, imperial, maritime, and military past, but in recent years it has also attracted considerable attention from those who explore art, cultural, and social themes within an historical context. The series will thus provide a forum for scholars from different disciplinary backgrounds, and for those who have interests in the history of Britain (London and the regions), India, China, Indonesia, as well as the seas and oceans.

The editors welcome submissions from both established scholars and those beginning their career; monographs are particularly encouraged but volumes of essays will also be considered. All submissions will receive rapid, informed attention. They should be sent in the first instance to: Professor H.V. Bowen, School of Historical Studies, University of Leicester, University Road, Leicester, LE1 7RH

The Twilight of the East India Company

THE EVOLUTION OF ANGLO-ASIAN COMMERCE AND POLITICS, 1790–1860

Anthony Webster

THE BOYDELL PRESS

First published 2009
The Boydell Press, Woodbridge

ISBN 978-1-84383-475-5

The Boydell Press is an imprint of Boydell & Brewer Ltd
PO Box 9, Woodbridge, Suffolk IP12 3DF, UK
and of Boydell & Brewer Inc.
668 Mt Hope Avenue, Rochester, NY 14620, USA
website: www.boydellandbrewer.com

A catalogue record for this title is available from the British Library

This publication is printed on acid-free paper

Printed in Great Britain by
CPI Antony Rowe, Chippenham and Eastbourne

CONTENTS

PREFACE

The East India Company and British imperialism in India have rightly attracted the interest of generations of historians. Britain's acquisition of the 'jewel in the crown' of its empire was a lengthy and complex process, involving subtle diplomacy with Indian powers and European rivals, outright belligerence and strategies to make this costly and vast imperial possession pay its way. Especially intriguing is the fact that it was not the British state which embarked upon this long process of imperial conquest, but a company of merchants dedicated, initially at least, to commerce rather than military adventures. One consequence of this has been that the development of the East India Company itself has attracted as much interest as its role in the acquisition and governance of the Indian empire. The transformation of this organisation, from privileged trading company, to an agency for the running of Britain's most important colony, has been a source of much analysis, and even more controversy. For some, it was the forerunner of the great multinational companies, combining economic strength with political power, becoming a player on the international stage in its own right. For others, it evolved into a framework for other commercial interest groups to develop their activities, and a forum increasingly for debates about wider imperial policy.

This book examines the last seventy years of the East India Company's active life as the governing agent for the British Empire in India. The aim of the study is to explore how new commercial interest groups emerged from within the shadow of the Company to compete for political influence in the determination of imperial strategies in Asia. The commercial methods of these new organisations are explored, as are their relationships with each other and with the East India Company. It is also a story of how British industrialists, merchants, agency houses, together with their peers in India and Asia itself, developed new political pressure groups first to challenge the privileges of the Company, and then later both to collaborate and compete with it in the determination of imperial policy. It is, in short, a study of British imperial politics in transition, from an era of mercantilism to one of *laissez-faire* and free trade. The aim is to show how the evolution of the new political landscape in respect of British policy formation in Asia during the early nineteenth century affected wider questions about the forces which shaped British imperialism, and the changing nature of the relationship between industry, trade, finance and government in Britain in the earlier phase of industrialisation.

In completing this work I would like to offer thanks to many people for the help and support they have given during this project. Peter Cain, Tony Hopkins and Ian Brown, who taught me at the University of Birmingham, shaped many of the ideas which are brought to fruition here, though any mistakes and faults are of course entirely my own. I would like to thank the British Academy South East Asia Committee, whose grant support contributed to many aspects of this book. Archivists at the British Library, the Bodleian Library, Oxford, and the Mitchell Library in Glasgow were unstinting in their advice and assistance. I would also like to thank Huw Bowen and Peter Sowden for their help in refining the manuscript. I would also like to express my gratitude to my old friend Stuart Bradbury, whose advice was as always invaluable and very amusing. This book was written during my first year as head of subject at Liverpool John Moores. It has been a busy time, but the good humour and support of my new colleagues has made managing the transition into my new role a real pleasure. One of the reasons I made such rapid progress with this book has been the atmosphere of enthusiasm for the subject which pervades the history team at LJMU, and the mutual encouragement which colleagues show each other. Finally, but not least, I thank Lesley, my wife, without whose kindness, love and tolerance of my tantrums at the computer, I would have achieved little.

Tony Webster
November 2008

One

INTRODUCTION: THE END OF THE EAST INDIA COMPANY, THE HISTORIANS AND THE EVOLUTION OF ANGLO-INDIAN COMMERCE AND POLITICS

THE EAST INDIA COMPANY has fascinated and divided historians, yet its importance for the development of the British Indian Empire is one of the few aspects of the Company's history on which there is some measure of consensus. Founded in London in 1600 as a monopolistic joint stock venture to engage in speculative trade with the Far East, the Company struggled through its first 150 years of existence. There were major problems both at home and abroad, notably the effects of civil war in the 1640s and, more seriously, the disintegration of the Mughal Empire from the late seventeenth century onwards. The latter development, however, precipitated major changes in the Company. Forced to defend itself against some of the new Indian states emerging from the fragmenting Mughal Empire, as well as older European rivals, the Company became a military as well as a commercial organisation. A turning point came in 1757, when hostilities with Sirajudaullah, Nawab of Bengal, prompted the annexation of that province by the Company. It set in train a process of expansion which by 1830 saw the East India Company establish itself as effective ruler of India. By then, recurrent financial crises had forced the Company to solicit the help of the British state, which was forthcoming, but at the price of government control over the organisation.[1]

In this way, the Company had become the agent of British imperial expansion in Asia, securing control not only of India, but also a chain of bases throughout south-east Asia, and a trading network which extended from China to southern Africa. The Company was both an instrument of rule and of commerce, specialising particularly in the export of opium from India to China and tea from China to England. In London, East India Company stock was highly coveted, and trade in it confirmed the Company as a central institution in the emerging money markets of the City of London. Company stockholders were diverse, but tended to be wealthy, influential individuals. This translated into formidable political clout. In addition to a phalanx of MPs in the House of Commons who were prepared to defend the East India Company's interests, the assertion of state control over the Company in the last decades of the eighteenth century brought leading Company directors into close contact with senior politicians, enabling them to shape policies towards trade and the new Indian empire. In this way, the Company became a power to be reckoned with in domestic British politics as well as international commerce and imperial policy.

Yet this political dimension of the Company's activities was insufficient to prevent a steady erosion of its power and status. Its monopoly of trade between Britain and India was breached under the Charter Act of 1793 and then lost under the Charter Act of 1813; and only twenty years later its remaining trade monopoly with China was also stripped away. The Charter Act of 1833 terminated the Company's commercial activities, leaving it solely as a bureaucratic machine for governing most of Britain's Asian possessions. The Great Indian Rebellion of 1857 sounded the Company's death knell, and in its wake the Company was abolished and its structures of rule replaced by a new administrative machine through which the British government would rule India directly. Perhaps inevitably, this strange and complex history has given rise to many different lines of enquiry and contrasting interpretations of the Company's evolution. At the heart of these debates lie fundamental disagreements over the nature of this peculiar organisation. For some, the Company was essentially a commercial organisation, in some respects the precursor of the great multinational corporations of the twentieth century. Others have argued that the conquest of India fundamentally altered its character, turning it into an organ of imperial rule, and an umbrella under which other commercial interests and entities came to dominate the Indian economy. These contrasting perceptions of the Company are central to this book and they will be explored shortly, but first it is important to set out the principal aims and themes of the present study.

The English East India Company has been the subject of an exhaustive literature, covering the vast array of its commercial and political activities. Much of this has focused on the debate about the nature of the Company mentioned above. Yet one important aspect of the Company's history has received surprisingly little attention, namely the processes of political and economic change by which the Company was gradually replaced by new organisations and structures which came to shape colonial policy and manage the increasingly complex commercial relationship between Britain and Asia. While the Great Rebellion of 1857 and the subsequent winding up of the East India Company's rule generally receives careful attention in most histories of British rule in India, the more subtle and gradual replacement of the Company by a new network of political interest groups seeking to influence

Britain's economic relationship with India and Asia has never received the attention it warrants. There has been a tendency for some to see the new structures of the British Raj, established in the wake of the end of Company rule, as 'a product of the Company's failure', effectively a brand new beginning for British rule in India, fortified by a recognition of earlier mistakes.[2] It is the contention here that while the new formal political structures for British rule in India were certainly the outcome of the rebellion itself, non-Company private enterprise in Britain and India had long been evolving new forms of commercial and political organisation which had already influenced British policy in Asia. For a long period these new commercial entities not only co-existed with the Company, some of them also worked actively through its political structures. Thus many aspects of the post-Great Rebellion imperial order in India can be traced back to a prolonged period of evolutionary change which had been in train from the last decades of the eighteenth century. To some degree this challenges the notion of 1857/58 as an unqualified sharp break with the past, a discontinuity in the development of British rule in India.

Of course, historians have not ignored the forces of change which, from the last decades of the eighteenth century, increasingly placed the East India Company on the defensive in respect of its privileges. Britain's rapidly industrialising economy threw up a new class of industrialists in the provinces, hungry for new overseas markets. As early as the early 1790s, Manchester, Glasgow, Liverpool and other emergent industrial centres were campaigning for access to the Asian markets under the East India Company's monopoly. Their anti-monopoly campaigns continued into the nineteenth century, and were at least partly responsible for the ending of the Indian and Chinese monopolies in 1813 and 1833. In tracing this struggle between the Company and its provincial rivals, historians have tended to see it in rather stark terms of implacable opposition between the two sides. In fact, the debates about the Company monopolies were blurred by the complex relations emerging between provincial manufacturers who wanted access to the Asian markets, London-based East India agency houses, which from 1793 traded independently of the East India Company and were becoming involved in the legal export of British manufactures, and the Company itself. Many of the partners in the London East India agency houses were prominent stockholders in the Company with a vested interest in its fortunes both as a commercial organisation and as an organ of political influence. Their attitude to the Company cannot be seen in simple terms of opposition; yet clearly they supported and benefited from the trend towards liberalisation of the Asian trade during the early nineteenth century. Whilst on the one hand they welcomed the opening of the India and China trades, on the other they still valued the political structures of the East India Company directorate and the Company bureaucracy as a conduit for lobbying government. This, it will be seen, was particularly significant in the years following the Charter Act of 1833, which effectively terminated the Company's commercial career. Even as it entered its twilight years in the 1840s and 1850s, the Company's links to government via the India Office, and its control of the complex administrative machinery for governing India, still gave it considerable influence over British imperial policy in the east. Many of those commercial interests, especially in London, who had supported the stripping away of the Company's commercial privileges, maintained a foothold in the Company's Courts of Proprietors and Directors in order to access its remaining channels of political persuasion. Thus the relationship between such key interest groups as the London East India agency houses and the Company was not one of outright antagonism. The East India Company directorate could be a powerful ally in campaigns to persuade government to adopt certain policies, or to veto unwelcome initiatives by rival interest groups. Even the provincial industrialists, probably the most vehement opponents of the Company during the anti-monopoly campaigns of the early nineteenth century, from time to time found it expedient to set aside their hostility to the great institutionalised symbol of 'old corruption'.

The complexity of the East India Company's relations with its erstwhile enemies in the first half of the nineteenth century has a wider significance than just the trajectory of imperial policy in Asia. It had a formative influence over the development of commercial politics in Britain itself and the empire more generally, shaping the development of the domestic and imperial commercial political networks which were eventually to outlive the Company. The rise of East India associations in Glasgow, Liverpool and London, and the emergence from the mid-1830s of Chambers of Commerce as far afield as Calcutta, Bombay, Madras, Singapore, Canton and Hong Kong, were a direct outcome of the development of relations between the Company and emergent commercial groups interested in Asia. These organisations continued, in one form or another, after the Company was wound up, and continued to exert an influence over colonial policy. In this respect, the manner by which the Company was displaced by its successor commercial organisations and their pressure groups casts a very long shadow indeed over the development of commercial politics in Britain and its empire.

Little of the existing historiography on the Company pays much attention to this period of transition, to the twilight of the East India Company and the rise of its successors. It is significant that several of the most important texts on the East India Company of the last fifty years end their surveys in 1833, with the termination of its trading activities and the last of its trading monopolies, with China. One of these, Philips' classic study, certainly explores the growing influence of such organisations as the London agency houses, but its terminal date means that perhaps the most crucial period for the formation of the post-East India Company commercial landscape is omitted.[3] The study of the management of the tea trade by Mui and Mui also ends in 1833, but in any case is not concerned with the issue of what succeeded the Company after its demise.[4] The most recent analysis of the East India Company by Bowen also ends in 1833, but is principally concerned with the Company itself, its operations, position within the City and relations with government, rather than the questions of legacy and succession.[5] Those studies which do trace the history of the Company to its bitter conclusion in 1858 tend to treat the last twenty-five years of the Company's life as a postscript of little significance. Lawson allows a mere four pages to summarise this final period of the Company's effective existence.[6] Robins' account of the Company as precursor to the exploitative multinational corporations of today is a little more generous in its treatment of the Company's final quarter century at twelve pages, but again the impression is of an afterthought, and that the period is of relatively little importance.[7] None of these accounts offer any detailed comment on the emergent system of commercial capitalism and associated political pressure groups which replaced the Company.

Plainly this question needs to be addressed, not least in view of new interpretations of British imperialism which have emerged since the 1980s. Perhaps the most influential theory to emerge in the last twenty years on the evolution of British imperialism during the eighteenth and nineteenth centuries is the 'gentlemanly capitalism' thesis of Cain and Hopkins.[8] This vast body of work traces the development of the empire, and the economic and political forces which shaped it, from the late seventeenth century to its demise in the late twentieth century. For Cain and Hopkins, the development of the British Empire can only be understood in the context of the domestic social and economic development of Britain following the Glorious Revolution of 1688. The usurpation of James II because of his suspected adherence to Roman Catholicism was not only a victory for Parliament; it also represented the establishment of the aristocracy as the dominant force in English politics. But the successor Hanoverian Protestant regime which was established by the early eighteenth century soon felt threatened by the great Catholic powers of Europe, especially France, which seemed dedicated to the restoration of the Stuart dynasty. The coincidence of these developments with the continuing expansion of European power in Asia and the Americas meant that this hostility manifested itself in a series of bitter colonial wars during the course of the eighteenth century. The Hanoverian monarchs and their aristocratic supporters were only too aware of the precariousness of their position, for their foes were not only external, as the Jacobite rebellion of the mid-eighteenth century demonstrated. Faced with enemies at home and abroad, military and naval strength became a priority for the regime. Of course, the dilemma was how to pay for a larger army and navy. Excessive taxation at home might easily drive the population into the Stuart camp. Fortunately, institutions and instruments had emerged at the end of the seventeenth century which offered a solution to this problem. The establishment of the Bank of England in the 1690s, and the creation of the National Debt in the same decade, allowed British governments to borrow in the City of London on long and generous terms, enabling them to expand military expenditure whilst limiting increases in taxation. Consequently the Hanoverian regime was able to triumph in successive global imperial confrontations (with the exception of the American War of Independence) without incurring fiscal or political meltdown. The contrasting and disastrous fate of the French regime in 1789 revealed the considerable political advantages which these financial arrangements brought for the Hanoverian dynasty.

But these arrangements came at a political price. The merchants, financiers, institutions and organisations within the City of London, who were instrumental in funding and facilitating government borrowing, required in return that their interests be safeguarded. Moreover, during the eighteenth century there was a growth of borrowing in the City by aristocrats, frequently to finance the modernisation of their estates. Cain and Hopkins contend that in effect an alliance was forged between the English (and subsequently the British) landholding elite and the leading mercantile and financial houses of the capital. This was more than a mere convergence of business interests. The relationships which developed between the two groups were social and personal as well as financial. Leading financiers were drawn into the social milieu of the aristocratic elite, and even found that their wealth occasionally rendered their lowly born offspring highly eligible for marriage to the children of aristocratic families, especially if the latter had money problems. Unlike on the continent, the British aristocracy was relatively open to newcomers, provided they had the money to pay for land, titles and the correct education for their children. Financiers and merchants soon found it advantageous to ape the behaviour, aspirations and material trappings of their aristocratic clients and friends, becoming 'gentlemen capitalists', men of trade and finance with aspirations and social values which were aristocratic in pretension. The ideal was to use the family's wealth to buy an estate and title, and to become assimilated into the aristocracy. In this way 'gentlemanly capitalists' came to exercise powerful influence within the British state, through the importance of the institutions of the City of London for government finance, and because of the social leverage and political connections arising from their relationship with the aristocratic elite.

Cain and Hopkins argue that gentlemanly capitalism was at the root of British imperial expansion from the eighteenth to the twentieth centuries. A sizeable portion of the business community in London were connected with overseas trade, notably in such fields as shipping, insurance and dealing in the bills of exchange which were increasingly central to the emergent international system of trade. As the nineteenth century progressed, the nature of the City's involvement in the international economy began to change, and the Stock Exchange and Merchant Banks of London emerged as a source of overseas investment, channelling funds raised in London into a wide array of overseas economic assets on every continent, including docks, tea plantations, gold mines and railroads. These overseas assets, which generated high profits for investors and City institutions alike, were simply too important to be left to the vagaries of imperial rivalry, local opposition or instability. They had to be defended, and as a consequence, the City and its leaders came to be central to both the expansion of the empire and the policies which governed it. In this way, gentlemanly capitalism lay at the heart of the British imperial project.

Two aspects of the Cain and Hopkins thesis are of particular importance for any consideration of the position of the East India Company and its eventual demise. Firstly, until the early nineteenth century the Company was probably the single most important commercial organisation in the City of London. In the mid-eighteenth century its stock was one of only a few that were regularly quoted in the London newspapers, and up to 1750 it had made loans in excess of £4 million to the British government to finance a series of major wars with European powers.[9] The *quid pro quo* of course was the privilege of monopoly enjoyed by the East India Company in British trade with Asia. The Company's importance for government increased still further after 1757, when Clive's conquest of Bengal launched the organisation as a major military power in Indian politics, thus beginning the convoluted and violent process by which the Company came to rule India. From this time, the Company's affairs and actions inevitably became an issue of major concern in governing circles. The imperial adventure carried a very high price though. Towards the end of the eighteenth century, the costs of imperial expansion and the internal corruption it brought in its wake, plunged the Company into a series of financial crises, ultimately rendering it a net debtor in its financial relationship with the British government. This did not, however, readily diminish its importance in the shaping of government policy. In order to ensure that its debts would be serviced, and the Company's policies in India kept under close scrutiny, Pitt the Younger's India Act of 1784 established a new government department, the Board of Control. This was to superintend all aspects of the Company's non-commercial affairs, and the Court of Directors of the Company was made answerable to the President of the Board of Control, a senior politician with high status in government. The first President and architect of the Act, Henry Dundas, epitomised the spirit of the new arrangements, which dictated that the Company would become an arm of state foreign and imperial policy. Of course the corollary of this was that the Company, in spite of the burdensome financial problems it now posed for government, had been institutionalised at the heart of the British state, with access to senior figures in government being enjoyed as a right by the 'gentlemanly capitalists' who ran the Company. In any case, the cost of the Company's debt to the state was at least partially offset by the customs revenues which the Company's trade brought into the Treasury.[10] Thus in spite of its waning fortunes in the early nineteenth century, the surrender of its monopolistic privileges and the emergence of new commercial organisations in the City, the Company remained a potent source of political influence over the government's policies in Asia, arguably up to its demise in the aftermath of the 1857 rebellion.

The second point which emerges from the Cain and Hopkins thesis in respect of the Company arises from their interpretation of the political and economic effects of British industrialisation. Industrialisation brought radical social change, creating harsh urban environments in which newly confident and wealthy industrial capitalists, together with discontented industrial workers, sought to extract policies from government which met their respective needs. For the industrialists, low taxation and free trade became the paramount demands, including a dismantling of the monopolistic privileges of such bodies as the East India Company. These new political interest groups could not of course be ignored, but Cain and Hopkins contend that their ability to shape government policy, in the face of the century-old alliance of aristocrats and gentlemanly capitalists, was limited and constrained by the existing configuration of power and influence. Whilst their demands required a response, they were in effect political outsiders, without the social and institutional channels of influence enjoyed by the landed elite and the men of the City. Cain and Hopkins contend that they never achieved the 'insider' status of the City gentlemanly capitalists in the determination of imperial policy. This did not mean that they were unsuccessful in achieving some of their most crucial objectives: the Corn Laws were repealed in the 1840s, and the East India Company had been stripped of its monopolies by 1833. But these were not victories which can be ascribed solely to the efforts of the new provincial industrial middle and working classes. Other factors certainly played an important part. The governing elite were not blind to the dramatic social and economic changes unfolding before them. They knew that industry's needs for new markets and cheap food would have to be accommodated if domestic conflict was to be minimised. In the case of the Corn Laws in the 1840s, the efforts of the Anti-Corn Law League were assisted by the emergence of politicians like Robert Peel who understood that the best way to protect the power of the ruling elite was by surrendering essential concessions to the new industrial capitalists.[11] In the case of the East India Company, the financial problems of the Company, and the emergence of new City-based organisations (The London East India agency houses) involved in trade to the east, persuaded governments that liberalisation of first the Indian and later the Chinese trades could be accomplished without jeopardising the good relations between the City and Whitehall, between the gentlemanly capitalists and the aristocratic elite.[12] According to this view, the diminution of East India Company privilege, the Company's displacement in commercial affairs by new City-based interests engaged in trade with Asia, its metamorphosis into an arm of imperial governance and eventual demise, and the creation of new governing mechanisms for India, were the result of processes which still reflected gentlemanly capitalist dominance.

The decline of the East India Company receives relatively little attention in the work of Cain and Hopkins. It was a process which arguably began in 1784 and took over seventy years to complete. In part, the purpose of this book is to provide the first dedicated examination of this process of decline and the transition to a new system of governance and commercial relations with India and Asia. One aim will be to test the notion that London-based gentlemanly capitalist interests were as dominant in the formation of colonial policy in Asia as suggested by Cain and Hopkins; to assess how effective the efforts of other groups to influence government were in industrial provincial Britain, and British commercial interests in Asia. There is also a tendency to see provincial industry, on the one hand, and the aristocracy and City finance on the other as quintessentially separate worlds, between which there was limited contact, and much mutual suspicion.[13] It was not only geography which set the money men of London apart from the factory owners of the north. The gentlemanly pretensions of the financiers were alien and frequently offensive to many of the self-made men of the provinces. Cain and Hopkins, together with historians such as W.D. Rubinstein, see the gulf as social as well as physical.[14]

But the accuracy of this depiction of social and political relations between industry and finance, at least in respect of policy towards British imperial interests in Asia, will be challenged. It is contended here that the relationships which existed in this field between the merchants and industrialists of the provinces and the financial interests of the City were much more complex and volatile than the Cain and Hopkins model would lead one to expect. In particular, the provincial men were not quite as prone to 'atomistic competition' nor as lacking in political cohesiveness as Cain and Hopkins contend.[15] The early nineteenth century saw the growth of political pressure groups in Liverpool, Manchester and Glasgow dedicated to the ending of the East India Company's privileges. These organisations were in perpetual contact with each other, and co-ordinated their efforts to lobby government and Parliament for change. Moreover, by the 1830s, this emergent provincial network of commercial and industrial interests had reached beyond the ocean to parallel organisations springing up in the great imperial cities of the east: the Chambers of Commerce established in Calcutta, Bombay, Canton, Penang, Singapore and eventually Hong Kong. Few historians have commented upon this global web of commercial interests. Only Ian Nish, writing in the early 1960s, really grasped the significance of this flowering of commercial pressure groups across the empire.[16] The connections even extended to London, which was not as divorced from the 'Gradgrinds' of the north as Cain and Hopkins suggest. It will be argued that the prolonged decline of the East India Company was accompanied by the emergence of this complex, trans-imperial network of firms and commercial/political pressure groups, which used the organs of the Company even as it undermined them. The latter included the Courts of Directors and Proprietors, the Company's London-based bureaucracy and its colonial administrations in India and the east, which together were responsible, under the scrutiny of Whitehall, for the running of Britain's Asian empire. British policy in Asia was thus a hotly contested arena, in which provincial and imperial commercial interests vied with the gentlemanly capitalists of the City.

A key theme in the decline of the Company and the emergence of a new order of commercial power in Britain's Asian imperial affairs was the changing nature of British business in the east, and its relations with the colonial administration and indigenous mercantile elites. Parallel to the growth of new firms and new pressure groups in Britain and the east was a revolution in the organisation of British firms in Asia, and the nature of British economic relations with Asia. As the East India Company retreated from trade, so it left a larger space for new firms to move into. But the prolonged process of Company decline meant that its continuing political and commercial importance exercised a powerful influence over the way in which the new organisations operated. For much of the second half of the eighteenth century the only strictly non-East India Company commerce was conducted illicitly by the Company's own servants, generating scandalous tales of corruption and greed which tarnished the reputation of Robert Clive and his generation of officials. Gradually the Company admitted into India a small number of independent traders, or 'free merchants', who were permitted to engage in the localised trade of India and south-east Asia (the 'country trade') provided that they did not infringe the Company's monopolies. The 1780s saw a major change in this non-Company presence, following the reforms of Governor-General Cornwallis, which excluded Company servants from engagement in commerce on their own account. The effect was to expand the scope for non-Company commercial activity by eliminating competition for the free merchants from the Company's own employees. Moreover, the increased salaries paid to Company servants in compensation for their loss of trading rights had to be invested. The more enterprising free merchants received deposits of the savings of Company men and soldiers, paying handsome rates of interest. This banking facility equipped the free merchants with an increased supply of capital for investment in agriculture, shipping and trade, and soon they were providing other financial services for their depositors, including acting as their agents. From this later activity arose the name of these new 'non-Company' organisations – the agency houses. They were assisted in their ventures by Indian merchants (*banians*) who were recruited specifically to conduct the agency house business with the Indian commercial community. As remittance to Britain of their depositors' wealth became an important service they provided, most of the Indian agency houses struck up partnerships with counterpart East Indian agency houses in London, which were usually established by men retiring home from service in the Indian house.

The agency houses enjoyed a complex relationship with the Company. Until 1813 they were subjected to the rigorous limits on trade with Britain imposed under the Company's monopoly. For their part the agency houses resented their exclusion from free commerce with home, while the Company viewed the agency houses with grave suspicion, especially when they gave voice to their free trade sentiments. Yet the relationship also became symbiotic. The houses, after all, depended upon attracting the savings of the Company's men. In return, the houses became an important source of loans for the Company in India, as the costs of its militarism and expansionist policies escalated. The agency houses also became instrumental in the trade between India and China, exporting opium and facilitating the Company's purchases of tea and other Chinese commodities in demand in London. But it was a relationship which had to endure turbulent times. The global nature of the Napoleonic Wars made trade perilous and uncertain, while conflicts within India itself compounded these difficulties. The ending of the Company's trade monopoly with India did not prove to be the panacea envisaged by many of the agency house men. It certainly brought dramatic changes in the balance of trade between India and Britain. India, for so long a supplier of cotton manufactures to the British market, soon became a vital market for Britain's own booming cotton industry. India began to evolve into a supplier of primary produce such as indigo, sugar and eventually tea. Exports of Indian opium to China financed the Company's lucrative exports to Europe of Chinese tea, silks and ceramics. But the liberalisation of the Indian trade also brought overstocking of the Indian market and depression, as well as unwelcome competition for the agency houses from a new wave of British merchants. The destabilisation of the Indian economy caused by the dramatic shift in India's economic relationship with Britain, together with the disruption of the enclosed and protected relationship between the Company and the agency houses, contributed significantly to a major crisis in the early 1830s. Between 1830 and 1834, all of the old agency houses failed, leaving a bitter legacy of insecurity and mistrust, not least on the part of the Indian mercantile community who suffered especially grievous losses.

The crisis coincided with yet another major reduction in the East India Company's power. The Charter Act of 1833 not only ended the Company's monopoly of trade with China, it also terminated its commercial activities. This left it as a most peculiar organisation indeed; in practice in India it had become an agency of British rule, an apparatus of state with responsibility for government, powers of revenue collection and control of a large army. But it still had stockholders to pay in Britain, regardless of the fact that it was no longer involved in trade or commercial activity. Once again new businesses and merchants moved into the vacuum left by the Company's retreat, most notably in the trade with China. The London East India agency houses, the sister organisations of the Indian firms destroyed in the crisis of 1830–1834, had with one or two exceptions, survived the fallout of events in India. They were now particularly well placed to expand their operations. Out of the confusion and hardship of the early 1830s there emerged a new commercial order which differed from the old in a number of ways. Firstly, although a number of new agency houses were established, many by former partners in the old firms which had failed, they operated on very different lines. Most were set up by agents from the London houses, and were subject to much closer scrutiny from the London firms. While this curtailment of independence was not total, it did mean that the new firms had to be much more responsive to the needs of their London parents, who in many cases had supplied the capital to create these new houses. Secondly, those of the new Indian firms which were not set up by representatives from London houses differed substantially in other ways, most significantly in their relationship with the Indian mercantile community. Some prominent Indians, such as the wealthy *zamindar* Dwarkanath Tagore, rejected the traditionally informal role of *banian* and insisted upon being full partners in the new European agency houses.[17] But regardless of origin, most of the new houses adopted a much more pro-active role in commercial activity than the older houses which had failed in the 1830s. Whereas the earlier houses had largely been content merely to advance cash to entrepreneurs, the new firms became involved in the running of the new wave of businesses which emerged in the 1830s, frequently taking over their management on behalf of the owners. 'Managing agency' thus became a major source of profit, in steam shipping, colliery management and the running of plantations. Its growth reflected the pursuit by British entrepreneurs of new and profitable avenues for investment. Most, though not all, of the new houses refused to become directly involved in banking, remembering all too clearly how it had exposed the older houses during the crisis of the early 1830s. Those dominated by London sister houses tended to rely heavily upon capital from home.

The advance of non-East India Company enterprise in the eastern trade was reflected in the emergence of new political networks which linked London, the British provinces and the commercial communities in the east. Pressure groups such as the Liverpool East India and China Association, and its sister organisation in Glasgow, which had been so active in attacking the old East India Company trade monopolies, established themselves as permanent guardians of the provincial industrial and mercantile interests.

They had developed close connections with some of the London East India agency houses, which in the 1820s had become involved in the export of British manufactures to India. One consequence was that by the mid-1830s, the provincial associations corresponded with a London East India and China Association, a pressure group set up in 1836. By the late 1830s, Chambers of Commerce had also been established in such eastern imperial cities as Calcutta, Bombay, Madras, Singapore, Penang and Canton, and these also shared intelligence and co-ordinated political activity with the British East India Associations. As the East India Company's central position in the politics of London and the Indian empire receded, so these new networks of power and influence emerged.

Yet it would be a mistake to regard the Company as a political irrelevance in these last decades of its existence. The Court of Directors continued to be regularly consulted on Indian affairs by the British government, and there remained an organic link between the bureaucracy of the Company and Whitehall. A substantial number of Company directors were MPs, and many City investors and merchants still held Company stock, and still used the Courts of Directors and Proprietors as a means of voicing opinions and exercising political influence over the government of the day. In this sense the Company was still an apparatus of the state, run by men of influence. They could still pose a formidable obstacle even against the new configurations of pressure groups and economic interests which had emerged in the early nineteenth century. It will be seen that in several debates during the period, most notably on the question of banking in India, and on the means by which the East India Company repatriated its tax revenues to pay pensions, dividends and other costs in Britain (the 'home charges'), the Company proved that it was still a major obstacle to proposed changes it did not welcome. The Company was certainly not as impotent an organisation as some accounts of its last years have suggested.

The next major convulsion to rock the fragile economic and political order left by the events of the 1830s was the great international economic and financial crisis of 1847/8. Excessive speculation in railway stocks was but one factor in what proved to be the worst economic crisis in living memory, with widespread failures of firms in the City of London and a sudden and severe depression descending upon the whole British economy. The impact upon the network of provincial, London-based and Indian firms involved in the Asian trade was especially savage. Twenty of the London East India Agency houses, the majority of them, failed within a period of twelve months.[18] Most of their corresponding houses in Calcutta also went under in what proved to be an even more serious debacle than the crash of the early 1830s. This time the full impact of the crisis was also felt in the British provinces, with serious failures occurring in Liverpool, Manchester, Glasgow and elsewhere. Just as the events of the early 1830s had stimulated new initiatives in the commercial world, so the crisis of 1847/8 brought in its wake a new wave of change. It was in the field of banking that the most radical innovations occurred. In the late 1830s and early 1840s, a combination of the East India Company, the leading London East India agency houses and provincial mercantile pressure groups had ferociously and successfully blocked a series of attempts to establish London-based banks designed to provide a wide range of financial services (including exchange banking) for those involved in commerce with and in India. The reasons for their opposition varied: the Company feared that such banks would interfere in and destabilise their arrangements for repatriating funds to service the home charges; the London houses feared the competition that such banks would bring, while the provincial merchants and industrialists believed the banks, as large and wealthy joint-stock organisations, would re-establish London's domination of the trade to Asia. But the demise of the London houses, and the nature of the crisis of 1847/8, effectively weakened this resistance. By the late 1850s, a string of new Chartered Banks had been established, including the Oriental Bank, the Chartered Bank of India, Australia and China and the Mercantile Bank of India, London and China all empowered to a greater or lesser degree to conduct financial activities in Asia. These large corporate organisations, with firm foundations in the City of London, represented a new phase of commercial organisation in the eastern trade, contrasting sharply with the small partnership structures which had characterised the old London East India agency houses. In size and aspiration they truly seemed to offer a clear vision of a future form of commercial organisation which would eventually succeed the East India Company and the constellation of small-scale enterprises which had co-existed with it in its last decades.

The economic development of India in the 1840s and 50s paved the way for this new generation of large companies. During this period, India became increasingly important as a primary producer, furnishing the British Empire and the world with a variety of raw materials and foodstuffs. Indian cotton, in spite of the problems its delicate fibres posed for the machinery and factories of the industrialising world, found new markets around the globe. In 1840, the East India Company's experimental tea gardens in Assam were purchased by the London-based Assam Company, and flourished into a major supplier for the world during the next two decades. By the early 1840s, the economic potential of India had attracted railway pioneers, and on the eve of the great crash of 1847/8 two railway companies were in the process of being founded: the Great Indian Peninsular Railway Company and the East Indian Railway Company. In spite of the uncertainties of the crisis, these new commercial leviathans survived and flourished, symbolising the emergence of the first joint-stock corporate capitalist firms since the East India Company itself had dominated the Indian economy.

By the 1850s, then, the East India Company had been reduced to a purely administrative wing of government, and though it still had a voice in such questions as the granting of charters to banks and railway companies, and determining the ability of companies to operate within the territories under Company control, the writing was on the wall. In June 1853 the East India Company's Charter was renewed, though the patronage enjoyed by the directors over appointments of officials in India was removed. During the debates about renewal, radical Liberal MPs such as Richard Cobden and John Bright argued vehemently that the Company was an anachronism and that it should be finally wound up. Though their arguments were unsuccessful in 1853, their views did capture a growing mood amongst politicians and business leaders that the organisation had had its day. When northern India was set aflame by the Great Rebellion of 1857, blame for the debacle was quickly and squarely placed on the shoulders of the Company, which was accused of maladministration, over taxation and general inefficiency. Within a year, new structures for the governance of the Indian empire were in the process of being constructed, which imposed a system of direct rule by the British government through the India Office and a newly constructed imperial bureaucracy in India. Within a few years, an entirely separate structure of government had been set up in the Straits Settlements (Malaya), which was placed under the authority of the Colonial Office. The Company was essentially a dead letter, though it was only finally wound up as an organisation in 1874.

But the slow death of the Company had shaped the commercial politics of Britain and its empire in profound ways. The fierce battles against the East India Company monopolies of the first half of the century gave rise to new pressure groups in the provinces and in the capital which, having won access to Asian markets, then sought to influence the development of imperial policy throughout the east. By the 1830s a network emerged linking not only merchants and industrialists in Manchester, Liverpool, Glasgow and London, but also their counterparts in Bombay, Calcutta, Madras, Penang, Singapore, Rangoon, Canton and Hong Kong. This movement gave birth to Chambers of Commerce in all of the great British-held Asian centres of trade, and furnished them with direct contact with their counterparts in Britain. Needless to say, this trans-imperial network survived the demise of the East India Company and continued to exercise an influence over the formation of colonial economic policy for the duration of Britain's imperial presence overseas. In Britain itself, the co-operation fostered by organisation around Asian affairs nourished alliances between cities and their business classes, especially in the provinces, a development which had implications for wider aspects of British political economy, including for example, the mid-nineteenth-century debate about protectionism versus free trade. While cities such as Glasgow and Liverpool saw the establishment of pressure groups specifically concerned with policy in Asia (both cities boasted their East India and China Associations), these were or became inextricably linked to Chambers of Commerce, which spoke on a much wider range of issues. In the case of cities such as Manchester, Asian policy was always conducted through its Chamber of Commerce. Thus the way in which the Company met its demise had profound consequences for commercial politics in Britain and its empire.

Inevitably this introduction has simplified a complex argument, and a complicated series of developments. The book will take the reader through the period, examining in detail key players, developments and events. The next chapter will set the context of the rise of the East India Company from mere trader in the seventeenth century to burgeoning imperial power at the end of the eighteenth century. It will show how the Company developed a symbiotic relationship with a number of British firms (agency houses) which became pivotal to the running of the Company's economic system in India. A principal theme will also be the emergence, outside the East India Company, of new business interests that wanted to challenge the Company's exclusive rights to trade with India and Asia. It will trace the role of these, and other factors such as war and Company financial difficulties, in setting the scene for the Charter Act of 1793, the first step in the reduction of the East India Company's power and privilege. The third chapter will then examine the effects of the Napoleonic Wars on the relationship between the British economy, the Company and the Indian empire, and how it created the circumstances for the Charter Act of 1813, which ended the Company's monopoly of trade to India. Chapter four will examine the impact of this liberalisation of the Indian trade to 1830, both on the Indian economy and British patterns of trade with Asia, and the emergence of new industrial and commercial organisations and pressure groups in Britain and Asia, who sought to exploit new opportunities. A key theme will be how these new players affected existing non-East India Company commercial interests in both locations, and how they came to relate to the East India Company itself. The fifth chapter focuses upon a period of five momentous years between 1830 and 1834, which saw the worst economic crisis in India in living memory, the demise of most of the older British agency houses in India and a period of great commercial uncertainty, bordering upon chaos. The chapter will focus upon the causes and consequences of the crisis. The other major development of the period was the victory of British commercial interests in ending the East India Company's remaining monopoly of trade with China, through the Charter Act of 1833, and the reasons for their success will be explored.

Chapter six then turns to the period between the two great crises of 1830–34 and 1847/8, during which a new order for commercial activity with India and the Far East was created following the demise of the Company as a trading organisation. The role of pressure groups representing non-Company interests, and the part played by the Company itself, in the formation of British colonial policy in Asia will be explored. The great opium war in China (1839–1842), rivalry with the Dutch in south-east Asia and continuing expansion in India itself were all major political developments in which these bodies had a major interest. The changing nature of British commercial enterprise in India and Asia will be also explored, with growing interest in the formation of new banks, commercial agriculture (indigo, tea and sugar) and the development of railways. The period of course ended with yet another major crisis in 1847/8, and the causes and effects of this, both in Britain and India, will be examined. Chapter seven will then outline the emergence of yet another new generation of non-East India Company commercial organisations, many of them large joint-stock companies such as banks and railway companies, and how the crisis of 1847/8 in many ways paved the way for the emergence of these new giants of eastern commerce. The reaction of the Company and those Company commercial firms to these new 'interlopers' will be a key theme, as will the effect of the rise of these new organisations on the trans-imperial network which had emerged in the 1830s. Finally, the book will conclude with an assessment of how the East India Company's protracted and complex winding up affected the development of British and imperial politics to 1860, and its subsequent legacy. It will also explore the implications of this study for historical debates about the East India Company and the nature of British imperialism.

Two

THE ORIGINS OF THE EAST INDIA COMPANY AND THE RISE OF NON-COMPANY COMMERCIAL INTERESTS IN BRITAIN, INDIA AND ASIA, 1600–1793

THE IDEA of an East India Company with exclusive trading rights between England and the east really emerged in the last years of the sixteenth century, at a time when England faced formidable opposition from powers like Spain and Holland, who were leaders in developing commerce with both Asia and the Americas. The defeat of the Spanish Armada in 1588 was still recent in the memory and, in spite of historians' depiction of her reign as a 'Golden Age', in truth Queen Elizabeth I and her Court remained deeply concerned by England's vulnerability to threats from the continent. Across Europe, the ideas on political economy which came to be known as mercantilism were ascendant, and were promoted in England by such eminent scholars as Richard Hakluyt. In essence, this school of thought postulated that the wealth of the world was finite and incapable of much expansion by human endeavour, and that nations which wished to strengthen themselves against rivals needed to amass for themselves a greater share of those scarce resources. In essence this meant the acquisition of colonies in the recently discovered 'New World' and the monopolisation of trade in commodities such as gold, silver, spices and other precious goods.

The England of Queen Elizabeth I was a beleaguered Protestant state, confronted by powerful Catholic enemies, notably Spain and Portugal, which already enjoyed a substantial lead in the quest for mercantilist and imperial dominance. In the wings, the Dutch were also a rising world power to be reckoned with, and English efforts to challenge rivals through state-backed piracy, or the pursuit of alternative land or sea routes to the east, had met with little success. By the 1590s, however, the international climate seemed more propitious for major advances to be made in this difficult field. It was apparent that the Portuguese were not as strong as they had once been, and that there was an opportunity in India and south-east Asia to establish English power. Furthermore, if the English did not act, it was likely that the Dutch would be the sole beneficiaries of this shift in the global balance of imperial power. This fact was underlined by a successful voyage by Dutch ships to the spice islands of south-east Asia in 1599. In this context, a consortium of London merchants met in autumn 1600 and successfully petitioned the Crown for a new joint-stock trading company with exclusive rights to trade to the east, and the controversial right to export bullion to fund its purchases of eastern produce. The English East India Company was thereby established by Royal Charter.[1]

The new Company was intended to be purely a trading organisation, with military powers restricted to the defence of its own vessels from attack. In fact, its first century of existence was a turbulent one. Although many of its voyages were profitable, and strong commercial (and diplomatic) links were made with the Mughal Empire in India, there were stark failures. The most serious of these was the massacre by the Dutch of ten East India Company servants on the spice island of Amboina, in south-east Asia in 1623. Thereafter, the English retreated from the region, and the main focus of their operations became mainland India. Meanwhile, at home the Company was as affected by the political upheavals of the English Civil War as other sections of society, suffering from the disruptions of commerce which it brought. Most alarming, however, was Oliver Cromwell's decision in 1653 not to renew the Company's monopoly, a decree which was reversed in 1657 following an unseemly free-for-all in the eastern trade which yielded little profit for the merchants or revenues for the government. After the restoration of the monarchy, the Company's exclusive trading privileges were reconfirmed by Royal Charter, and the next thirty years saw its profits and trading activities flourish. By this time India had clearly become the main theatre of the Company's operations. During the course of the century the Company established bases in four main locations. Its first acquisition was at Surat on the east coast in 1617, granted by the Mughal emperor following the defeat of a Portuguese naval force by the English two years earlier. The Company's trade in the Bay of Bengal and on the Coromandel Coast led to the establishment of a trading factory at Madras and the formal acquisition of the settlement in 1646. Then, in 1661, the island of Bombay was acquired by the English Crown as part of Catherine of Braganza's dowry to her husband Charles II. It was rented to the Company. In 1690, Job Charnock established a base at the tiny Bengal village of Calcutta. These last three – Madras, Bombay and Calcutta – became the three great presidencies from which the Company would conduct its operations in the east for the next century and a half.[2]

It is important to recognise that the East India Company's exclusive right to trade with India and Asia was always controversial. England's steady growth as a mercantile economy inevitably threw up individuals and consortia of merchants who viewed the Company's privileges with envy and a sense of injustice. From time to time their voices were raised against the monopoly, notably during the Cromwell regime. The political upheavals following the Glorious Revolution of 1688 and the demise of the Stuart dynasty provided yet another opportunity for the Company's rivals to move against it. Part of the problem was that the Company had allied itself very closely with the Stuarts and their foreign policy in the non-European world. In addition to making generous loans to members of the royal family, with the encouragement of James II the Company had adopted an increasingly aggressive stance in their relations with the Mughal dynasty. In the 1680s and 1690s this policy had backfired, as in Aurangzeb (ruled 1658–1707) the Company found a Mughal emperor with the power and will to resist them. In the 1690s the Company had to retreat quickly from their aggressive policy. These setbacks and the fall of the Stuarts opened new opportunities for the enemies of the Company to challenge its privileges. The 1690s saw an abortive attempt to set up a Scottish East India Company, which was thwarted only by the new monarch's prohibition against English money being invested in the new organisation. This was followed by a much more serious, and initially successful, attempt to set up a new rival English East India Company. Whig hostility to the bribery and corruption fostered by the Company in its relations with the Stuarts, and a sudden and pressing need for the Crown to raise money because of war with France resulted in the Crown effectively inviting open bids for a new charter carrying exclusive rights to trade with the east. The winners were a new company, the English East India Company Trading to the East Indies, which was granted a monopoly to the eastern trade in September 1698. The old Company looked doomed, but practical problems faced by the new organisation left open an escape route. In order to secure the charter the new Company had promised to lend the Crown £2 million out of its paid-up share capital.[3] But although the new Company was not short of financial support, it soon became clear that it simply lacked the commercial expertise to move quickly into the trade with Asia, and this resulted in a delay in the commencement of trade. The old Company moved quickly to exploit this delay. In 1699 it secured legislation which allowed it to continue in business beyond the normal statutory period for winding up of three years. This allowed it the breathing space to make an audacious bid to buy into the new Company, and it quickly established itself as the leading shareholder. From here there was only one direction in which matters could move satisfactorily, and that was towards a merger between the two enterprises.[4] After prolonged negotiations, in 1709 the United Company of Merchants Trading to the East Indies was formed, incorporating shareholders and supporters from both companies. Its establishment marked the end of a difficult period in relations between leaders of the trade with Asia and the British state, and also the beginning of one of security for the new organisation. It had effectively absorbed those in the City of London who had felt excluded by the privileges of the old Company, and as such inoculated the new Company against the jealousies and protests which for some time had sporadically threatened the exclusive privileges of the old organisation. The setting of the eastern trade on fresh foundations together with the establishment of the Bank of England and the inauguration of the National Debt may be seen as part of the wider financial revolution which followed in the wake of the new settlement of 1688. Of course, the unification of City interests did not extend to commercial interests in the outports, who continued to resent the privileged position of their metropolitan peers. Nonetheless, it would be almost a hundred years before another major challenge to the idea of an East India monopoly would be mounted.[5]

There can be little doubt that the early eighteenth century represented the zenith of the Company's fortunes, and its profitability, prominence in national life and importance to the British state rendered it nearly invulnerable to would-be rivals. The Company's activities in the east captured both the public and political imagination. The growing presence of tea, Indian textiles and a range of other eastern commodities in the homes of the elite (and later, further down the social order) generated a wide awareness of the Company and its importance for everyday comforts as well as the national interest. A voluminous literature was published on the activities of the Company and the Orient, which appealed to the curious as well as the intellectual. East India Company stock was prized by all of the financial classes in London because of its stability, reliability and high returns.[6] But it was in the hard world of national finance that the Company's importance was most marked. By 1744, the Company had lent £4.2 million to the British state, contributing significantly to its ability to fight and win a series of wars against rival European powers.[7] The East India Company had become part of the Hanoverian political, economic and cultural establishment.

But developments in India were to transform dramatically the Company and perceptions of it in Britain, in ways which were initially exciting and promising, but ultimately problematic. The first half of the eighteenth century saw a series of major crises within the Mughal Empire, caused by a combination of factors, including invasions of northern India by tribes from Central Asia and the emergence of powerful regional polities prepared to challenge the authority of the emperor. These, ironically, resulted partly from the economic buoyancy of the Indian economy, which enabled local rulers to maximise their revenue collection.[8] The upshot was the emergence of rivalries between new regional states competing for control of vital resources, trade routes and other sources of revenue, which frequently erupted into localised warfare. Even though the East India Company's bases were restricted to the coastal presidencies, the organisation could not avoid the effects of the disruptions of trade caused by war, or the increased revenue demands and interference in their affairs by new local rulers. Appeals to the emperor in Delhi became progressively a less effective remedy for the resultant grievances. The presence in India of major European rivals, notably the French, further exacerbated the Company's problems, as the rival European companies tried to exploit local instability to their own advantage through alliances with regional rulers in exchange for preferential treatment in matters of commerce. Much of this early rivalry was focused in the south-east of the sub-continent, on the Coromandel Coast, and both the French and English East India Companies found themselves paying for troops to defend themselves and honour agreements with Indian rulers in local military confrontations. Thus began the process of militarisation of the European companies, and their engagement in internal Indian politics. But it was in Bengal in the 1750s that matters took a dramatic and decisive turn. In 1756 the Nawab of Bengal, Sirajudaullah, seized Calcutta, an action which sprang from suspicion about a possible British conspiracy with disaffected interests at the Nawab's court to overthrow him. The death of a number of Company servants in captivity (the 'Black Hole' incident) was used by the Company to justify a draconian response. Robert Clive was sent to Bengal to restore the Company's rights, by force of arms if necessary. Clive carried out his instructions to the extreme, and when the Nawab's armies were defeated at the Battle of Plassey in 1757, the Company were installed as effective rulers of Bengal.

The events marked the beginning of a succession of wars and conquests which resulted, by 1840, in Company rule over most of the Indian sub-continent. It represented a metamorphosis of the East India Company from trading firm to agency of colonial rule for the British state. In the process, the Company acquired an army, a foreign policy, and a large bureaucracy (in London as well as India) for revenue collection, law enforcement and the governance of the Indian people. A key development came in 1765, when Robert Clive accepted for the Company the Bengal *diwani* (right to collect revenues) from the emperor, Shah Alam II. A similar pattern followed elsewhere. Where it did not conquer, the Company established alliances with Indian states, offering military protection in return for rights of revenue collection. The burgeoning cost of the Company's sepoy army made such lucrative 'subsidiary alliance' arrangements increasingly attractive for the Company, but the new commitments involved pushed up those costs still further. A cycle was set in train of Company expansion in pursuit of more revenues to meet escalating military expenses, described by one eminent historian as 'military fiscalism'.[9] Military adventures against the Indian states were further complicated by continuing rivalries with other European powers as the intermittent eighteenth-century conflicts with France and Holland spilled into the colonies, culminating of course in the Napoleonic Wars of 1793 to 1815.

The hubris of imperial dominance and plunder soon gave way, however, to an alarming and sudden realisation that the costs of expansion were outrunning the benefits and income it brought. At the time of the acquisition of the Bengal *diwani* the mood in London and Calcutta was bullishly optimistic; it was believed that Indian revenues could finance a huge expansion of the Company's trade, particularly the purchase of tea in China, a beverage for which the British seemed to have an insatiable thirst. But the Company had simply not reckoned with the sheer cost of its new political and military role, or the untrammelled avarice of its own employees. Company servants were permitted to engage in trade on their own account, and the growing military and political power of the organisation dramatically increased their opportunities to feather their own nests at the expense of Indians and their employer. They even used Company bills of exchange to transmit home the proceeds of their private adventures, an arrangement which helped precipitate a severe financial crisis in 1771. In that year, the costs of the Company's militarism, declining sales of Indian produce in London and a sudden rise in outgoings to pay shareholders and the excessive bills issued on behalf of Company servants in India all converged to undermine the Company's liquidity in London.[10] It was forced to seek emergency financial help from the government, which was forthcoming under Lord North's Regulating Act of 1773, but at a price. Although the Company received a loan of £1.4 million, the government imposed a regime of Cabinet supervision of its affairs. A new system of government was created for India, comprising the Governor-General and his Council of four, who were to be jointly appointed by, and answerable to, the British government and the Company's Court of Directors. Other impositions included reforms of the elections for the directorate (the introduction of a rotation system under which a quarter of the directorate came up for election each year, rather than all being subject to annual elections) and of the voting rights of Company stockholders. These later changes tended to increase the power of the largest stockholders, and to reduce the vulnerability of the directorate to sudden shifts of opinion within the Court of Proprietors, both of which reduced the pressure upon the Company's leaders to pay unreasonably large dividends and created a more politically stable environment in which they could operate.[11]

But none of this was enough. Problems arising from Company servants attending to their own interests rather than those of their employer did not abate, and in spite of a clear brief to stamp out corruption and to curb the Company's expansionist tendencies, the first Governor-General, Warren Hastings (1773–1785) proved unable to restrain his new subordinates. Defeat for the British in the American War of Independence strengthened the government's resolve to reform the Company for once and for all and, in 1784, Pitt the Younger's administration forced through new East Indian legislation. Pitt's India Act established the Board of Control, a government department with the final say over all political decisions in the east, and the President enjoyed a seat in the Cabinet. Appointment of the Governor-General and his

Council would, from now on, be the exclusive preserve of the President and Board, and these Indian officers would answer directly to the new government department. But Henry Dundas, who designed the new structure, was determined to go much further. In 1785, a new Governor-General, General Charles Cornwallis, was appointed to replace Warren Hastings with instructions to eliminate for once and for all the ability of Company servants to engage in private trade on their own account. This was accomplished in 1787, and Company servants received a substantial increase in their salaries in compensation. Cornwallis also reformed the taxation system in Bengal through the Permanent Settlement of 1793, which set for all time the taxes to be paid by the *zamindari* landholders, who were the main collectors of revenue. It was a major step towards modernising the Company's system of government in India. In addition, Cornwallis curbed, for a few years at least, the trends towards territorial expansionism, though he too found himself drawn into war with Tipu Sultan of Mysore in 1790.[12]

The 1770s and 1780s were thus a turning point in the affairs of the Company, and in many respects can be regarded as the beginning of the process which would lead to the stripping away of its privileges, and its eventual demise in the middle of the nineteenth century. The financial difficulties and the need for government to intervene in the Company's affairs raised considerable doubts about the validity of the Company's privileges, and its competence to use them in the national interest. For the first time since the beginning of the century, the Company's favoured position began to be questioned. Wider economic and intellectual trends also served to open debate. The early stages of the industrial revolution saw the emergence of manufacturing firms (especially in textiles) which were eager to find new markets for their produce and fresh sources of raw materials. Increasingly they came to see India as a potential market, and while the Company certainly purchased substantial quantities of manufactures for export, there were those who began to see advantage in a liberated trade regime with the east.[13] They were encouraged by the new political economy espoused by Adam Smith, whose *Wealth of Nations*, published in 1776, condemned monopolies of trade as harmful to the national interest, and called for the promotion of free international commerce. In this respect, the intellectual tide was turning against the East India Company. By the early 1790s, provincial merchants and manufacturers would be a significant voice against the renewal of the Company's Charter.

But it was Cornwallis's reforms of the Company civil service in India which were to stimulate perhaps the most dramatic change in the position of non-Company interests in India. During the eighteenth century, the Company in India had become an umbrella for the pursuit of private commercial adventures by its own servants. P.J. Marshall's ground-breaking study of the mid-1970s, *East Indian Fortunes*, showed how the assertion of Company rule in Bengal opened new opportunities for Company servants already heavily engaged in trade on their own account.[14] Before Plassey, their involvement in the internal trade of Bengal and northern India was quite limited, but once control was established, it flourished dramatically.[15] Marshall also shows how the conquest encouraged British involvement in the production of indigo by individuals such as John Prinsep.[16] In addition to Company servants trading privately, there were a restricted number of 'free merchants' and other private entrepreneurs who were permitted to conduct their own businesses, provided of course that they did not infringe the Company's monopoly of trade. They were allowed to engage in agricultural or industrial ventures such as producing indigo or growing sugar. They were also allowed to engage in the intra-Asian trade between India, south-east Asia and China (the 'country trade'), so long as they did not breach the Company's rights and privileges in this field. One important observation is that the Company in India had become an apparatus through which its own employees could conduct their own business affairs. In effect private interests which otherwise would be separate from and possibly in competition with the Company were incorporated into the latter's system of governance and trade. In this way, in India the Company accommodated and tolerated a multiplicity of separate business interests. One effect of this was to prevent the emergence before the 1780s of any dissent in India against the Company's privileges. There were echoes of this approach in arrangements at home; as probably the most important private company in the City of London, the East India Company attracted investment from a range of commercial interests in London, especially the great ship-owners, whose vessels the Company hired.[17] There was also a licensed private trade (the 'privilege trade') which was conducted by the commanders and officers of East Indiamen, which allowed a considerable volume of non-Company trade to be conducted between Britain and Asia. This was utilised by the agency houses and Company servants to transfer wealth from Asia to Britain, as well as generate the usual profits arising from trade.[18] This meant that many of those who might have otherwise challenged the Company's privileges were placated by their share and vested interest in its fortunes.

One of the most important consequences of the Cornwallis reforms was effectively to break up the Company's system for accommodating separate commercial interests. No longer could Company servants or soldiers openly feather their own nests whilst ostensibly serving their employer. The effect was to create more opportunities for the free merchants operating outside the Company, and several moved swiftly to take advantage of the situation. The increased salaries of Company servants, combined with their exclusion from private commerce, enabled the free merchants to adopt a form of commercial organisation ideally suited to the new administrative arrangements – the agency house. The key innovation was the provision by the new agency houses of personal financial services for the army of Company servants and soldiers, including financial advice, arrangement of wills, trusts and invest-

ments, remitting wealth to families in Britain, and, crucially, banking facilities. By providing these, the agency houses made themselves indispensable to
those who ran the Company in India, including some of the highest placed
members of the administration. This ensured a sympathetic hearing for their
problems and needs. The savings of Company servants deposited with the
houses constituted a rich source of capital for investment by the houses in a
wide range of commercial ventures which did not infringe the Company's
monopoly. Thus, from the 1780s, agency houses were established in all three
company presidencies, and extended their activities into the country trade
to south-east Asia, the purchase and export of Company opium to China,
investment in indigo factories and plantation agriculture, shipbuilding, salt
production as well as the various private financial services described earlier.
Typically an agency house was owned and managed by four or five European
partners, each of whom took responsibility for managing one of the lines of
business. Virtually all the houses depended on close relations with the Indian
commercial community, and so they all employed *banians*, Indian agents who
dealt with this aspect of the business, and who were effectively unofficial
partners in the agency house. Relations with leading Indian merchants and
Company servants who were house clients were quite intimate, and agency
house partners were expert network builders, cultivating friendships and
commercial relationships all over India and the east.[19] The need to deal with
clients' interests in Britain, and the desire of agency house partners to eventually retire and invest their wealth in a flourishing business in the City of
London, led to the establishment by partners retiring from the Indian houses,
of 'sister' agency houses in London. These were separate firms, and each
of them sustained a close relationship with the Indian agency house from
which their partners had been drawn. The London houses eventually became
involved in the importation and exportation of commodities to and from the
east, as the East India Company's India monopoly was relaxed by the Charter
Act of 1793, and ended in 1813. They also bought East India stock, and by
the 1820s they had become a powerful interest group within the East India
Company's Courts of Proprietors and Directors.[20]

   One of the first agency houses to achieve prominence was that of Scott,
Tate & Adamson, based in Bombay. Little is known of the origin of the house,
but its most senior figure, David Scott, son of the Laird of Dunninald, left the
Bombay firm in 1786 to set up David Scott & Co. of London.[21] By 1788 he
was an East India Company director, and two years later MP for Forfarshire.
By the 1790s he had become an outspoken critic of the East India Company's
monopoly, and a spokesman for the agency houses in the directorate. Perhaps
inevitably, he attracted the hostility of supporters of the Company's privileges.[22] His career was a prototype for many successful agency house men
who came later: modest beginnings, the making of a fortune in India and
the cultivation of powerful and eminent friends in the East India Company,

followed by return to London, the establishment or membership of a London agency house, the purchase of a landed estate, a seat in Parliament and one on the Company directorate. Similarly, Sir Charles Cockerell rose from being a lowly writer in the East India Company's service in the 1770s to a senior partnership in the Calcutta firm of Paxton, Cockerell & Trail in the 1790s. In this capacity he helped Governor-General Richard Wellesley to finance his war against Tipu Sultan of Mysore in 1798/9, a service for which he was granted a baronetcy in 1809. On his return to England in 1801 he joined his former Bengal partners in the new and separate London firm of Paxton, Cockerell & Trail. A few years later he married the daughter of John Rushout, Baron of Northwick. He acquired a country house and estate at Sezincote near Evesham, decking it out in oriental splendour. Like Scott, a parliamentary career followed, and on his death in 1837 he was a Commissioner of the Board of Control.[23] In this way, the new Indian and London agency houses became a ladder to the heights of influence, wealth and power in London and in the East India Company. As a result, they were to emerge as a powerful interest group within the Company and an increasingly fierce critic of its privileges. Thus some of the earliest and most strident challengers to the Company emerged in India and out of the reforms of the 1780s.

The progress of the agency houses in Calcutta, the capital of British India, was especially rapid. There were fifteen agency houses by 1790, and twenty-nine by 1803.[24] But five or six principal firms came to dominate Calcutta business, notably such prominent houses as John Palmer & Co., Fairlie, Fergusson & Co. and Alexander & Co.[25] Tracing the development of the agency houses is a task made complicated by the renaming of the firms on the retirement of older partners and the accession of new ones. This drafting in of partners for old made for a high degree of continuity. The relationship between the Company and the agency houses in London and India was a complex one. On the one hand there was a general ideological difference between Leadenhall Street and the agency houses on the question of the monopoly, but on the other there was the fact that the Company was powerful and that the latter's interests were closely linked with it. Broadly speaking, most of the agency house men were free traders by belief and self-interest. They argued that national prosperity would be best assured by free and open competition, and they naturally believed that they would benefit from an abolition or relaxation of the Company's monopoly. Key figures like David Scott were committed and outspoken in their criticisms of the East India Company, but they frequently found it prudent to tailor precise demands for change for reasons of political expediency.[26] The reason was that many of the London houses, as holders of East India stock, had a vested interest in the organisation's profitability. Whether they liked it or not, the price of influence within the Company was a practical acquiescence in its monopolistic privileges. Furthermore, the considerable influence of the Company in Parliament and politics generally, which remained formidable in spite of the problems of the 1770s and 1780s, was not something to take lightly, as Scott was to discover to his cost. Attacks on the Company, or key interest groups within it, could have severe repercussions in the form of legal action or a loss of key clients who were employed by, or stockholders in, the Company. This ambivalence amongst those business interests that co-existed and co-operated with the East India Company, but who fundamentally opposed its privileges, was a theme which ran throughout the last three quarters of a century of the organisation's life. For much of this period, the Company was resented, occasionally opposed, but more frequently obeyed by some of its most implacable commercial opponents in London and India. This was a key reason why the Company's decline was so protracted.

In India, this contradictory relationship between the East India Company and non-Company commercial interests was even more striking. The Indian agency houses and the East India Company became so close that they were effectively partners in the imperial project. Both partners found the co-operation of the other indispensable. The agency houses depended upon the goodwill of the East India Company in attracting the deposits and custom of the Company's employees. They relied upon the willingness of Company ships' captains to sell their own privileged cargo space to allow the houses to conduct a limited trade between Britain and India. At crucial moments of financial difficulty, the Company acted as lender of last resort, bailing out the agency houses on several occasions in the 1820s.[27] In addition, of course, Company rule also provided protection and security through its military infrastructure. In return, when the Company needed to borrow in order to meet commercial expenses or to fight wars, the agency houses were a major market for the issue of government securities.[28] The personal and financial services provided by the houses to the Company's servants and soldiers undoubtedly helped maintain morale and loyalty within the organisation.[29] The agency houses also helped supply Company military expeditions, such as to Java in 1811, and outposts of imperial authority such as Ceylon after 1795.[30] But it was in the China trade that the agency houses proved their supreme value to the East India Company.

Supplies of tea had first been brought back to England by exploratory expeditions in the seventeenth century.[31] By the 1770s and 1780s, the growing British thirst for the beverage offered the prospect of a very lucrative market indeed, especially after the Commutation Act of 1784 had significantly reduced the duty on the commodity.[32] In the context of the financial crises of the 1770s and 1780s, the Company quickly recognised that the development of the China trade might go a long way to solving it problems. There were, however, some formidable obstacles to be overcome. Not only were the Chinese authorities inclined to view foreign traders with hostility and suspicion, Chinese consumers also showed little interest in British produce, save musical novelty toys ('sing songs'). Without substantial exports of goods to China, tea could only be purchased by the export of bullion, which would render the trade unprofitable and impractical. The solution lay in the growing Chinese appetite for raw cotton and opium produced in India, the latter of which was a branch of agricultural production that was soon declared an East India Company monopoly. But an additional difficulty was the extreme hostility of the Chinese authorities to the trade, and the British soon found that the only way into the market at Canton (the only port open to British traders) was through smuggling, with the help of a syndicate of Chinese merchants known as the Hong.[33] The Company, which possessed a precious trading station in Canton, could not afford to jeopardise it by antagonising the Chinese authorities, and so it needed others to conduct the trade in opium. The agency houses soon stepped into the breach. They purchased opium off the East India Company in India, and shipped the drug to Canton, smuggling it into the city with the help of the Hong merchants. They then paid the receipts from the sales into the Company treasury at Canton, in return for bills of exchange payable in India or London. In this way the Company was furnished with the Chinese currency to pay for tea, which was shipped back to Britain on its East Indiamen, and the agency houses obtained a safe form of remittance of their sales receipts to Britain or India. Altogether, the relationship between the agency houses and the East India Company amounted to one of symbiosis from the 1780s until the demise of the houses in the early 1830s. But at times it was a fraught relationship, partly because this was a very turbulent period indeed, in which the war with France (1793–1815) was compounded by conflict with Indian states (the war with Burma 1824–26 was especially disruptive to Company finance). At other times the Company and the houses found themselves in competition for capital, and were on fundamentally different sides on the question of the Company's monopoly. This exemplified the complex relations which existed between the Company and the plethora of separate commercial interests connected with Asia which emerged in the last eighty years of its life.

The emergence of the Indian and London agency houses, shaken government confidence in the competence of the East India Company to manage the nation's commerce with Asia, the rise of British industry and a new wave of economic thinking which extolled the virtues of free trade, all converged in the 1780s to bring into question, for the first time in living memory, the validity of the Company's monopolistic privileges. Of these factors, the consequences of the Company's dire financial situation was the most immediate in fuelling the opposition to monopoly. By the mid-1780s, on the eve of Cornwallis's reforms, such were the Company's local debts that it found it increasingly difficult to fund the 'Investment', the regular purchase of Asian commodities to be sold in Europe to generate the Company's commercial profit. Its borrowings from the European and Indian communities escalated, as it sought to fund its trading operations and sustain its military commitments. The effect was that European free merchants, early agency houses and the Company's own servants found themselves in receipt of substantial interest payments on their loans to the Company; funds which many wanted to remit back to England. At the time, the Company's facility for allowing private remittance via the privilege trade was extremely limited indeed, allowing for only £180,000 in value per year. Limits on the overall value of the privilege trade in Indian commodities were compounded by almost equally strict rules dating from 1773 on the employment of Company bills of exchange by private merchants to facilitate remittance. These confined the issuing of such bills to no more than £300,000 per annum.[34] The only alternative was to remit illegally by engaging in the 'clandestine trade', that is by exporting commodities through the Danish, Portuguese, Dutch or American merchants who called at the Indian ports from time to time, with arrangements for sales receipts in Europe to be paid to a nominated agent in Britain.[35] The East India Company was particularly hostile to this practice, as the goods shipped were in direct competition with its own sales in Europe. In August 1787, just over a year after coming to office, Cornwallis revealed that many Company servants in the Bengal administration's Board of Trade were involved in the clandestine trade, one of the factors prompting his prohibition of private trade by the Company's employees.[36] This did not of course solve the problem of remittance for the free merchants and agency houses who, wishing to repatriate their profits and the savings of their clients, also frequently took advantage of the clandestine trade. For them, while in the late 1780s an end to the Company's monopoly might have seemed unachievable, reform which increased the provision of space on Company ships for their goods seemed a feasible goal.

By the end of the 1780s, as the date for the renewal of the Company's Charter loomed on the horizon, a range of forces and circumstances coalesced to ensure that a measure of reform of the Company's privileges would be a real possibility. One important factor was the bitter struggle experienced by Henry Dundas and Pitt's administration when it forced through the India Act of 1784, and in the period which followed. The passage of the legislation was only the beginning of five years of tough confrontations with the Court of Directors and the 'Indian interest' in the Company (the coterie of Company directors and proprietors who had made their fortunes in India as Company servants or soldiers and had retired as wealthy *nabobs* to England, where they bought stock in the Company).[37] By 1790, Dundas had managed to exert his authority through a judicious mix of cajoling, bullying and threats of more punitive legislation, but principally through building a strong group in the Courts of Proprietors and Directors who owed their rise to Dundas's patronage. By then, he was well placed to contemplate the possibility of reform, and the bitterness of some of his battles with the Company provided a personal motive to cut down to size some old adversaries within it. Of course, the huge wealth of the Company, and the fact that many influential people possessed a vested interest in it, was a check on how far Dundas could go. Moreover, Dundas was far from convinced that an end of the Company's monopoly would be beneficial to the national interest. The Company's trade, he believed, was the best way to remit the surplus tax revenues of the Indian empire to Britain for the benefit of the Company's stockholders and the national economy in general. As such, he held the view that, broadly, the Company's privileges should be upheld but with greater opportunities for other mercantile interests in Britain and India to engage in a significant but limited trade with the territories under Company control.[38] Besides, having won many of his battles with the directors of the previous few years, Dundas believed that, more or less, there was now a practical and workable system of state-supervised governance in India, and that too radical an attack on its privileges might undo all the hard work of the late 1780s. Within these constraints, he was able and willing to make concessions.

As shown, there were of course interests within and outside the Company which desperately wanted reform of the Company's commercial system, specifically to liberalise the export and import trade with India. Of enormous significance was the elevation of David Scott to the Court of Directors in 1788, with Dundas's assistance.[39] As the head of the London East India agency house of David Scott & Co., Scott swiftly established himself as spokesman for the non-Company private trade interest in India and London, consolidating his political influence by becoming MP for Forfarshire in July 1790.[40] Scott's position reflected a more general ambiguity in the agency house interest's relationship with the Company which persisted almost to the end of the organisation's life in the 1850s. On the one hand Scott, like the other agency house men, wanted liberalisation of the Company's trading monopoly, a conviction which evolved in due course into a full commitment to its abolition. But on the other hand, he was a prestigious figure within the Company's ruling councils, and with a substantial personal financial stake in its fortunes. He also recognised, and indeed was to experience, that the wrath of the Company and its powerful interest groups was something to be feared. This meant that while Scott was outspoken about what he saw as the inequities and inefficiencies of aspects of the Company's monopoly, there were boundaries which he would not cross. As a result, Scott focused his criticisms at specific targets which he judged would not set him too much at odds with the Company, but would attract the support of the government. Thus, from 1787, his efforts were aimed at increasing the facilities for private trade between Britain and India, short of abolition of the monopoly, for the benefit of both non-Company traders in India, and manufacturers in Britain.[41] Scott played on the fear of senior politicians, including Pitt himself, that the inadequacy of existing arrangements for private trade effectively drove large quantities of goods and wealth into the clandestine trade, to the cost of both the nation and the Company.[12] Crucially, in mid-March 1793 Scott was the principal author of a memorial to Pitt and Dundas which claimed that since the mid-1760s approximately £10 million had been remitted illegally to Europe through this channel.[13] Scott was supported in this view by his principal business connections in Bengal, the agency house of Fairlie, Fergusson & Co., which openly admitted to having used illegal means of remitting to Europe because of the want of legitimate facilities through the Company.[14] In 1791 William Fairlie had requested space aboard Company ships to export 500 bales of Indian piece goods to London, but had been refused. Fearful of heavy losses, Fairlie sent them illicitly to Ostend and Lisbon. Fairlie claimed to speak for all the agency houses when he wished for a more direct route into the British market:

> It will give all of us in India who have any connection with the trade to Europe the greatest pleasure to be enabled to communicate with London direct and not be forced to seek other foreign markets[15]

A second memorial was issued by Scott later in March, which provided compelling evidence of the scale of the clandestine trade and the pressing need for a greater facility for private trade.[16] These efforts were to bear fruit in the terms of the new Charter enacted later in the year.

Other interests joined Scott in the clamour for the Charter to meet the needs of non-Company commerce. An important group was composed of shipowners and masters who wanted to break the near monopoly of providing Company ships enjoyed by a coterie of London men who used their power to keep freight costs high.[17] They included men such as John Fiott and Anthony Brough, who had purchased stock in the Company to secure influence within the Court of Proprietors in pursuit of this aim.[18] They threw their weight behind David Scott's attack on the Company's restrictive limits on the private trade, effectively forging an alliance with the private trade interest of the London and Indian agency houses.[19] But perhaps most significant was the emergence of British manufacturers as a voice in the Charter debate. Bowen's ground-breaking work on the Company's export of British commodities in this period demonstrates that the organisation was a major purchaser of certain British commodities, notably woollen goods such as long ells (a type of serge), broadcloth, tin, copper and iron. By 1791/2, shortly before the passage of the new Charter, the Company purchased £1,298,551 worth of British manufactures for export to India and China.[50] There was, however, a general perception that the Company was inefficient in its operations and unfairly exploited its monopoly of trade to charge excessive freight rates.[51]

As a result, the Charter negotiations in spring 1793 were preceded by a flurry of petitions and delegations to the government, pleading for a variety of adjustments of the new Charter terms which would promote their diverse interests. In early March 1793, manufacturers of long ells in Exeter complained that the East India Company's heavy purchases in Devon of the commodity for the China market had so increased prices that Exeter's manufactures were being priced out of its European markets. The problem for the Exeter men was that the long ells purchased by the Company were 'in their raw state', that is, unrefined by the processes used by the Exeter manufacturers. They demanded that the Company undertake to purchase their refined long ells for the China trade.[52] Later in the month, a delegation representing cotton manufacturers in Manchester met Pitt and Dundas in Downing Street with their own list of demands for the Charter. They wanted a complete prohibition of the import of Indian cotton goods into Britain, except for re-export, and the increased import by the Company of cotton wool as a raw material for the British cotton industry.[53] The call for a ban on the import of Indian cotton goods was repeated at a meeting of muslin and calico manufacturers in Manchester early in April.[54] Two other delegates from Manchester, Messrs Gregg and Frodsham, asked Pitt and Dundas for limits on Company freight charges, the exemption of British manufactures from all import and other duties on entry into the Company's territories, and the re-export to China from India of British manufactures.[55] In November 1792, a group of Liverpool merchants had set up a special committee on the question of access to markets east of the Cape of Good Hope. On 8 March 1793, the Liverpool merchant Thomas Earle wrote to the Privy Council Committee on Trade on their behalf, stressing the desire of Liverpool ship-owners to participate in the shipping of freight to and from the east.[56] Eleven days later, the Glasgow manufacturer John Dunlop wrote to Dundas to represent the demands of his peers. They wanted the Charter to be limited in duration for a period 'considerably short of twenty years', the import of Indian cotton goods to be prohibited, except for certain classes of expensive and ornamental muslins which would not compete with domestic British manufactures, and a ban on the export of cotton machinery to India. Most controversially, they wanted all British merchants to be given the right to export manufactures and import raw materials from Asia on their own vessels, paying the East India Company the equivalent of the duties charged on the vessels of other nations. These ships would only be allowed to use the dock facilities of the Company in London.[57] At the same time, Lord Falmouth, on behalf of a group of Cornish tin-mine owners, pressed for the right to export tin and import return cargoes on their own account, using East India Company ships. He was particularly keen to secure access to the Chinese market.[58] Thus the government was pressed by various demands from the emerging manufacturing and mercantile interests of the provinces, and Dundas made these known to the East India Company directors immediately, in order to strengthen his hand in the debate on Company reform.

But there were several reasons why these efforts by provincial lobbyists achieved only limited results in respect of the terms of the 1793 Charter Act. Firstly, there seems to have been no communication or co-ordination between the various provincial commercial centres demanding reform. This was demonstrated by the varying and sometimes conflicting demands made by different commercial interest groups, and the absence of a common line on crucial areas of reform. While David Scott tried to champion the cause of the manufacturers as part of his campaign for greater facilities for the private trade, this was undermined by the sheer diversity and occasionally contradictory nature of their demands.[59] This exasperated the most ardent supporters of reform. Even a dedicated and outspoken supporter of free trade like John Cochrane had to concede that:

> Self interest and oppression are the prominent features throughout. Each individual or company, not only conceive the idea, but insist that their interest alone is to be attended to, to the injury both of the foreigner, and the bulk of the people of this country[60]

He then went through the demands of the various interest groups, including the Cornish tin-mine owners, the Exeter long ells manufacturers, and the cotton manufacturers of Glasgow and Manchester, showing that many of these were not only contradictory but also grossly unjust. Cochrane was disgusted by calls to open the Indian market for British cotton goods whilst closing Britain to the import of Indian cottons. He lamented the fate of the 'poor natives of India', whose interests were not represented in this debate about the eastern trade.[61] He was damning of British manufacturers in general, who he said, 'have more of the savage about them than any other class of men'.[62] Their only mitigation was the fact that the East India Company was no better in its ruthless pursuit of self-interest.[63]

Secondly, the lack of co-ordination meant that it was relatively easy for opponents of the manufacturers' demands to offer counter arguments against proposals which could easily be depicted as the isolated whims of selfish and localised commercial interests. Even Cochrane robustly attacked the injustice of the calls by Manchester and Glasgow to impede the Indian cotton industry by import prohibitions and an embargo on the export of cotton machinery. A significant point here was that the efforts to ban imports of Indian cotton goods directly opposed the aspirations of the leading Indian agency houses. Fairlie in particular had called in 1792 for a reduction of duties on imports into Britain of Indian textiles, complacently suggesting that:

> The manufacturers at home I think would also be satisfied as they are making such rapid improvement in the machinery for their manufactures they ought to be able to cope with the sales at the India House on these terms[64]

Clearly, had closer co-ordination between the provincial manufacturers and the London and Indian agency houses been attempted, there would have been major disagreements within the reform camp, weakening it still further. Cochrane also condemned the Cornish tin interest's demands as unreasonable, while he accused the Exeter long ells producers, especially those involved in dyeing, of conspiring to discredit their competitors in London in the eyes of the East India Company.[65] In early April 1793, Thomas Brown, Chair of the Committee of Merchant Drapers in London, emphatically rejected the Glasgow and Manchester demands for an import prohibition on Indian cottons.[66] Dundas had asked them to consider the impact of such a policy on the British economy, and Brown estimated that it would result in a loss of £100,000 in government customs revenue.[67] Brown depicted the northern manufacturers as rich and ambitious men, but with little knowledge of India. He warned Dundas against exposing tried and tested commercial men such as those Brown represented, to the 'wild theories' expounded by the men of Manchester and Glasgow.[68] As Brown pointed out, Dundas himself had judged that the northern manufacturers were generally 'acting in too narrow a view of the subject'.[69] Indeed, in personal interviews with manufacturers, Pitt and Dundas had been eager to squash what they saw as unrealistic or unreasonable demands. For example, when Gregg and Frodsham, the two Manchester delegates, called for ceilings on the Company's freight rates at £4 per ton out to India and £12 return, Pitt and Dundas rejected these demands, pointing out that they exposed the flawed nature of the Manchester delegation's understanding of the Indian trade.[70]

In any case, the nature of the provincial demands betrayed a lack of ambition and confidence. The only petition which offered any challenge to the principle of the Company's privileged monopoly was that from Glasgow, which mentioned in passing that the petitioners 'were not sanguine with regard to the advantages to be derived by the country from a trade to India regulated by an exclusive Charter'. Significantly, however, they went on to waive opposition to such a Charter, provided the Company meet their list of demands.[71] In the main, most of the demands presented by the various provincial lobbies required only limited adjustments to Company practice or the terms of its monopoly. The principle of monopoly itself was not really challenged. Indeed, some of the demands, notably the proposed prohibition of Indian cotton goods imports and the export of cotton manufacturing machinery, were inconsistent with any spirit of free trade or fairness. For the manufacturers campaigning for change in 1793, opportunistic self-interest was the guide to proposed reform, rather than the new principles of Smithian free trade political economy. It was a position which on the whole weakened their efforts. Although a full frontal assault on the principle of monopoly would have rallied the might of the Company and its metropolitan allies in its defence, it would at least have provided the basis for a co-ordinated and consistent common front amongst the provincial reformers. Defeat would still have been likely, but the show of strength made possible by a disciplined campaign based on common ideological ground might have wrung more concessions from government and Company. The absence of such a common front made it easy for the Company and its allies to dismiss the provincial demands as incoherent, confused, and guided by narrow self-interest. In short, they presented an ineffective challenge which government and Company could contain without surrendering too much.

The Charter of 1793 therefore made few substantial concessions to provincial merchants and manufacturers. Almost from the outset, Dundas made it clear to the East India Company that most of their privileges would be safe. Nonetheless he stressed that what he wanted was 'regulated monopoly', which would enable the merchants and manufacturers of Britain to export sufficient quantities of goods to meet the demand of India, and to import sufficient amounts of raw materials to satisfy their own needs, at reasonable rates of freight.[72] The Company's monopoly of trade was therefore renewed for a further twenty years, on condition that it provide 3,000 tons of shipping annually for private traders to ship exports and imports to and from India. This was by far the most important concession to the private trade interest, and measures were embodied in the Act by which the Company could regulate the export from India of certain goods which it shipped itself as part of the annual Investment. These were subject to a system of appeal to the Board of Control which merchants and manufacturers could use if they felt Company restrictions were unfair. Freight was reduced to £5 per ton to India and £15 on return voyages, subject to special conditions which would allow the Company to increase these in the event of war or other contingencies. The Company was permitted to increase the Investment from India substantially to facilitate increased dividend payments to its stockholders, and to allow a payment to the public exchequer of £500,000 per annum.[73] The feeling was that most interested parties, with the possible exception of the 'old shipping interest' of the Company, had gained.

Who among the non-Company private trade interests in Britain and India were the principal architects and beneficiaries of this change? As shown, the muddled and incoherent campaign conducted by the provincial manufacturers and merchants in Britain can hardly be credited with the limited concessions to non-Company trade secured by the Charter Act, though they did impress government with the need to help Britain's emerging industrial sector. The manufacturers certainly welcomed the concessions granted under the new Charter. But essentially they represented a victory for the London and Indian agency house interests, led by their tireless champion, David Scott.[74] During the Charter negotiations of spring 1793, Scott and representatives of the London East India agency houses made several telling interventions which convinced Dundas that substantial concessions to the private trade interest were needed to curb their resort to the clandestine trade. Scott's memorials on the clandestine trade in March 1793 have already been mentioned, but he was not a lone voice among the London agency houses. In March a committee of London merchants representing clients in India stressed the dangers of the clandestine trade for British national interest, but they complained that many Indian merchants had no alternative but to use this channel because of the absence of a legitimate means of trade under the existing monopoly regulations. They repeated Scott's arguments, and were almost certainly working in collusion with him. Several partners in the London houses, Richard Muilman, William Thomas Raikes and Edmund Boehm, were the leading figures in the committee.[75] Early in April, as stockholders in the Company, all three of the firms represented by these men pressed their case in the Court of Proprietors.[76] These London and Indian interests proved more effective than their provincial counterparts for several reasons. Firstly, the fact that they were based in the City of London allowed them easier access to senior politicians and leading figures in the East India Company. Secondly, as proprietors in the Company, the London merchants were well placed to press their demands within its internal political and management structures as well as through direct exhortations to Dundas. These were no small advantages, given the enormous importance of the Company to the financial centre of London generally. They were strengthened further by David Scott's seat on the directorate of the Company, and his close relationship with Dundas. Effectively, Scott and the London private trade interest were insiders in the London establishment, able to exert influence at the very heart of the political structures which would decide the nature of the Company Charter. Finally, unlike the provincial interests, the London men seem to have presented a consistent and co-ordinated case, which was calculated to convince Dundas of the urgency and practicality of better provision for the non-Company private trade, without eliciting an excessively hostile response from the more conservative elements in the Company who opposed reform.

The fact of the matter was that although by 1793 significant commercial organisations with an interest in the Asian trade had grown up outside the East India Company, the dominant position enjoyed by the latter within the financial centre of the City of London ensured that any major assault on its privileges was almost certain to fail. This was regardless of the fact that the Company had been in serious financial trouble in the previous decades, and that the practices and behaviour of its servants had caused so much disquiet. As Bowen shows, the Company was still a very important source of wealth for influential and powerful men in the City and in the world of politics. This was a formidable barrier for any would-be reformer to overcome.[77] Moreover, as the ruler of an expanding empire in India, the Company was beginning to be seen by politicians and the public as an important agency of the British state, a perception reinforced by the assertion of state surveillance and control over the Company's political activities in the Acts of 1773 and 1784. Its complex machinery for collecting and recording information about India, and its army of experienced servants in London and in India, all affirmed the Company as the principal source of expertise in Indian affairs. By comparison, the credentials of provincial manufacturers with no experience of the east seemed poor. The great advantage of the London East India agency houses, and their leaders like Scott, was that they were insiders within the formidable citadel of knowledge and power which the Company still appeared to be in 1793. But there were limits to how far even they could go. At this stage of the Company's development, those who sought more space for non-Company men to make inroads into the Asian trade needed to work from within the Company and the political establishment in London. In addition, war with France in 1793 persuaded the government to err on the side of caution on the question of reform, and probably made the private traders and manufacturers less ambitious in their demands. For example, Dunlop, the Glasgow manufacturer, was prepared to postpone the Charter debate until after hostilities ceased.[78] But, as will be seen, the Napoleonic Wars of 1793 to 1815 would further undermine the status of the Company and create an opportunity for much more far-reaching reform than was possible in 1793.

Three

WAR, POLITICS AND INDIA: THE BATTLE FOR THE EAST INDIA COMPANY TRADE MONOPOLY, 1793–1813

THE REFORM of the Company's trading practices under the Charter Act of 1793 represented a limited but significant success for non-Company commercial interests in Britain and India. The requirement that the Company provide 3,000 tons for private trade was an important victory because it recognised certain rights for those interested in the trade to India who were outside the East India Company. At the time, however, the achievement was seen by supporters of the Company as a modest and pragmatic response to the specific problem of the clandestine trade, and as a sop to the incoherent demands of provincial manufacturers and merchants. The reality was that the Company monopolies of trade with India and China remained intact, and senior politicians still regarded the Company as the best instrument through which to conduct commerce and political relations with the east, albeit with the safeguard of state supervision. The Company remained a formidable political and economic power. It was still, notwithstanding its financial difficulties of the 1770s and 1780s, a central pillar of the City of London. A phalanx of MPs was closely connected to the Company, and could be called upon to defend its interests. This was a valuable asset in a period of political instability in which party loyalties were flimsy, and the votes of key interests frequently essential for the survival of governments. In the immediate aftermath of 1793, leaders and defenders of the Company were reasonably confident that non-Company commercial interests had been largely placated, and would remain amenable in the future.

Events were to prove this a mistaken perception. War in Europe and India, and the persistence of industrialists and private traders combined to undermine the Company's position. Ultimately, the result was a successful challenge to its monopoly of trade with India during the negotiations for the Charter Act of 1813. It was a dramatic fall from grace, and has been heralded by some historians as a victory for the growing power of non-Company commercial interests, especially the industrial capitalists of northern Britain, who lobbied assiduously during the period immediately before the Charter negotiations of 1812–1813.[1] This has led some historians to see the 1793 Charter as the thin end of a wedge, presaging the inevitable triumph of industrial interests over the forces of commercial monopoly.[2] In fact this view oversimplifies what was a very complex process, which was by no means an untrammelled victory for industrialism. As one historian aptly put its: 'no single causation theory appears viable'.[3] This chapter will explore the developments behind and reasons for the weakening of the Company's position, and the role of non-Company commercial interests in that process.

It is important to realise that government curbs on the Company's independence since the mid-1780s, and the reforms of the 1793 Act, angered some powerful vested interests in the Court of Proprietors, who were hostile to state interference and anything which threatened the Company's privileges. One such section was the 'old shipping interest', a group consisting of wealthy ship-owners, managers and captains who had enjoyed a virtual monopoly of the provision of shipping to the Company since the early eighteenth century. The Company did not own its own ships. Instead it hired them from a small number of wealthy ship-owners, who had ships for the India and China trades (the famous *East Indiamen*) built to unique specifications, and charged high rates of freight for their vessels. The rigours of the eastern trade meant that these ships usually needed to be replaced after only four voyages, and under a longstanding agreement the owner of a ship going out of the East India service had the right to provide its replacement, a practice referred to as 'the system of hereditary bottoms'.[4] Although the ship-owners were barred from membership of the directorate, they nonetheless maintained a formidable presence in that body through their allies and ciphers. They also organised their own pressure group, the Committee of Managing Owners, which lobbied the Company and the government. Effectively the ship-owners operated a kind of cartel within the Company, one which ensured that freight rates would be maximised through their oligopoly of the provision of shipping. Here was an example of a discrete commercial interest group in London which found supreme advantage in operating within and through the governing mechanisms of the East India Company and its privileges.

Of course, among the constellation of forces which brought about the Charter Act of 1793 were men who had broken into the provision of shipping for the Company. This 'new shipping' interest took advantage of the Company's increased demand for ships in the wake of the Commutation Act of 1784 which, by dramatically reducing import duties on tea, had facilitated a rapid growth in Company imports of the commodity from China.

Thus by the early 1790s, new shipping magnates, such as Brough and Fiott, were allying themselves with leaders of the private trade interest like David Scott, to challenge the privileges of the 'old shipping' interest, especially the high rates of freight they were able to command and the system of hereditary bottoms. For this alliance, the 1793 Act was but a first step in a more comprehensive challenge to the Company's monopolistic culture. Between 1793 and 1796, with the support of Scott and Dundas the new shipping interest pressed for reform of the shipping system. They demanded that the system of hereditary bottoms be replaced by open competition to supply new East India Company ships. They also wanted to end the sale of ship commands, which had enabled the old shipping interest to build a solid body of support among ships' captains.[5] By rallying the private trade interest and supporters of Dundas in the Court of Proprietors, the new shipping interest won the day early in March 1796. In fact Scott and others wanted to go further, by compelling the Company to admit smaller ships into the eastern trade than existing regulations allowed. Nonetheless, the reform seemed to offer bright prospects for those aiming to diminish still further the privileges of the Company. But in fact it helped to consolidate a faction around the old shipping interest within the Company, which would emerge as implacable and formidable opponents to further reform.

The outbreak of war with France in 1793 created problems for the Company's commercial operations, as French privateers attacked its shipping and the British country traders in south-east Asia and China. Yet, ironically, the volume of Company sales of Indian commodities in London increased by about a quarter between 1793 and 1800, as the war in Europe disrupted the supply of goods such as silk, and India emerged as an alternative source.[6] Unsurprisingly, Leadenhall Street sought to capitalise on this opportunity by increasing the size of the Investment of Indian commodities, by increasing its exports of bullion to India for increased purchases of locally produced goods.[7] But what should have been a boon to the Company's commercial fortunes was undermined by the outbreak of war in India. There were major conflicts with Tipu Sultan of Mysore in the late 1790s, and later against the Marathas between 1803 and 1806. These wars, and the need to increase the Company's military strength in India, pushed up its costs beyond all expectation. As a result, many of the resources intended to expand the Investment were actually used to finance military engagements and an aggressive policy of imperial expansion in India, especially under the Governor-Generalship of Lord Richard Wellesley between 1798 and 1805. To meet the exigencies of spiralling military costs and the need to fund the Investment, the Company had to borrow heavily, principally though the issue of government securities in India. The Company's debts soon escalated out of control. At the beginning of 1793, total Company debts in India were about £9 million.[8] By 1802 they had grown to £18 million and by 1808, a staggering £32 million.[9]

During the period 1810–1812, the Company was forced to borrow £4 million from the British government. This brought home to senior politicians that further reform was necessary, and it had an important influence over the outcome of the negotiations for the renewal of the Company's Charter in 1813.[10]

The deterioration of the Company's finances weakened it politically in its relations with the British state, and this was compounded by the growing importance and confidence of the agency houses in India and in London. The Charter Act of 1793, with its promised facility of 3,000 tons of shipping for non-Company private trade between Britain and India, had been welcomed by these merchant firms, but they were soon claiming that it was inadequate for their needs. In fact, take up of tonnage for export from Britain was initially very slow, use of the 3,000 ton limit only being reached in 1805. Non-Company traders were principally concerned, however, by the uptake of the tonnage from India, which was indeed quickly used up.[11] During the 1790s the Indian agency houses became central to the functioning of the Company's commercial system, and their leaders acquired considerable political influence. Singh shows that up till the early 1790s most agency houses confined themselves to agency acting on behalf of others on a commission basis. But during the 1790s they began to trade on their own behalf, and to branch out into banking, insurance and ship-owning.[12] Six of the houses emerged as wealthy and dominant players in Calcutta, exercising an increasing degree of influence in governing circles. These included Fairlie, Fergusson & Co., Paxton, Cockerell & Delisle (later Trail), Lambert & Ross, Colvin & Bazett and Joseph Barretto.[13] It can be difficult to trace the development of individual agency houses over time because the names of firms changed to reflect the admission of new partners to replace retiring ones. For example, the firm of Paxton, Cockerell & Delisle in 1790, evolved through several partnership changes to become John Palmer & Co. by 1810.[14] Palmer's career embodied the spectacular rise of the agency house men during this period. In 1791 he was the unemployed son of General William Palmer, a former aide of Governor-General Warren Hastings and diplomat at the Courts of Lucknow and the Maratha confederacy.[15] By 1793 he had secured a partnership in the Calcutta agency house of Burgh & Barber, which in 1801 merged with Paxton, Cockerell & Trail, then one of the major agency houses in Calcutta. By the mid-1810s, John Palmer had been dubbed 'the prince of merchants' by the then Governor-General, Francis Rawdon, Marquis of Hastings.[16] Palmer enjoyed business connections all over India, as well as in Canton, London, Batavia and even the USA. As early as the 1790s, the agency houses in Calcutta and the other presidencies were emerging as a political force to be reckoned with. The decade in particular saw a steep growth in their exports of opium to China, consolidating their pivotal role in the East India Company's commercial system in east Asia.[17] Their links with their 'sister houses' in London even extended their political reach to the Court of Directors and the India Board.

The agency houses quickly took full advantage of the 3,000 tonnage allocated for private trade aboard the East India Company's ships bound for Britain from India. From 1793, the Company's Board of Trade in Calcutta was inundated with applications from agency houses to send home cargoes on their and their clients' accounts.[18] The latter included a range of individuals and commercial firms who used the agency houses as intermediaries to export their produce to Britain. In April and June 1796, for example, the agency house of Barber & Palmer applied for space to export indigo, bandanas and sugar belonging to the firm of Hamilton & Aberdein.[19] In the same period they also exported substantial amounts of indigo for a Mr Cheap, an indigo producer.[20] Other firms represented by Barber & Palmer included Mercer & Co., a leading indigo producer and dealer until its demise in the late 1820s. They also shipped for Nason, Tod & Co., another major indigo firm.[21] In December 1797, Cockerell & Trail exported 11 tons of cloth to the Cape aboard a Company vessel for the firm of Pringle & Quieros.[22] Prinsep & Saunders was another of their frequent clients.[23] In respect of the private trade, the agency houses did not merely speak for their own interests, they legitimately claimed to represent the wider European commercial communities in India. This undoubtedly lent weight to their efforts to liberalise trade. In addition, some prominent Company officials profited directly from the new facility. In 1798, Barber & Palmer made a number of shipments to England on behalf of Sir John Shore, the Governor-General. In January they requested space for a shipment of rice on his account.[24] In February they asked for a ton of space for further cargoes, and additional provision for six pipes of Madeira wine.[25] Shore's successor, Richard Wellesley, also exported madeira through the offices of Barber & Palmer.[26] Both Shore and Wellesley have been identified as sympathetic to the demands of the private merchants.[27] In Shore's case this has been seen as arising from his loyalty to Dundas and Scott, strong promoters of the private trade cause. For Wellesley, it was more a product of an ideological leaning towards the private traders, and a desire to alleviate the difficulties for trade caused by war in India. But it is also clear that these men benefited personally from the private trade. How far this influenced their leanings towards the interests of the agency houses, one can only speculate.

Certainly the supporters of the private trade interest were soon dissatisfied with the concessions of 1793. Many merchants in India had anticipated much more for the private trade from the Charter Act, some even anticipating that their own Indian-built ships would be admitted into the trade with Britain. Several merchants had even increased their investment in shipbuilding in anticipation of such a concession. As a result, almost from the moment that news of the Charter reached India, the agency houses and their allies were pressing for further concessions, most notably the admission of Indian-built ships into the trade with Britain. Various schemes were suggested, the most popular being that the Company should hire Indian-built ships for their own trade and for re-letting to private merchants, who would be permitted to trade with Britain on their own terms.[28] Other complaints were voiced about Company privileges in India, notably its monopolies of the production of salt and opium.[29] At first, Shore resisted these overtures, especially pressure from the firm of Lambert & Ross, which wanted the Company to hire its ship the *Lachmi*.[30] But the situation in Europe was extremely volatile. Indeed the high price for Indian produce in Europe, induced in part by the uncertainties of war, was one of the reasons for the clamour of the Bengal agency houses for further concessions. East India Company ships were being requisitioned for service with the Royal Navy at the same time that the Company needed to increase the Investment of goods it imported from India. To alleviate the resulting shortage of ships, in 1795 the Court of Directors gave Shore permission to hire several private Indian-built ships to carry Company goods to Britain, and to carry private goods, all at freight rates lower than normally charged by the Company. Two ships, the *Warren Hastings* and the *Caledonia*, were among those hired, and the principal beneficiaries were the Calcutta agency houses of Fairlie, Fergusson & Co. and Lambert & Ross.[31] The concession was only ever intended to be a 'one-off' arrangement to meet an unusual emergency, but from the agency houses' point of view it had established an important precedent which it was clearly in their interest to exploit. It was, for them, the thin end of a wedge – a perspective shared, but from the opposite point of view, by the 'old shipping interest' in London. The scene was set for a major confrontation in the years which followed.

The problem for the agency houses was that within the Company the balance of power in the Courts of Directors and Proprietors began to shift decidedly towards the old shipping interest. In the early years after the passage of the Charter Act of 1793, the network of allies which Dundas had built up within the Company offered the prospect of reform remaining in the ascendancy, an impression which seemed to be confirmed by the early successes of the new shipping interest in the three years following the Act. David Scott's installation as Chairman in 1796 also seemed to bode well for those interests committed to diminishing the Company's privileges. But already developments were afoot which favoured a revival of conservative fortunes. The war against France in particular stemmed the tide of reform. Suddenly aware of the need for the co-operation of the Company both to supply ships to the Royal Navy and to help resist French power in the east in what was becoming a global conflict, the British government was reluctant to compromise its relationship with the East India Company by further reforms which might antagonise key groups like the London ship-owners and shipbuilders. Furthermore, from 1794 Dundas, who had been the main promoter of reform, became increasingly preoccupied with his new role as Pitt's War Secretary. This inevitably limited his involvement in Company affairs.[32] As the battle between reformers and conservatives within the Company unfolded during the period 1795–1805, the latter were assisted by political changes at Westminster. The government fell suddenly and unexpectedly in February 1801 over Catholic emancipation and Ireland, and Pitt was replaced by Addington, whose extraordinary difficulties in forming an administration further weakened the ability of ministers to assert themselves over the Company. Crucially, Addington found himself having to appease a coterie of MPs in the House who represented the interests of the East India Company. He was thus in no position to adopt the robust stance of his predecessor's administration in East Indian affairs. In addition, the old shipping interest and those eager to defend the Company's monopoly were quick to counter allegations that they were concerned primarily with their own sectional concerns rather than the welfare of the Company with some accusations of their own. They had noted that Dundas's chief ally on the directorate, David Scott, was just as vulnerable to the claim that he put his own interests before the Company's. As the head of David Scott & Co. in London, there was a potential conflict of interest between his agency house role and his position as a senior director of the East India Company. In 1794 the opponents of reform forced through a ruling that no director be allowed to engage in trade with India on either his own account or as an agent. This compelled Scott to hand over control of his London house to others associated with the firm, in the name of his young son.[33] But this separation of Scott from his house was vulnerable to the accusation that this was a mere technicality, that in fact Scott senior remained the real leader of the firm. A campaign of rumours was conducted against Scott until 1799, when a much more serious attempt was made to destroy him with the accusation that he was engaged in a range of illegal trading activities. Early in February, Jacob Bosanquet, then Chair of the Court of Directors and closely connected with merchants in the City of London and the old shipping interest, claimed that Scott had supplied goods on the ship *Helsingoer* to refit French privateers operating out of the Philippines, through his firm's connections with the Copenhagen firm of Dunzfeldt & Company. Bosanquet was accusing Scott of treason as well as engagement in illicit trade. Scott defeated these allegations in an acrimonious and lively debate in the General Court of Proprietors in March 1799, by demonstrating that he had not been personally involved in David Scott & Co. since renouncing his position, and that the London firm were unaware of the intentions of Duntzfeldt & Co. in respect of the goods supplied to them.[34] But the potential for all kinds of mischief by the agency houses against both the Company and the national interest had been revealed to all involved in Company affairs. While Scott survived and secured personal exoneration, the engagement of his former firm in apparently illicit trade dealings with a Danish firm had been proven. As a result, the London and

Indian agency houses now appeared to be just as self-interested as those, such as the old shipping interest, against whom they had levelled that very same allegation. The case had cost the promoters of free trade their command of the moral high ground. These factors greatly assisted the old shipping interest and other opponents of the private trade and new shipping lobbies.

Nonetheless, in the mid-1790s, the private trade interest remained confident of victory. The presence of Dundas, albeit distracted by the war, and the sympathy of some key Company officials in Bengal sustained the resolution of the Indian agency houses and their allied organisations in London. The appointment in 1798 of Richard Wellesley as Governor-General certainly promised to help. Wellesley combined an aggressive policy of imperial expansionism with a growing conviction of the benefits of free trade. As the Earl of Mornington, Wellesley had served on the Board of Control since 1793 and had been strongly influenced by the trade liberalising sympathies of Dundas, Pitt and David Scott.[35] He was inclined to side with the agency houses whenever he could, especially in loosening the Company's grip on trade between India and Britain. Wellesley was particularly receptive to the claim of the private traders that the Company's monopoly merely fuelled the clandestine trade to the benefit of Britain's rivals. Throughout his Governor-Generalship he spoke consistently for the private trade interest and for trade liberalisation, a stance which won him the enduring hostility of the Company's conservative interests.

Inevitably, it was the question of the limited opportunities for the Indian agency houses to export their goods and remit their capital to Britain which provided the battleground for the two sides. The difficulty for the agency houses was not merely that tonnage aboard Company ships for their goods was restricted to 3,000 tons; it was also that the freight rates charged by the Company (£35 per ton on average) were also cripplingly expensive compared to those of foreign ships. The Americans and other neutrals not involved in the war with France, unencumbered with the need to travel in convoy or the burden of wartime rates of insurance, could freight at about £20 per ton.[36] The problem was compounded by a deepening financial crisis in the Company's affairs. Ever since the start of the war, the Company had been trying to increase the quantity of Indian goods it shipped home as part of the annual Investment. This was in response to a surge in the European price of Indian silks, cottons and other commodities, brought about by the uncertainties created by the European conflict. In fact the Company did increase the value of Indian goods sold in London by £2,301,465 between 1793 and 1800, an increase of 36%.[37] But the general costs of running the Company's Indian empire began to spiral out of control during this period. War in India, particularly against Mysore, swallowed up any surplus revenues available for the purchase of Indian goods for export to Britain. To compensate for this, between March 1798 and March 1800 the Court of Directors sanctioned the export of about £2.5 million in bullion to pay for Indian produce.[38] But this too was swallowed up in the heavy expenses of Wellesley's expansionist policy in India: having defeated Tipu Sultan of Mysore, he now began to prepare for war against the Marathas. The high expense of insuring shipping added to these increased costs. Consequently by 1799–1800 the Company was simply unable to fill its own ships with Indian produce. The Indian agency houses, desperate for shipping space for their own goods, were enraged by the situation, and most had no alternative but to use the illegal clandestine trade to conduct their business. As a result, by 1799–1800, the clandestine trade again flourished, with the volume of foreign traders visiting Calcutta doubling compared to the previous year.[39]

The loss of trade to rival European powers and the general crisis in Company affairs worried Dundas and Pitt, and matters came to a head in the years 1798–1800. The agency houses and their allies in India and London campaigned for the right to export Indian produce on their own, Indian-built ships, effectively a permanent adoption of the temporary arrangement of 1795. Some supporters of private trade went further in their demands. In March 1799, John Cochrane, that champion of the private trade interest and an active member of the Court of Proprietors, warned Dundas that on a recent visit to Leadenhall Street he had discovered both a deep hostility to the private trade interest, and also a plot to incriminate some of the leading agency house merchants allegedly involved in the clandestine trade.[40] Cochrane outlined the split in the Court of Directors between Scott and his pro-private trade allies, and the more conservative elements, led by the old shipping interest. He accused the latter of seeking 'to crush and ruin the free merchant in India, whom they erroneously considered as their adversary and opponent'.[41] Cochrane wanted an end to the India monopoly, restricting the Company's privileges to the China trade alone.[42] In May 1799, a memorial was issued by the Exeter cloth merchants who had clamoured for the assistance of the Company in exporting long ells to the east in the early 1790s. This time they rejected the 1793 Charter as inadequate for their needs and called for the opening of the India trade.[43] In July, John Prinsep, a proprietor who had built his reputation and fortune in the indigo trade in India, argued in the Court of Proprietors for shipping space for the private trade, to prevent its commerce falling into the clandestine trade.[44] He repeated these pleas in October to Stephen Lushington, then Chairman of the Court of Directors.[45] But the effective leader of the private trade interest in London, David Scott, had targeted his efforts on persuading the Court of Directors to increase the tonnage available for the Indian agency houses to export their Indian produce, by permitting the authorities in India to hire Indian-built ships and then re-let them to merchant firms for the purposes of private export. Scott had stipulated that the ships should be re-hired only at the Company's rate of freight, a proviso which persuaded the Court of Directors to cautiously adopt this policy in May 1798.[16] The trouble was that, in Calcutta, Wellesley had also been on the receiving end of pressure from the agency houses to allow them to export to Britain on their own ships. In light of the fact that the escalating costs of his military operations left Wellesley with little cash to fund the Investment, and following his own leanings towards free trade, he reasoned in autumn 1798 that the only way to ensure that stocks of Indian produce piling up in India did not find their way into the holds of foreign ships was to allow the merchants in India to ship home aboard their own vessels. Thus far Wellesley's calculations mirrored those of Scott in the latter's efforts to persuade the Court of Directors to admit Indian-built ships. But there was one important difference. Whereas Scott stipulated that the Company rates of freight should be applied to Indian-built vessels, Wellesley allowed the owners of the Indian ships to set their own rates of freight, which were significantly lower than the Company's.[17]

News of what Wellesley had done reached London in March 1799, just when the allegations of illicit trade and treason against Scott were being debated in the Court of Proprietors. It inevitably inflamed the hostility between the old shipping and private trade interests, and hardened the attitude of the former against Wellesley's measures, which they saw as yet another sinister attempt to undermine the Company's privileges. After heated debate in the Court of Directors, Wellesley was instructed to adhere strictly to the terms of Scott's original plan for the use of Indian-built shipping. The reversal prompted complaints from agency houses in India, who now claimed that Scott's plan was too bureaucratic and expensive for the private merchant.[18] Dundas and Scott did not surrender on the issue, and in April 1800 Dundas again tried to move the Court of Directors to accept Wellesley's aborted arrangement of 1798, on the basis of the continuing size of the clandestine trade. He stressed that the arrangement would be temporary, and that it did not represent a threat to the Company's privileges in the long run. Meanwhile in India, ongoing financial difficulties persuaded Wellesley to defy his orders from the Court and to enlist a number of Indian-built ships to carry home part of the Company's Investment as well as private cargoes, on the terms he had introduced in 1798. By this time, the agency houses had become vitally important for Wellesley's administration and his expansionist policies. They provided loans and acted as provisioning agents for the Company's Indian army. In return, Wellesley was very much inclined to support them on the question of Indian shipping and better access to the British market.[19] By the summer of 1800, the agency house and private trade interest in India and London seemed to have firm grounds for optimism about their cause.

But this was an illusion. In fact, the balance of opinion within the Courts of Proprietors and Directors was swinging back in favour of the defenders of the Company's privileges. Wellesley's defiance of instructions from the Company, and the willingness of Dundas and his allies to indulge this disregard for the Court of Directors' wishes, helped trigger a backlash against the supporters of reform. Two key figures emerged as leaders of this conservative rearguard. Jacob Bosanquet II came from a wealthy London merchant family of German, Huguenot stock. His grandfather, Jacob I, had built a large fortune and considerable political influence within the City, and both his son Richard, and grandson Jacob, had risen to prominence in the Company directorate.[50] Jacob II had been an outspoken defender of the old shipping interest and the Company's monopoly since the mid-1790s, and he used his influence within the City to rally a wide range of London financiers and merchants behind him. By 1800, this was already beginning to turn the tide against the private trade interest within the Company's governing institutions.

The other major conservative figure was Charles Grant, a Scot who had served the Company in India and, following his return to Britain in 1790, initially supported Dundas, Pitt and the free trade interest.[51] With Dundas's support he entered the directorate in 1793, and for a time remained loyal to his patrons, but in 1798 he underwent a major change of conviction. While some historians see Grant's defection to the pro-monopoly and anti-reform faction as motivated by careerist opportunism, based on a calculation that the balance of power within the Company was swinging against the forces of liberalisation, Grant's devout evangelical Christianity was probably a more crucial factor.[52] Porter shows that Grant believed that the conversion of the Indian population to Christianity was the only way to make British rule in India permanently secure. By the late 1790s, he believed that only the East India Company possessed the organisation and political clout necessary to implement such a policy, and that consequently the preservation of its economic power and its commercial monopoly were essential prerequisites for it to be achieved.[53] Grant quickly became a most eloquent intellectual defender of the benefits of monopoly. He argued that the extent of the clandestine trade had been exaggerated, and that a loosening of the Company's control over the movement of goods, capital and people to India would inevitably lead to the colonisation of India by the British, to the detriment of the Indian population.

Bosanquet and Grant rallied supporters in the Courts of Directors and Proprietors against Dundas, Scott and Wellesley, and the 'Trojan Horse' of Indian-built shipping. The outcome was that, in 1800, the Court of Directors set up a special Select Committee to consider the question of Indian-built shipping, the clandestine trade and other aspects of the management of commercial relations with India. Grant, with Bosanquet's and the conservative lobby's support, became the mouthpiece for the committee, writing two reports which responded to Dundas on the question of Indian-built ships. In essence these asserted that the problem of providing a channel of export to Britain for the goods of private traders was caused by wartime disruptions of commerce combined with excessive speculation by the agency houses in such items as indigo. As such, it was a temporary phenomenon which would resolve itself in due course. Grant claimed that the size of the clandestine trade had been overestimated by the private trade interest, a calculated swipe at David Scott, who was still a prominent figure in the Court of Directors. Wellesley was fiercely criticised for his unilateral admittance of Indian-built shipping on terms not approved by the Court of Directors in London.[51] But the committee did offer one concession. In spite of its view that the size of the clandestine trade had been exaggerated, it proposed that the Company should provide additional shipping over and above the 3,000 tons allotted for the private trade, at a lower rate of freight than usual, to deal with any existing glut of private goods in India. But Indian ships were only ever again to be admitted into the trade in circumstances where the Company's additional supply of ships was demonstrably inadequate.

The committee's proposals became the subject of prolonged debate, culminating in their official acceptance by the Court of Proprietors in June 1801. The London agency houses and their allies did their best to refute the committee's findings and recommendations, and held out for the admittance on a permanent basis of Indian-built ships for the export of their goods. The most eloquent critic of the committee was Thomas Henchman, who published a pamphlet refuting the claims of the reports, particularly what he saw as a gross underestimation of the size of the clandestine trade.[55] But matters really came to a head at the end of May 1801, when the Court of Proprietors began to debate the committee's proposals. On 28 May, a memorial signed by forty-three proprietors, which included prominent London agency house men such as Charles Cockerell, William Lennox, Charles Lambert and Edmund Boehm, as well as sympathisers such as Henchman, was submitted to the Court of Proprietors, calling for the question to be referred to a committee of the 'great and the good', comprised principally of former Governors-General of India.[56] They also subsequently demanded a ballot on this proposal when it was rejected by the Court. The nature of the proposal itself, which was essentially a stalling tactic to play for time, suggests that the agency house men had little confidence that they could win by pressing for outright rejection of the committee's recommendations. Certainly the conservatives in the directorate now felt that they held the whip hand. On 1 June 1801, they issued a printed letter to the proprietors condemning the idea of consultation with previous Governors-General as 'invidious' to the men themselves and insulting to the Courts of Directors and Proprietors.[57] They accused the agency house petitioners of being motivated entirely by their own self-interest. Constrained by the convention of collective responsibility, even David Scott, who had been Chair of the Court of Directors since April 1801, felt compelled to sign the letter. Ominously, the proprietors supported the committee's recommendations and rejected the overtures of the agency house interest. It was an important turning point.

*

The private trade interest appealed to the Board of Control, and even raised the issue of Indian-built shipping in Parliament in June 1801. But the political climate had shifted decisively against them.[58] Pitt's government had fallen in February 1801 over disagreements with the king about Catholic emancipation and Ireland. Addington had managed to form a ministry, but with huge difficulties in assembling sufficient support in the Commons. Philips suggests that this amplified the power of the East India Company's MPs, and therefore made the new administration reluctant to challenge the Company on the issue of Indian-built shipping.[59] As the summer of 1801 progressed, the conservatives in the directorate consolidated their position and, in August, a demoralised David Scott resigned the Chair. Briefly it appeared that the private trade interest had found an ally in the new President of the Board of Control, Lord Dartmouth, who was influenced by Dundas and Scott. But, in November, Addington undercut him and accepted the Court of Directors' position on Indian-built shipping, forcing Dartmouth to resign, eventually to be replaced by Castlereagh, an ambitious politician who had learned that it was inexpedient at present to challenge the conservatives who now dominated the Company. The victory of the old shipping interest and the conservatives was embodied in an agreement about revised provisions for private trade between the Directors and the government on 17 November 1801. In essence, this allowed for an extra 5,000 tons of shipping for the private trade, aboard vessels built for the Company in England or India, but with the proviso that after 1 April 1803 the use of Indian-built ships would cease.[60] Wellesley, who had been identified by the conservatives as the Company's mortal enemy as a result of the private trade question (and also the high expense of his expansionist policies) struggled on as Governor-General for several more years, constantly at loggerheads with his masters in London, before he was eventually forced from office in 1805.

The frustration of the agency houses of India and London in 1801 had a profound effect on their subsequent behaviour and political strategies. Their disappointment was deep and the defeat of their efforts came as a shock after they had enjoyed the initiative for so long. The material costs were very heavy for some, especially those in India who had speculated in shipbuilding on the assumption that Wellesley's efforts to engage Indian-built ships on a permanent basis would be successful. In 1803, the Calcutta shipbuilder Henry Archer lamented the parlous state into which the industry had fallen since the Company's ruling on Indian-built shipping, and expressed his anger at the 'duplicity' of the Court of Directors in the harshest terms.[61] The leadership of Scott and the sympathetic disposition of such figures as Dundas and Wellesley had led many of the agency house men, in London and India, to believe that they could liberalise the trade between India and Britain by working almost solely through the Company's internal structures.

The concessions secured in 1793 were a direct result of this approach, and the meteoric rise of prominent agency house men like David Scott within the Company, bolstered by support from a faction among the proprietors and the Company's own servants, seemed to attest to its effectiveness. But the defeat of 1801 suggested that this would not be enough to secure further concessions. Other, more powerful interests had proven themselves to be more than a match for the parvenu agency houses in a contest confined to the Company's own structures of power. The sympathy of government ministers, which had been so evident under Pitt and Dundas, was less forthcoming from Addington's administration because of its weakness in the Commons and its vulnerability to the anger of the Company's parliamentary supporters. Many agency house merchants in India and London began to recognise that they needed to organise themselves more effectively outside as well as inside the Company. They needed to win wider support from politicians and public opinion to supplement their continuing complex and arcane struggle within Leadenhall Street. In 1803, E. Watts of the Madras agency house of Harrington & Co. advocated closer political co-operation between the agency houses at the three Indian presidencies, a suggestion which met the Calcutta shipbuilder Henry Archer's hearty approval.[62] In this respect the legacy of 1801 was to impress upon the agency houses and their London allies the need for much closer co-ordination of their efforts. An example came in November 1807, when nineteen Calcutta agency houses petitioned the Court of Directors in protest against a reported increase in Company freight rates from £14 to £22 15s a ton.[63] But in the aftermath of the reassertion of the power of the old shipping interest and their allies such appeals carried little weight. There would need to be a political sea-change before the agency houses and others seeking to weaken the Company's privileges could hope to succeed.

In fact, the global conflicts of 1793–1815 did eventually bring about a shift in political attitudes towards the Company. In part this arose out of the deteriorating state of Company finances caused by Wellesley's aggressive forward policy in India. As shown, between 1793 and 1808 the size of the Company's debt more than trebled. By the end of the first decade of the nineteenth century, the Company's claim that its privileges were being managed effectively and that its financial position was fundamentally sound had lost all credibility. On several occasions it had to petition the government for financial aid, and between 1807 and 1812 the Company borrowed £6 million through bond issues.[64] The urgent need to borrow stemmed from the spiralling cost of the expanding Indian empire, the consequent growth in Indian government debt, and a variety of schemes to transfer these to Britain.[65] By 1808, the Company's plight was so severe that a Select Committee of the House of Commons was appointed to investigate its financial affairs. Its work was long and gruelling, and the committee produced four reports between 1808 and 1812. Whilst these stopped short of condemning the Company's handling of its commercial affairs, they all highlighted the central problem of the Indian debt. The demands of war also exacerbated the financial burdens on the Company during this period. In 1808, the island of Mauritius was seized from the French, and added to the costs of the expedition were the expenses of administering the island. Then, in 1811, Governor-General Minto ordered the costly occupation of the Dutch possession of Java to prevent it falling into French hands. The upshot was that by the time discussions began for the renewal of the Company's Charter (due in 1813), the prevailing political mood was one in which some loss of privilege by the Company seemed inevitable to most observers outside the Company itself.

The last few years before the scheduled renewal of the Charter saw a number of developments which contributed further to the new mood. If the Company's affairs and commerce seemed in disarray, the private trade and the agency houses offered a picture of rude health. Since 1793, the exports of Indian commodities via the privilege trade grew dramatically, doubling in the eight years after 1803.[66] All in all, between 1793 and 1809 the total value of the privilege trade from India exceeded £21 million.[67] It seemed at last that there were others beyond the Company who were now sufficiently competent to be entrusted with the trade to India. Furthermore, British economic fortunes became critical in the period 1808–1812, as the commercial problems caused by the European war were exacerbated by rapidly deteriorating relations with the USA. The roots of the latter conflict lay in the spread of warfare between Britain and France to the economic sphere. Napoleon's military successes delivered into his control large tracts of continental Europe, with which the British had enjoyed a flourishing export trade in manufactures and colonial produce such as sugar. To counteract British economic might, in 1806 Napoleon had issued the Berlin-Milan Decrees, which imposed an embargo on all continental trade with Britain, effectively an economic blockade. French successes later in the decade, particularly in Holland and northern Germany, dramatically increased the effectiveness of this strategy, and helped to precipitate a serious crisis in the British economy. Britain experienced rising unemployment and accelerating inflation. The British government responded by issuing the Order in Council of November 1807, which forbade all French commerce with the United Kingdom, and also imposed tough regulations on French trade with neutral powers. These required that all neutrals trading with the French be routed via British ports, and that they pay substantial taxes for the privilege of engaging in trade with territories under the control of the enemy. It was a provision which hit directly at the then flourishing American trade with continental Europe, exciting bitter resentment in the USA and prompting retaliatory measures against the British, including the Non-Intercourse Law of 1809, which forbade direct trade between America and Britain.[68] In both Birmingham and Liverpool there were major agitations against the Orders in Council, so important had the trade with the USA become by this time. By 1806 the USA was the second largest market for British exports, the value of which reached a peak in that year of over £8 million.[69]

Ultimately the trade dispute with the USA led to the war of 1812, but indirectly it also influenced the outcome of the debate about the renewal of the East India Company's Charter, by deepening the already serious crisis which beset Britain in the period 1810–1813. These were desperate years indeed. Virtually all the major industrial cities saw unemployment, hunger and rumblings of political discontent. In 1810, in Birmingham, a number of firms trading to South America failed, causing much distress and political anxiety.[70] In Liverpool, the Orders in Council came at a time when there was already severe concern about the likely consequences of the 1807 abolition of the slave trade, worries which seemed confirmed in 1811 by a rash of failures of smaller firms engaged in the American trade.[71] Furthermore, these were years of serious disorder in the industrial regions generally, with the violent resistance of the Luddites to the introduction of new technologies in the Nottinghamshire stocking industry and the Yorkshire woollen cloth industry. Industrialisation was changing the face of British society profoundly, creating fast-growing urban areas in which industrial workers' distress and discontent translated quickly into politically dangerous strikes, protests and violence. In this context, high food prices, extreme fluctuations in the economy and general uncertainty about the future all helped create a political climate of volatility and fear. Memories of the French Revolution of 1789 were still fresh, and the Tory governments of Spencer Perceval and Lord Liverpool were much exercised by how to prevent internal economic and political collapse. One consequence was a significant change in government priorities in economic affairs, and shifts in policies to meet new objectives. Cookson describes how the severity of wartime economic and political crises prompted a shift away from defending the interests of large privileged trading corporations like the East India Company, towards meeting the needs of British industry, including new markets, affordable labour and cheap raw materials.[72] This reorientation of policy was also prompted by the emergence of vociferous organisations representing British manufacturers on such questions as the Orders in Council and, in the years immediately before 1813, the East India Company's monopoly. Cookson shows how this shaped what came to be known as 'Liberal Toryism', a political strategy associated with Lord Liverpool's administration, but which was already emerging under Perceval. Under this, the government sought compromise solutions for conflicts within society over such issues as manufacturers' demands for freer trade, and an end to the protectionism of well established interest groups such as the East India Company and the landed interest. This meant resorting to free market solutions, or a version of them, to appease strong pressure groups in areas of particularly acute political sensitivity, as manufacturing industry had become by the latter years of the war.[73]

Given the dire position of East India Company finances, and the Company's dependence upon government loans, it is therefore unsurprising that when initial discussion of the renewal of the Charter took place in November 1811 between the President of the Board of Control, Lord Melville (Robert Dundas, son of Henry), and Jacob Bosanquet and John Inglis, the Chairs of the Court of Directors, it quickly became apparent that the government's view was that the export trade to India should be thrown open.[74] Added to the Company's financial weakness was deepening government concern about trouble in the manufacturing districts and a growing awareness that manufacturers and merchants in Liverpool, Birmingham, Glasgow and Bristol were mobilising local opinion in favour of opening the Indian trade. Compared with the provincial agitation which preceded the 1793 Act, the movement of 1811–1813 was much more formidable. Whereas the provincial petitions of the early 1790s had been isolated efforts by the merchants and manufacturers of separate cities, demanding different and frequently contradictory concessions, the agitation which was unleashed in the spring of 1812 was much more carefully planned and co-ordinated. In fact, collaborative efforts by the leaders of the various provincial cities had been going on for a number of years, assisted by such rising political stars as Henry Brougham, the barrister and aspiring radical Whig politician. Brougham became an early champion of free trade and a vocal campaigner against the Orders in Council and the East India Company's trading privileges. He also assiduously cultivated some of the emerging leaders of the merchant and manufacturing classes in the provinces. As early as December 1808, Brougham was advising the prominent Liverpool merchant, William Roscoe, that the financial difficulties of the Company and its dependence upon government loans could be turned into 'a favourable opportunity for attacking the Company on several grounds'.[75] The abolition of the slave trade had created potentially acute problems for the Liverpool merchants, and an opening of the East Indian trade was seen as one way of compensating those in the city who had suffered because of it. In April 1807, another leading Liverpool merchant, William Rathbone, stressed the importance of this to Roscoe, who had been a supporter of abolition, and thus likely to incur the wrath of those who had been hurt by abolition.[76] A year later, like Brougham, Rathbone also cited the financial predicament of the Company as providing an ideal chance to challenge its trading privileges.[77] Like Brougham, Rathbone had been speaking to like-minded people in other cities, notably London and Bristol. As the question of Charter renewal loomed on the horizon in February 1810, Brougham urged Roscoe to not only organise in his own city, but also to reach out to his counterparts in other provincial cities when drawing up petitions against the renewal of the Company's privileges:

Now the importance of an opposition by petitions of evidence needs not be pointed out. In fact it is the only effectual way of giving weight to a cause against which the ministry musters its strength. I do therefore urge you to destroy the Company (for you may do it) by this fair and prudent method. A petition to be heard by evidence cannot be refused – and such a petition coming from Liverpool would proceed from the proper quarter. If joined by Bristol, Glasgow and Cork it would be decisive.[78]

Brougham also cultivated links with industrial leaders in other cities, promoting opposition to both the Orders in Council and renewal of the Company's privileges. His connections with Thomas Attwood and Richard Spooner in Birmingham were especially close.[79] As a result of all this activity, by the time the Charter question came to the fore early in 1812 the provincial merchants were ready to unleash a co-ordinated campaign of lobbying through petitions and deputations to the capital. In several of the major provincial cities, large public meetings were attended by the great and the good from the local commercial community. There was a general meeting of merchants and industrialists in Birmingham on 4 March 1812, led by Attwood and Spooner.[80] Attwood was already acting as something of an unofficial co-ordinator of activity, and he urged his counterparts in both Bristol and Glasgow to encourage the smaller towns around those cities to join in the campaign.[81] Glasgow held their meeting on 23 March, and the same month saw a gathering of forces in Liverpool, Bristol, Hull, Plymouth and Sheffield. Early in April, deputations from all of these cities converged on London, and prepared to negotiate with government for free trade to the east and the effective end of the Company's commercial privileges. In fact, the aims of the different city delegations varied considerably. While for Glasgow, Liverpool and Birmingham the primary concern was with opening the east for the export of British manufactures, Hull, Bristol and Plymouth wanted a share of the import trade and to challenge London's dominance of shipping involved in the eastern trade.[82] Neither were the various deputations particularly knowledgeable about the realities of trade with, and conditions in, the east, a fact exposed by some of their testimonies to the parliamentary Select Committees set up to consider the Orders in Council and the Charter question in 1812–1813.[83] The real success of the agitation during this period lay in the maintenance, regardless of these differences, of a coherent and consistent line on key points such as the need to open both the import and export trade. What made this possible was the development of effective channels of communication between the various cities and deputations.

The eruption of the provincial campaigns certainly had an immediate impact, though not on the question of the opening of the export trade to India, which had effectively been conceded by the Company in private during their negotiations with Melville and the Board of Control between November 1811 and March 1812. Melville and the Company Chairs had reached a tentative agreement on 21 March that the import trade would be opened to non-Company merchants, but restricted to the port of London.[84] But there then followed a dramatic change of government policy. A Cabinet reshuffle in early April saw Melville moved to the Admiralty to make way for the Earl of Buckinghamshire at the Board of Control. Buckinghamshire had been a much criticised Governor of Madras in the 1790s, and was certainly an embittered critic of his former employers.[85] He lost no time in announcing that, after all, the import trade from India would be opened to the provincial ports.[86] This decision galvanised a number of London merchants into action, who thus far, because of the indications that London would be granted an effective geographical monopoly of the import trade, had found little reason to engage in direct political lobbying. On 21 April, Thomas Brown, representing London buyers of Indian piece goods, argued in a letter to the Chairs of the East India Company against the opening of the import of Indian cotton goods to ports outside London. His questionable case was that Indian cotton manufactures would prove damagingly competitive to the cotton textiles produced in provincial Britain. The letter was signed by a number of prominent men involved in the trade, including George Ranking, James Cazenove and Thomas Wilson.[87] A day earlier, a different group of London businessmen had met, consisting of merchants and manufacturers engaged in the export trade to India. Chaired by John Atkins, Alderman of the City of London, these men petitioned Parliament, arguing that the Indian and Chinese markets were simply too small to absorb additional imports from the British outports, and that the effect of opening the export trade to the east would be to ruin, through excessive competition, those merchants and manufacturers in the capital who had developed expertise in making and exporting those commodities demanded by the eastern markets.[88] On 25 April, Thomas Brown wrote to Spencer Perceval, the Prime Minister, deploying a number of arguments against opening the import trade from the east to the provinces. He claimed that the collection of customs duties would be endangered by allowing the outports into the import trade, and that working class unrest in the provinces would erupt once cotton operatives learned that they would soon be faced by competition from imported Indian cotton textiles.[89] Philips describes how from April 1812 there was a concerted effort to mobilise the capital against the opening of the Indian and China trades. The Common Council of the Guildhall and the East India Company united in a pamphlet campaign to resist the efforts of the outports to liberalise the East India trade.[90]

But the governments of both Perceval and his successor Lord Liverpool were adamant that the trade of India at least would be thrown open to the British provinces. Whereas in 1793 the arguments of the Company and their allies in the capital had been sufficient to contain the demands of outsiders for a freer trade regime, in 1812/13 the tide had moved decisively in favour of challengers to the Company's privileges. Three developments had brought about this shift towards a more pluralistic strategy for the protection of Britain's eastern empire and its economic fortunes. First, by 1813 the state of manufacturing industry in the British provinces was much more prominent in the concerns of politicians, both as an essential component of British economic power at a time of global war, and as a potential source of internal social and political unrest should lost markets, depression or inflation be allowed to go unchecked. This sensitivity to the needs of the provinces was sharpened by the confidence of a new generation of provincial business leaders, men such as Finlay in Glasgow, Roscoe and Rathbone in Liverpool, Attwood and Spooner in Birmingham and George Schonswar in Bristol, who proved themselves adept at unifying the disparate commercial interests of their cities into an effective lobby for reform. They were relentless in their efforts to maintain the pressure for change on government, and throughout the summer of 1812, and into 1813, they continued to lobby Parliament and ministers through petitions, letter and deputations.[91] Indeed, in Liverpool mercantile organisation on East Indian affairs subsequently became a permanent feature of the political life of the city. As soon as the provinces got wind of the move to try to confine the import trade to London they addressed the issue directly in their petitions and activities. One notable Glasgow petition of 19 March 1812 condemned any effort to confine the Indian trade to London as 'unnecessary, unjust and impolitic'.[92] A recent and insightful PhD thesis by the Japanese scholar Yukihisa Kumagai, on the provincial campaigns against the East India Company monopolies in the periods immediately before 1813 and 1833, has shown just how skilful the political leaderships within the cities of Liverpool and Glasgow were in bringing together disparate interest groups to support the cause of free trade.[93] Kumagai shows how, in Glasgow in 1812–1813, West Indian merchants and cotton manufacturers, amongst other groups, were unified against the Company's monopoly in a concerted public campaign of petitioning and deputations in support of the cause.[94] The Liverpool men also created a similar state of unity out of varied elements during this period.[95] In general, Kumagai's work brings back to the centre of the argument the role of provincial interests in persuading government in 1812–1813 that the India monopoly had to end. In particular, Kumagai shows that these groups were instrumental in convincing government ministers, especially in the Board of Trade, just how politically dangerous were the social ills caused by the wars with France and the USA, and just how pressing was the need to open all facets of the Indian trade, including the import trade, to ports in the provinces as well as London.[96] Kumagai's work has certainly persuaded the present author to accord the provinces a much more important role in the campaigns of 1812–13 than was previously the case.[97]

But it would be a mistake to see government as being merely reactive to the demands of the provincial industrialists and their allies. A second factor in the abandonment of the old notion that Indian and eastern commerce should be exclusively or even predominantly the domain of the East India Company was the emergence of the 'Liberal Tory' philosophy described by Cookson. This in essence recognised the need to placate emergent new interest groups such as provincial industry and commerce by limited economic concessions. It also embraced the utility of a more liberal trading regime for ensuring supplies of essential raw materials at a time of war and potential national crisis. In the case of the East India trade, these general notions were translated into very specific policy prescriptions which militated against the continuance of the India monopoly. A key figure in the governments of both Perceval and Liverpool was George Rose, Vice President of the Board of Trade. When Rose became aware in early April 1812 of Melville's agreement that the import trade from India would be confined to London he persuaded Melville that the Board of Trade should have an input into the debate. Kumagai correctly identifies the importance of provincial lobbying activities in persuading Rose and the Board of Trade to act on this question, but there was rather more to Rose's perception of the problems of monopoly than an awareness of the hardships experienced in the new industrial urban centres.[98] Some of his concerns addressed the methods and structure of the Company. For example, Rose ferociously criticised the East India Company's record of restricting commerce through its bureaucratic commercial practices, notably at Canton.[99] Rose's rejection of the notion that the import trade should be confined to London was made clear in June 1813, when he vehemently opposed an attempted amendment to the new Charter which would have confined the import trade to London.[100]

Rose's intervention in the issue was in response to several specific and severe national economic problems, some of which were indeed highlighted by the provincial interests, as Kumagai shows. But what is also important is that Rose believed a new approach to East Indian trade could provide some amelioration of these difficulties. These difficulties included food shortages and inflation as well as shortages of essential raw materials for industry, such as raw cotton, a problem particularly associated with the crisis in Anglo-American relations. Food inflation had become a desperate problem by 1812. During the course of 1811, wheat prices had soared from 96s to 106s per bushel, and continued to rise in 1812.[101] The latter year saw food riots in a number of British cities. For Rose, a liberated import trade from India offered new sources of essential commodities, which could alleviate shortage and help curb rising prices. The origins of this perception did not lie with the provincial lobbyists of spring 1812, and it was no mere hunch on Rose's part. Rose's ideas were shaped by the contributions of a wide body of people, but particularly by interests in London who had enjoyed long experience of the Indian trade and who could offer much more expert opinion on the potential of India than could the merchants and manufacturers of Glasgow, Liverpool and Birmingham. The latter may have established in the minds of Rose and other politicians just how politically explosive the economic difficulties of provincial industrial Britain were, but the feasibility of an Indian solution to them emerged from metropolitan and colonial sources.

This latter point is evident from a range of sources of information at the disposal of Board of Trade ministers. The parliamentary Select Committee on East Indian Affairs, which had been sitting for a number of years, interviewed a very wide range of merchants involved in the 'privilege trade', and a number of London agency house men stressed that India could become a major supplier to Britain of a range of commodities, especially raw cotton and sugar.[102] All that was required was that the stifling bureaucracy and privilege enjoyed by the East India Company should be lifted. In 1813, another prominent London agency house merchant, William Fairlie, offered exactly the same argument to the Committee of the Whole House on East Indian Affairs, and was supported by Colonel Thomas Munro, a senior East India Company soldier and administrator.[103] In fact the Select Committee on East Indian Affairs produced four reports between 1808 and 1812 containing much detailed evidence of the problems posed by the East India Company's commercial practices. It heard how the Company's vast warehousing capacity enabled it to release eastern commodities for sale to the British public only when a certain minimum price could be secured for them.[104] The government had always approved of this system because it tended to maximise tax revenues, but the committee pointed out that it could only exacerbate the problem of inflation.[105] The Company's high freight charges had also been cited to the committee by London agency house merchants, and the inflationary consequences of these were also now brought to the government's attention.[106] Other voices reinforced this emerging picture of India as a potential source of cheap essentials, given a more liberal trading environment. The silk manufacturers call in 1812 for increased imports of Bengal silk to help their ailing industry implicitly criticised the Company's record in this field.[107] The Chairman of the Board of Excise for Scotland claimed there was a large unfulfilled demand for Indian goods north of the border.[108] Hemp and shipping cable were also cited as Indian produce for which there was much domestic British demand.[109] There were even anonymous claims passed onto the Board of Trade in April 1812 that large supplies of Indian rice could be procured to help alleviate domestic food shortages.[110] While Henry (Earl) Bathurst, then President of the Board of Trade, was sceptical, he nonetheless passed on the suggestion to the Prime Minister.[111]

The result of all this was that the governments of Perceval and Liverpool came to regard India as a useful source of essential raw materials and food at a time when high inflation and shortages threatened to exacerbate problems of domestic unrest. They no longer felt that the Company monopoly of trade with India was the best way to maximise these supplies; instead it was better to allow the free market to ensure both ample supply and minimised prices. Government ministers were under no illusions about the scale of Indian imports. They did not believe that India would become the principal supplier of cotton, sugar or other commodities; but it could supplement the main traditional sources. For example, from this time onwards India began to be regarded as a useful alternative source of raw cotton at times when supplies from the United States were interrupted by war or other factors.[112] In short, traditional government thinking on trade with the east, which in the past had favoured the principle of exclusive monopoly as the foundation for policy, had moved towards a much more pluralistic and open premiss. An important shift had taken place in official state political economy which, though tentative and pragmatic rather than overtly ideological, was to change the whole framework within which the commercial interests involved in economic relations with India would operate.

Another factor in the emergence of this leaning towards free trade rather than protectionist policies in respect of India was the abysmal failure of the Company and its allies in London to defend their Indian privileges effectively, or to secure preference for London in the import trade. To some extent this is explained by the longstanding financial difficulties of the Company and its dependence on state support, which undermined the credibility of the Company's claims that its monopoly offered the most efficient method for managing commerce with India in the national interest. But there was another significant reason. Despite the efforts of the Company to rally London against the provincial demands for free trade with India, especially in respect of confining the import trade into London, the London East India agency houses did not support this agitation. They were a key group within London commercial circles. In fact, as shown, senior figures in the London houses such as Henry Trail, Henry Fawcett and R.C. Bazett and William Fairlie were eagerly impressing upon various parliamentary Select Committees the advantages likely to accrue to the British economy from a general opening of the import trade in a variety of Indian commodities. The only figure connected with the private trade with India who seems to have defended the Company's privileges was Alexander Baring of Baring Brothers, and even then only half-heartedly.[113] As relations with the USA deteriorated in March 1813, eleven London East India agency houses petitioned the Board of Trade to impose a complete embargo on the import of American cotton, arguing that a freed import trade from India would ensure adequate supplies of Indian raw cotton for the British provincial textile manufacturers. Among the signatories were such prominent houses as Paxton, Cockerell & Trail, Prinsep, Saunders & Co. and Fairlie, Bonham & Co.[114] Though the petition failed it was clear that the London East India agency houses did not support continued restrictions on the import trade, a point reiterated in a subsequent petition to Parliament in May 1813, which contended that the end of the East India Company's import monopoly would pave the way for the expansion of production of raw cotton in India and its improvement to meet the necessary standards of quality.[115] Though the London houses had not matched the provincial men in terms of pressure-group organisation and speed of response to a volatile political situation, they had belatedly joined the fray in favour of free trade. Crucially, their unwillingness to support the Company and other London merchants' demands for privileged treatment had served to divide and weaken the capital's lobby at a crucial time, and helped ensure that the trade to and from India would be thrown open.

By the autumn of 1812 the future of the Company looked very shaky indeed, and the survival of any of the Company's privileges was in question. It seemed as though there would be no need for any renewal of the Company's Charter. Certainly throughout this period the provincial delegations kept up a relentless pressure in favour of complete free trade with Asia. But the Company had not lost all of its influence, and ministers were hesitant to peremptorily dismiss the needs of what was still, both politically and economically, a very important organisation in the City of London. In March 1813, the Company's supercargo at Canton, Sir George Staunton, delivered a detailed paper to the Court of Directors, arguing that the Company's monopoly of trade with China should be preserved, regardless of what happened to the India trade.[116] Staunton held a number of interviews with Buckinghamshire on the subject, and convinced him that the China monopoly should, after all, be preserved.[117] The key arguments centred upon the fact that the China trade was one of the few profitable commercial lines of activity for the Company, and it followed that if this were opened up to free trade, the state might in the end have to find yet more resources to keep the Company afloat. In addition, Staunton went to great lengths to explain the deep suspicion of Chinese rulers towards European traders, and the system of restrictive practices controlled by the Chinese Hong Merchants at Canton. An uncontrolled free trade with China would be likely to incite Chinese hostility, and destabilise the whole of British commerce with the empire. Preserving the Company's monopoly was vital to avoid this. Whatever its merits, Buckinghamshire and the British government accepted this argument, and a new Charter was indeed passed by Parliament in 1813, one which opened the trade between Britain, India and south-east Asia to ships of 350 tons and above, with the main proviso that they should call only at the main Company settlements in the east. One clause sought to defend the industrial provinces of Britain from competition from Indian cotton textiles, by confining the import of the latter into London, and imposing heavy duties on them, against which the Company's government in India could not retaliate. It was another nail in the coffin of the Indian cotton industry, which was already destined for extinction because of competition from cheap British manufactured textiles. However, the Company retained its monopoly of trade with China, and was permitted to continue trading on

its own account with India, on the condition that it reform its auditing procedures to ensure that its commercial accounts were properly separated from
those recording its political and territorial dealings. In essence, the Company
would have to ensure greater transparency in its commercial activities, and
therefore greater accountability and profitability.[118] The Company had just
about survived as a commercial organisation, but its role in governing India
would henceforth become increasingly its principal *raison d'etre*.

The Charter Act marked a turning point in the role of non-Company
commercial interests in India and the east, and in the evolving relationship
between the British state and the Company. In essence, the Charter Act and
the political developments leading to it marked the arrival and legitimisation
of non-East India Company commercial interest groups connected with Asia
as significant players influencing colonial policy in that region. No longer
would the prevailing assumption of the British state be that the Company
should be the sole or even prime mover of imperial economic policy in India
and the east. Given the expertise of its staff, its role in the actual governance
of India, its enduring presence as a voice in the City of London, and the
existence of a body of MPs linked to Leadenhall Street, the Company could
not of course be ignored, and it remained a potent influence. Indeed, key
non-Company interest groups such as the London East India agency houses
continued to hold Company stock and, if anything, they were to use this
even more after 1813 to exert an influence within the Courts of Proprietors and Directors in an effort to shift Company policies in directions which
suited them. In this respect, the agency houses came to develop a 'twin-track'
approach to influencing colonial policy in Asia, operating both within and
without the institutions of the Company. Thus, while 1813 heralded a new
era of pluralism in the determination of British commerce and policy in India
and Asia, it was not a regime in which all the new arrivals offered an outright
challenge to the bastions of the old order. Instead, a rather complex picture
emerged in which, from time to time, some of the new interests, particularly
those in London with a stake in the Company, found it politic to side with the
men and machinery of Leadenhall Street, sometimes against others amongst
the ranks of the newcomers. Whilst a new political and commercial environment had been created by the Charter Act of 1813, the institutions and men
of the old order were not yet done in their desire and ability to shape policy
towards India and the east.

Four

ACCOMMODATING FREE TRADE: INDIA, THE EAST INDIA COMPANY AND THE COMMERCIAL REVOLUTION OF 1814–1830

THE PASSAGE and implementation of the Charter Act of 1813 coincided with a period of great political turbulence in Europe and North America. Global events overshadowed what would amount to a revolution in Britain's commercial relations with India. Tensions with the USA erupted into war by the time the Act passed through Parliament. The tide of the conflict in Europe turned decisively in 1812 following Napoleon's disastrous invasion of Russia. Victory followed swiftly in 1814 and Napoleon was exiled to Elba. But Napoleon's escape led to a resumption of hostilities until his final reckoning against his enemies at Waterloo. There then followed the complex diplomatic negotiations at the Congress of Vienna, which redrew the political contours of Europe and the European empires in India and south-east Asia.

Without question the British had emerged from the war as the most powerful nation in the world. This was not merely a consequence of victory on the battlefield. Britain's impressive economic growth, already commented upon before the war, accelerated during the conflict. This was most evident in the continuing rise of British manufacturing industry, which was already conquering the markets of the world. But Britain had also established itself as the most important mercantile and financial centre in Europe. Indeed, one of the reasons for Britain's victory had been its ability to fund the campaigns of allies on the continent. In spite of the social and economic difficulties caused by the war, the British emerged stronger than ever, especially in respect of their empire. Whereas before the war the British had suffered great anxieties about the threat posed by other powers in Asia, after 1815 these were subsiding; and with the final defeat of the Marathas in 1818 the Indian empire seemed secure at last. Moreover, the British were well placed to dictate a peace that would suit their political and economic interests. Their main aim was to prevent any power ever again dominating Europe as Napoleon had done. France was seen as the principal threat and so British policy was designed to contain French power and ambitions. The vital region was the Low Countries, the infamous 'cockpit of Europe' over which wars had been fought for centuries, and which the French had occupied during the wars of 1793–1815. The long stretch of Channel coast in this part of Europe meant that enemy control of it would present the British with a threat of invasion. British post-war diplomacy therefore sought to strengthen the Netherlands as a northern bulwark against French expansionism. But the Dutch had suffered greatly during the French occupation. Their colonies in south-east Asia had been seized by the British to prevent them falling into French hands.

British policy in post-war Europe was to have important implications for their strategy in Asia. In order to assist Dutch recovery, all of the occupied colonies, namely Java, Malacca and the spice islands of the Moluccas, were to be returned to the Netherlands as soon as possible. It was indeed a sign of new British confidence in their superiority in Asia that such a move could be contemplated. The Dutch had been bitter colonial rivals before 1793 and there had been several Anglo-Dutch wars during the eighteenth century. The Dutch could be treated generously precisely because they were no longer a serious threat to British interests. While this made perfect sense to the Foreign Office, there were those in the East India Company, and others interested in trade with south-east Asia, who were dismayed by the decision. They felt that an opportunity to advance British commerce in the region had been surrendered.

For all these reasons, the commercial changes wrought by the Charter Act of 1813 did not at first attract the interest that one might expect, but they were no less important for that. For the first time, independent British traders could hire their own vessels and trade freely with the main presidencies of India. They could ship out British manufactures on speculation, and purchase Indian commodities for the home and European markets. The 'privilege trade', through which the Indian agency houses had conducted their private trade with London, was obsolete. The Indian firms too were now free to engage in their own speculative commercial ventures with Britain. It was, however, impossible in 1813 to assess the impact of this new liberalised trading regime on India, or indeed on the British economy. In order to appreciate how the changes affected India, it is necessary to revisit the nature of the Indian commercial system which had grown up under Company rule since the 1780s.

What were the principal features of British commerce in India before 1813? In particular, what relationship had developed between the Company and the agency houses? Firstly, since the late 1780s most Company employees had been debarred from private trade on their own account, a restriction for which they were compensated by higher salaries. From that time, the agency houses began to provide banking facilities for Company servants and soldiers, who deposited their savings and salaries with the houses. These deposits were then utilised by the houses as capital for the considerable range of commercial activities permitted within the confines of the Company's monopoly. These included investment in the production of local commodities such as indigo, sugar, salt and Indian cotton piece goods. The houses were also permitted to engage in the 'country trade' with south-east Asia, China and other ports in the Indian ocean, provided they did not infringe the Company's monopoly of trade with Britain. As a consequence many of the houses became involved in ship-ownership, usually joint partners with the captains of the vessels.[1] This branch of business became especially important for the East India Company because the houses played a vital role in the China trade, the single most profitable branch of Company commercial activity. The trade to China involved the export of Indian and south-east Asian produce in exchange for Chinese tea and other commodities for sale in Britain and Europe. Opium became the single most important commodity in this export trade, though raw cotton also produced lucrative returns. But the illegality of opium imports into China made it impossible for the Company to engage in this trade directly. Instead the opium made by the Company in India under its monopoly over the production of that commodity was sold to the agency houses, who smuggled it into China aboard country ships. Receipts were paid into the Company's treasury at Canton in exchange for bills of exchange payable in India or London. These bills were much valued because of the difficulties and risks involved in the remittance of funds to Britain. In this way, the Company secured local currency for purchasing Chinese tea and other luxuries for sale in London.[2] It is important to recognise that the export of opium became very lucrative indeed during the last years of the eighteenth century. The total value of opium exports to China between 1796/7 and 1799/1800 was recorded as Rs2,657,189. But in the period from 1805/6 onwards the total annual value was usually in the region of Rs4 to 5 million a year, rising as high as Rs7 million in 1814/15.[3] In volume this trade amounted to a regular supply to China from India of around 3–4,000 chests of opium a year.[4]

This relationship between the agency houses and the Company had developed and matured in the two decades before 1813. A generation of leading partners in the Indian houses had retired to Britain to join London sister houses, establishing themselves as men of importance in the City or in politics. As shown earlier, a retired agency house man like Charles Cockerell was able to marry into the Gloucestershire gentry and acquire an elegant country house and a baronetcy within ten years of his retirement to Britain in 1800. By 1820 his firm of Paxton, Cockerell & Trail had become one of the leading London East India agency houses, moving in 1819 into premises in Austin Friars, close to the Bank of England and at the heart of the City.[5] During this period, Cockerell and the firm became major creditors for the

Wellesley family, including the Duke of Wellington. Henry Trail, a partner in the same firm who had also returned from India in the early 1800s, bought an estate in Fife and briefly served as MP for Weymouth and Melcombe Regis in 1812–1813.[6] William Fairlie, an associate of David Scott and widely regarded as the most important and wealthy of the Calcutta agency house men in the first decade of the nineteenth century, returned to Britain in 1812, and became an active partner in the London firm of Fairlie, Bonham & Co. He was an outspoken figure on East Indian affairs, offering important testimony during the Charter debate of 1813.[7] The second decade of the century saw a substantial growth in the vote of these London East India agency house men in the Court of Proprietors, and in their presence on the Court of Directors, strengthening their position within the Company's kaleidoscope of competing interest groups.[8]

But agency house influence within the Company went beyond the election of London partners onto the Court of Directors. By the time of the 1813 Act the Indian houses had other means of persuasion at their disposal. Central to these were the personal and financial services the houses provided for Company servants. These are evident in the few business and personal records of the agency houses which have survived. Perhaps the best example of this was John Palmer & Co., which became by reputation the most wealthy and important house after the return of Fairlie to England in 1812.[9] So influential was Palmer in India, particularly in his relations with Francis Rawdon, the Marquis of Hastings and Governor-General from 1814 to 1823, that he earned the nickname of 'prince of merchants'.[10] The sources and methods of Palmer's political influence are most illuminating. The most obvious was his deliberate cultivation of senior Company civil servants like Hastings and other members of the Bengal Council, through personal acquaintance and by providing personal financial services. But the Palmer papers show that the methods of persuasion used were much more sophisticated and varied than mere personal ingratiation with the powerful.

The agency houses provided banking and financial services for a very wide range of men in the Company's service, from senior servants or officers in the Company's forces, down to the lowliest young writer, newly arrived from London. Agency house merchants like Palmer took the greatest care to ensure that their relationships with these men and their families were not merely financial. Many of the young men who came to India to work for the Company found themselves taken under Palmer's wing, even being invited to the prince of merchants' home for social occasions. They received generous loans, but also stern lectures on the need for frugality and caution.[11] As the career of the young Company servant developed further assistance would be provided through the establishment of wills or trusts to help support the young man's family, both in India and Britain. Palmer employed the services of one Augustus Frederick Hamilton, a leading Calcutta lawyer, to draw these up, usually tying the client's funds into Palmer & Co. on terms which made it difficult to withdraw them in future.[12] On occasion, Palmer even used his influence to secure promotion for his acolytes. Thus a generation of Company men grew up, rising in power and influence within the organisation, who felt a strong sense of loyalty to John Palmer. This was used on occasion to deliver advantages for the latter's firm. For example, in 1813, Palmer got Lieutenant-Colonel Nesbitt, an old client and Company officer serving on the island of Mauritius, to persuade his fellow Company officials to order supplies from Palmer & Co.[13] In the same year, when rumours that Palmer & Co. was in serious trouble began to circulate on the island of Java, where Palmer & Co. had substantial commercial interests, Palmer got two of his clients in the Company's service, Lieutenant-Colonel Dewar and Lieutenant Eckford, to reassure the firm's clients of Palmer & Co.'s continuing health.[14] Lucius O'Brien, an East India Company soldier, rose from being a cadet in 1794 to the rank of Lieutenant-Colonel in the Bengal Light Cavalry in 1822. The pinnacle of his career was his appointment to lead the administration of Nagpur, central India, in 1818.[15] O'Brien had risen under the watchful patronage of John Palmer, who had acted for Lucius's father in managing the son's financial affairs, sought promotion for him on various occasions, and used Lucius as an agent for the firm.[16] In this way the agency houses won considerable support within the Company's ranks. Even if many of these servants lacked the rank decisively to promote the interests of their agency house patrons, their support did affect the general ambience of beliefs and assumptions within the Company's service on key issues, which in turn influenced the perceptions of its leaders.

Moreover, the agency houses used these subtle methods in their dealings with East India Company directors. Palmer struck up particularly close relationships with several directors, to great mutual advantage. Colonel Sweny Toone, who served intermittently on the directorate between 1798 and 1831, exchanged favours with Palmer. In the mid-1810s, Toone secured a Company writership for one of Palmer's sons.[17] In return, Palmer promised to use his influence to help Toone's son to rise in the East India Company's army.[18] There were numerous other examples of Palmer exchanging favours with other directors, either for himself or on behalf of others.[19] While such deals were the day-to-day realities of Company life, and by no means guaranteed a director's support for causes cherished by the agency houses, these relationships persuaded many in the Courts of Directors and Proprietors that it was not in their self-interest to deny the houses on all issues. This must have muddied the waters for many otherwise staunch defenders of the Company's privileges, impressing upon them that the houses were vital for aspects of the Company's operations. Agency house influence, applied on a small scale, and on matters which touched the personal interests of directors, promoted ambiguity where outright hostility towards non-Company businessmen might have reigned. Conversely, in spite of their longstanding desire for a freer trade regime between Britain and the Company's territories, the frustration of the agency houses at the Company's intransigence never degenerated into the outright hostility displayed by some of the industrialists and merchants of provincial Britain. Their links with Company servants, both in Britain and India, were too close and too profitable for this to be allowed. It followed also that for the agency houses in both India and Britain, relations with the Company were managed both from within and without the Company. The wide range of methods used included quiet lobbying, the cultivation of directors' and Company servants' self-interest, and the building of a strong agency house presence in the Courts of Proprietors and Directors. When necessity so demanded, more assertive tactics could be employed, notably through independent organisation outside the Company and the public lobbying of politicians. This ambivalence towards the Company amongst the Indian and London agency houses set them apart from the provincial industrialists in Britain, and largely explains the subdued hesitancy of the London agency houses during some of the debates about the Charter in 1812–1813. They could never quite make up their mind about the East India Company. Whilst on the one hand they resented its stifling restrictions on trade with Britain, which limited their trading opportunities and made remittance home of their and their clients' wealth so difficult, on the other they had grown up under the wing of the Company and had flourished by serving it and its employees. It was an attitude amongst the London agency house partners which persisted into the middle of the nineteenth century.

One should never lose sight of the fact that the agency houses had emerged within the confines of the East India Company's monopoly. Whilst many of them were eager to weaken the Company's privileges so that they could capture a larger share of the trade with Britain, the monopoly in fact shielded them from the competition of interlopers. Before 1813 the relatively small number of houses had a complete free reign in the intra-Asian country trade, and privileged access to the fortunes of the Company's servants, as well as the limited 'privilege' cargo space aboard Company ships. Their pivotal role in the China trade, and the services they supplied to Company servants and soldiers ensured that the Company was sensitive to their needs. But even before the opening of the British trade to India, competition was intensifying, with an increase in the number of houses from sixteen in 1803 to twenty-five in 1812.[20] Thus while a prominent figure like John Palmer chided his London corresponding agency house, Paxton, Cockerell & Trail, for their misgivings about throwing open the trade between Britain and India, arguing that increased trade would flow naturally to the existing agency houses, others were not so sure.[21] Their apprehension proved to be well founded. In reality, the position of the agency houses was fragile even before the end of the Company's India monopoly. Their dependence upon capital deposited by

Company servants and, on occasion, funds supplied by Indian merchants made them extremely vulnerable to crises of confidence and changes in the general financial and political climate in which they operated. The Company's bellicose policy of expansionism drew it into expensive military adventures which it had to finance through the issue of public securities in India. This meant that occasionally it was competing with the agency houses for the funds of its own employees, forcing the houses to pay higher rates of interest to retain funds. In addition, the partners in the agency houses regarded their involvement in the Indian firms as a necessary but temporary route to a better future in Britain. The ideal was to make one's fortune as quickly as possible and transfer one's interest to the corresponding London agency house at the earliest opportunity, in the process taking as big a share as possible of the Indian house's capital. This meant that the Indian houses were frequently subject to sudden and destabilising drains on their capital, making them vulnerable to crises in liquidity and confidence. Such transitory loyalty among the partners to their Indian agency houses did not make for good management or trusting relationships between the agency house men. In addition one should remember the other perils of commerce during this period: the vulnerability of early nineteenth-century shipping and agriculture to the vagaries of the weather, and the damage inflicted upon commerce by the global European war and more localised conflicts in the east. The exposure of the houses to a new wave of competitors from home increased these dangers, even if some could see new opportunities.

When the Indian trade was thrown open in 1814 few appreciated how it would affect the commercial communities in India. Some agency houses, like Palmer & Co., urged their London agents to seize the initiative, imploring them to seek business with merchants and industrialists in Liverpool, Limerick, Glasgow and Dublin, with a view to exporting British manufactures to India on a commission basis.[22] But when his London contacts hesitated, Palmer took matters into his own hands. By 1816 he had developed trading contacts with several Liverpool merchants, notably John Gladstone, one of the most eminent commercial men in that city.[23] To celebrate this new connection, he even named one of the vessels in his growing fleet, *Liverpool*.[24] Others followed suit, eager to take advantage of their new ability to export Indian produce to Britain. Indeed, 1813/14 saw frantic speculation in Bengal produce as the agency houses prepared to exploit the newly liberalised trade regime with the home country. One consequence was that the Rupee rose sharply in value against Sterling, just when the Company needed to borrow heavily in India to fund the Investment. Company bills and securities, normally able to tempt the agency houses and other investors, were suddenly unattractive, as the rate of exchange they offered for the Rupee was worse than could be had in private transactions.[25] Thus the opening of the Indian trade initially caused severe financial problems and uncertainty for the Company in Bengal.

But the Company was not alone in facing difficulties. In spite of the anticipated benefits of free trade with the home country, the agency houses soon discovered to their dismay that the 1813 Act had unleashed an unwelcome deluge of freebooting adventurers into India, eager to win a share of the Indian trade. Sole traders, some owning only a single vessel, now chanced their arm in the trade to the Indian presidencies. The effect was to quickly swamp India with a large quantity of British manufactures, which, in spite of competitive price and quality, were unable to find a market. The value of produce imported into Bengal rose from Rs15.9 million in 1813/14 to Rs29.7 million by 1818/19.[26] One British official reported that the value of imported British manufactures in Bengal rose from Rs5.3 million in 1813/14 to over Rs15 million by 1818/19.[27] For the first time, the outports in Britain were benefiting from trade with India, and the growth was quite spectacular. For example, one estimate suggested that the export of British goods from Liverpool to India had risen from Rs2,264,317 in 1817/18 to Rs5,149,203 just a year later.[28] As these newcomers sought return cargoes from India for the British market, the agency houses had to compete with them for the purchase of Indian commodities. The prices of Indian produce rose spectacularly during this period, and the value of imports into Britain from Bengal alone rose from Rs46.4 million in 1813/14 to Rs65.1 million in 1817/18.[29] Liverpool's share of these imports rose in value from Rs1,873,549 in 1817/18 to Rs2,224,405 in 1818/19.[30] Thereafter there was a glut of Indian commodities coming onto the British market, causing falling prices and financial difficulties for those involved in the trade.[31] In addition, many agency houses had invested heavily in shipping in the years preceding the 1813 Act, anticipating that they could then take advantage of the freer trade regime with Britain likely to be created on renewal. To their dismay, they found that the supply of shipping suddenly outstripped demand, as some of the new traders were tempted into encroaching on the agency houses' traditional preserve of the country trade. By 1817/18 difficulties were very severe indeed. John Adam, the private political secretary to the Governor-General, noted that by 1819 freight rates were dropping rapidly as there 'was little employment for funds in shipping'.[32] After all the high hopes for the expected benefits of free trade, by 1819 it had brought bitter disappointment for many of the Indian agency houses.

By the end of the 1810s the problems caused by the Charter Act of 1813 were reaching a crisis. The overstocking of the Indian market with British manufactures, the glut of British shipping at the Indian presidencies and the competition for Indian goods for re-export to Britain severely reduced the agency houses' opportunities for profitable investment. John Crawfurd, a keen observer of Indian commerce, noted that the houses responded to this shortage of profitable avenues for investment by applying their funds to increasingly precarious ventures such as coffee and spice plantations, rice mills and house-building.[33] The only field in which the agency houses were reluctant to speculate was the import trade in manufactures from Britain, which was regarded as treacherously uncertain because of the experience of the previous few years. John Palmer's change of heart about dabbling in the import of British manufactures in India typified the deep suspicion now felt by the Indian agency houses for this branch of commerce. So eager to court firms in Liverpool in 1813, by July 1818 he complained bitterly that freight rates had been brought disastrously low by competition from the new traders from the British outports.[34] In August 1819 he publicly demanded that two ships belonging to the firm of John Gladstone of Liverpool be debarred from engaging in the country trade of Asia, traditionally the exclusive territory of the Indian agency houses.[35] Gladstone had been an important trading contact since the end of the India monopoly, and Palmer's new obstructive attitude was a clear signal of his disillusionment with the outport trade. Then in October 1819 there was a failure of a Liverpool firm with whom he had enjoyed a close commercial relationship, resulting in losses both for Palmer & Co. and Paxton, Cockerell & Trail and Co. in London.[36] Within a few years, Palmer had severed all links with Liverpool and the import of British manufactures, asserting that the new merchant firms who sold British manu-factures could never threaten the position of the established Indian agency houses because of their limited capital resources.[37] Bitter experience, and the expense of diversifying into new areas in the face of new competitors, meant that the rest of the Indian agency houses also turned their backs on the trade in British manufactures.

But in the long run this aversion was not shared by their sister firms in London and others waiting in the wings. Wary at first of dealing with the export trade in British manufactures, the London East India agency houses, like their Indian connections, were initially put off by the chaotic overstocking of the Indian market during the years immediately following the 1813 Charter Act. By the early 1820s however, some of the more adventurous London firms began to export British manufactures on a commission basis. One of the first was the London agency house of Duncan & MacLachlan, which in 1821 told the Select Committee of the House of Commons on Foreign Trade that they exported British goods to their sister house in Calcutta, McIntyre & Co.[38] The early 1820s saw the rise of more widespread interest in this trade among the London houses, especially the export of cotton textiles. The prominent Glasgow industrialist Kirkman Finlay, identified 1820/21 as a key period in which the London agency houses became involved in the systematic export of British cotton goods.[39] George Larpent, a fast rising member of the firm Cockerell & Co., the firm descended from the London sister house of John Palmer's firm in Calcutta, revealed how his firm had also moved into the export of British manufactures during the 1820s.

Larpent outlined the financial arrangements which his firm made with manufacturers, and which were duplicated by the vast majority of the London houses involved in the export trade to India. These involved the London houses advancing money to the manufacturers, frequently up to half the value of the commodities to be shipped. The London firms charged interest and commission on these advances. The goods (usually cotton twist or cotton cloth) would be shipped to India, most often to one of the new houses set up by men who had gone out to India since 1813, and from there they were sold on the Indian market. The receipts were subsequently repatriated through bills of exchange or by the purchase of return cargoes for the British market, providing the means for the manufacturer to settle his debts to the London house.[40] By the end of the 1820s Cockerell & Co. were very substantial exporters. Larpent boasted that between 1830 and 1833 alone his firm had exported 850,000 pounds of cotton twist, and that he had 'not lost a single shilling' upon the advances made to the various manufacturers. The firm dealt with manufacturers in a range of provincial centres, including Glasgow, and Larpent offered some important insights into his methods and principles of business. He had dealt consistently with a fairly constant body of manufacturers, whom he had come to know and trust. When evaluating risk, Larpent assessed a manufacturer 'upon my knowledge of his means and of his general character'.[41] Larpent's personal relationships with these provincial factory owners were very close, and they were on the whole men of substantial capital means, even if they were trading on elaborate credit arrangements.[42] Larpent took pride in acquainting himself with the ways in which his clients ran their businesses, and his knowledge of the cotton industry was thus considerable. What emerges is a picture of growing intimacy in the 1820s between the London East India agency house men and the cotton industrialists of provincial Britain. In the case of Larpent's firm, this move into the export trade in British manufactures was only part of a wider diversification into a range of new activities, including carrying passengers to India.[43] During this decade, some London commercial firms even found ways to export British manufactures to China, circumventing the East India Company's remaining monopoly. Joshua Bates, the prominent American partner in Baring Brothers, told a parliamentary Select Committee in 1830 how that London firm procured British manufactures on commission for a US commercial house based in Boston, which then exported the goods to China. Between 1826 and 1829 alone Bates estimated that about £547,000 worth of British woollen goods had been exported to China via this route.[44] He estimated that during the same period about £30,000 worth of cotton manufactures were exported each year. Another commission agent involved in the American trade to China in British manufactures, Charles Everett, estimated that most London firms made about 2.5% in commission on such transactions.[45] Everett's own dealings in supplying British manufactures to American merchants exporting to China were very extensive. Between 1818 and 1828 he purchased £762,118 worth of British manufactures, including £207,784 worth of cotton manufactures.[46] Clearly, during the 1820s, not only were the commercial links between financiers and provincial industry becoming well established, but they also made a mockery of the last vestiges of East India Company commercial privileges in China.

London and American merchants were not alone in exploiting the liberalised trade to India in British manufactures, or in flouting the China monopoly. In Liverpool, particularly, well established business firms moved swiftly to export British goods for commission on a more systematic basis than in the speculative period of the late 1810s. In fact, some London East India agency house merchants had chosen to channel a portion of their Indian trade through Liverpool rather than London. On 27 June 1821, John Forbes Mitchell, a partner in the London agency house of Smith, Inglis & Co., revealed that his firm had sent a number of ships trading with India to Liverpool rather than London because freight and dock charges in Liverpool were as much as £1 or £2 per ton cheaper. It also took just an average of ten days for a ship to deliver its cargo and clear the port, compared to a month in London.[47] The East India agent and ship-owner George Lyall supported this claim.[48] In 1819 there were thirty-eight Liverpool ships involved in trade with India on a regular basis.[49] A year earlier John Gladstone, a prominent West Indian merchant up till that time, owned six ships which were involved in the Indian trade.[50] The trade became so important to Gladstone that in 1825 he dispatched two of his employees, Thomas Ogilvy and F.M. Gillanders, to Calcutta where they established the firm of Ogilvy & Gillanders.[51] Ogilvy was no mere employee, as his father was married to Gladstone's sister.[52] Following the establishment of the Calcutta firm, Ogilvy returned to Liverpool where he set up a sister firm, initially with the same name, but changing it to Gladstone, Ogilvy & Gillanders when John Gladstone's brother David joined the firm as senior partner in April 1826.[53] Though David left the Liverpool firm in 1833, his dominating presence indicated that Ogilvy & Gillanders was inextricably linked to the Gladstone family. Although few of the firm's early records have survived, a letter-book covering the firm's business correspondence during the last two months of 1836 gives a clear outline of the commercial activities which the firm had developed since the late 1820s. It was exporting a variety of British manufactures to India, including Glaswegian textiles and Staffordshire pottery.[54] The tone and content of the letters show that these were longstanding business arrangements. Ogilvy & Gillanders went to great lengths to try to communicate the tastes of the eastern markets. They advised the Staffordshire firm of Messrs Charles S. Mason & Co. that the patterns on earthenware they had sent to Calcutta were simply too old fashioned for the market's tastes.[55] Ogilvy & Gillanders also imported sugar from Mauritius, and by 1836 commanded such expertise in this branch of trade that they were even advising a prominent London sugar dealer.[56] The firm was also heavily involved in the re-export to Europe of eastern commodities such as indigo and coffee, particularly to Le Havre and Bordeaux in France.[57] The Liverpool firm had developed a long reach by the mid-1830s, which encompassed Scotland, the Midlands and the French coast.

Liverpool's existing links with the USA also assisted this breakthrough into the markets of Asia, particularly in respect of the still-forbidden Chinese market. In the 1820s, like Barings and Everett, the Liverpool firm of William J. Brown & Co. became heavily involved in procuring British manufactures for American merchants exporting to China. The scale of Brown's operations demonstrated the extent of Liverpool's involvement in undermining the Company's China monopoly. Between 1821 and 1829 Brown supplied £805,257 worth of exports to his American clients, consisting almost entirely of British manufactures.[58] Brown revealed the deception necessary for the carrying out of this illicit trade. Ships bound for China clearing out of Liverpool named Batavia in Java as their destination in all official correspondence.[59] The trade was certainly lucrative for Brown. He received 1% commission on the value of all goods shipped, and additional charges on top of this per shipment.[60] Brown argued that the China trade should be thrown open, and predicted that if this were done, British merchants would soon drive out their American rivals by virtue of their greater capital resources.[61] Thus, after the free-for-all and instability of the immediate post-1813 Charter period, the 1820s saw the emergence of a much more sophisticated and systematic network of commercial transactions and alliances which joined British manufacturers with Liverpool, London and American merchants and financiers, in a concerted effort to develop access to the Indian and Chinese markets. One consequence was that the bonds between the London agency house merchants and their sister firms in India became severely weakened as the latter eschewed engagement in the trade in British manufactures, leaving this to the newer and smaller firms (such as Ogilvy & Gillanders) who had emerged in the period after 1813. In the long run this was a grave development for the fortunes of the Indian agency houses.

Just as the 1813 Act eventually gave rise to new channels of commerce between Britain and Asia which undercut what was left of the East India Company's commercial system, so it also paved the way for new political organisations to represent commercial interests connected with Asia. These amounted to rather more than the *ad hoc* movements which attacked the privileges of the Company before 1793 and 1813. In the provinces the most important of these was the Liverpool East India Association. Initially established in the period before the passage of the 1813 Charter Act, the organisation was unique in that, unlike its peer associations in other provincial cities, it continued as an active body after the Act became law. The main reason for this was that the Liverpool merchants were deeply dissatisfied with the terms of the 1813 Act, which still imposed a number of limitations on trade. The continuing activity of the Liverpool association reflected the fact that, after London, Liverpool was fast becoming the principal British port trading with Asia. On 9 May 1822, responding to parliamentary reports on overseas trade published a year earlier, the association held a general meeting to express their continuing dissatisfaction with the laws governing the Asian trade.[62] The meeting cited numerous unresolved grievances, including the restrictions which confined British ships to specified ports in the east, and prohibited ships of less than 350 tons. The system of licensing ships and people was also criticised as excessively cumbersome.[63] But the main concern of the meeting was the punitive level of duties imposed upon sugar imported from the East Indies compared with those levied on the trade with the West Indies.[64] Little wonder then that it was the Liverpool association who launched a new campaign against the privileges of the East India Company at the end of the 1820s, targeting its remaining monopoly of trade to China.[65] The unbridled confidence of Liverpool's merchants was on display for all to see, with prominent men such as John Gladstone and William Rathbone taking the lead. Gladstone remarked upon the divisions amongst Liverpool merchants which had stifled the city's commercial and political influence in the past:

> but on the present occasion he was happy to think that they would all be found to be in one mind, all desirous to promote the principles of free trade and equal rights, not only for their own particular advantage as merchants of Liverpool, but for the benefit of the kingdom at large, of their fellow subjects generally, and those of the other outports[66]

But it was another merchant, Samuel Hope, who revealed the full extent of Liverpool's mercantile and political aspirations. For him, the possibility that the city would soon overtake the capital in its economic importance and political clout was real and achievable within a brief span of time:

> The port of Liverpool has been raised to its present proud pre-eminence by the enterprise of its merchants, and within its own time, has been elevated from the rank of a third or fourth rate town to that of a second. Though Liverpool has a leg tied up, she is now running a race with the Metropolis; they are neck and neck, and let but that leg be untied which now restricts the motion of one of the competitors, and we may venture to anticipate that the same enterprise which has carried Liverpool so far, will soon lead her beyond the port of London herself[67]

The applause which Hope received for this rallying call showed that he was not alone in believing that the Charter question held great moment not only for the future of British commercial fortunes, but also the geographical spread of wealth and power in Britain itself. With hindsight, the belief that Liverpool could replace London as the pre-eminent British centre of commerce might be dismissed as hubris. But it was a sentiment which was to be repeated during the course of the nineteenth century, and did not seem to be as unrealistic an aspiration then as it appears now. The city's sustained attack on the Company's privileges thus came to be seen as integral to challenging the political and economic dominance of London; such was the growth of the confidence of Liverpool's political leaders after 1813.

The other group of business interests connected with Asia which had been emerging as a force in its own right for even longer that the Liverpool men was, of course, the London East India agency houses, who had made their political presence felt as early as the 1790s. But their relationship with the East India Company was much more intimate than any enjoyed by Merseyside or other outport interests. Bowen shows that there were few in Liverpool, Glasgow or Bristol who owned stock in the Company and therefore enjoyed a voice in its Courts of Proprietors and Directors.[68] It was no coincidence that these cities gave vent to the most outspoken criticisms of the Company, and generated fiercely independent movements in favour of an end not only of that organisation's commercial privileges, but also London's dominance of trade with Asia. For the London East India agency house merchants the situation was much more complex. In his classic study of the internal politics of the East India Company, Philips shows that after the 1813 Act these men, who had been accumulating Company stock as their fortunes grew, began to emerge as a powerful faction within the Courts of Proprietors and Directors.[69] He argues that the 1820s in particular saw a rapid escalation of the power of this faction, its representation on the directorate rising from eight in 1826 to seventeen by 1831. The increasingly prominent role the agency houses played in the internal politics of the Company meant that their attitude to it stopped short of the unbridled hostility of Liverpool and Glasgow. Their stake in the organisation and their power within its councils muted whatever private animosities they nurtured. Instead, they came to see the Company as a tool of commercial politics in its own right, which could profitably be used to influence state economic policy in the east. Philips shows, for example, how they mobilised opinion within the Company to wind down the Company's engagement in trade with India, an objective which was adopted as policy by the directorate in 1826.[70] The London agency houses, with their longstanding business in importing Indian goods, and growing stake in the export trade of British manufactures, could only gain by this decision. Philips is sharply critical of the 'Private Interest', as he styled it, arguing that the agency house men were largely ignorant of India. By the 1820s many of the later generation of men inducted into these firms had never served in the east, and cared little for it save the profits it generated. Moreover, their efforts to impose their own agenda for the governance of India upon the Company were to fail. Philips attributes this to the lack of ability within the agency house faction in the directorate, who he dismisses as 'an undistinguished and ill-informed set of men'.[71] This is perhaps too harsh a judgement of a group of merchants who were less homogeneous than Philips assumes. In addition, the tasks of guiding the Company in the 1820s and protecting its remaining privileges in the face of the problems of war and economic crisis in India, and the swing towards political radicalism and pressure for free trade at home, would probably have been too great for even the most gifted and united leadership.

In fact on some issues the agency houses were more successful in defending their interests, and their methods of operation more varied, than Philips suggests. As useful as their growing representation within the Company in London was, the agency houses did not rely solely on it. On at least one key question of foreign policy in the east they proved themselves just as adept as the Liverpool merchants in organising an effective campaign outside the Company, though they were able to combine it to amplified effect with simultaneous lobbying within the Company's internal structures. The issue concerned British policy in south-east Asia in general, and their recent acquisition of the island of Singapore in 1819. As shown, the return of the Dutch colonies in the region following the end of the Napoleonic Wars was part of the British strategy of bolstering the Netherlands against the threat of future French expansionism, but it was also a source of great concern for the East India Company, the Indian agency houses and their allies in London. During the war, the British had built up substantial commercial interests in occupied Dutch possessions such as Java, including coffee and spice plantations as well as trading interests.[72] Revived Dutch power and inclinations towards protectionism might easily undermine these. They also feared that the Dutch would quickly resort to the commercial practices they had followed before the war, namely the imposition of treaties with the local states of the Malay Archipelago, which tied those states to trade exclusively with the Dutch. In January 1819 the London and Indian merchants and agency houses with interests in Java used the London-based Ship-owners Society to raise their concerns with the British government. In February the British Foreign Secretary, Lord Castlereagh, duly brought the matter before Baron Fagel, the Dutch ambassador in London, complaining specifically about recent increases in trade duties at Java.[73] But it was in India that the agency houses were especially active in alerting the Company's administration to the dangers posed by Dutch revival.

In November 1818, the British Governor-General, the Marquis of Hastings, met with Thomas Stamford Raffles, Governor of Bencoolen, in Calcutta. Hastings gave Raffles instructions for a mission to several locations in the Malay Archipelago.[74] Raffles' orders were to establish a new British port at the southern tip of the Malay Peninsula, and to explore a possible diplomatic solution to the civil war between rival contenders for the throne of the Sultanate of Aceh, in northern Sumatra. The most famous outcome of the mission was of course the British acquisition of Singapore in February 1819 as a result of Raffles' agreement with a senior minister of the Malay state of Johore. Though the Dutch bitterly contested the legality of this agreement and the new possession, British ownership of it was to be confirmed by the Treaty of London agreed between the Dutch and the British in 1824. Raffles' mission was in part the result of lobbying by the Calcutta agency houses to defend their commercial interests in south-east Asia. The disruptive effects of the opening of the Indian trade have been described, and the need to protect export markets for such Indian produce as cotton cloth and opium, and to find employment for agency house shipping, were especially pressing concerns for both the houses and the Company administration in Bengal.[75] A key figure in persuading Hastings of the need for urgent action was John Palmer, argu- ably the wealthiest and most influential of the Calcutta agency house men.[76] Tarling shows that Palmer took a very keen interest in the dangers posed by Dutch power to British commercial interests, and that he explored possible solutions with British and Dutch officials and merchants in Penang, Malacca, Batavia and elsewhere.[77] Palmer was Hastings' close confidante, and it is clear from Palmer's own correspondence of November 1818 that he was not only aware of Hastings' instructions to Raffles, but that he had also exercised some influence over their content.[78] Thus the close personal links between the Indian agency house men and Company officials in the east were brought to bear to shape British policy.

After Singapore had been established, the London East India agency houses were instrumental in ensuring that Singapore remained British. They employed various strategies to achieve this aim. In essence, they convinced senior British politicians such as Castlereagh and Canning that the port was simply too commercially and strategically valuable to surrender. The exper- tise of the agency house merchants on the Asian trade proved to be decisive in the ensuing debate. In 1821 two parliamentary Select Committees were convened to review British trade to the East Indies and China, one in the Commons and the other in the Lords.[79] Amongst the issues discussed were the consequences of the 1813 Charter Act, the effects of restoring Dutch authority in south-east Asia, and the question of the continuing Company monopoly of trade to China. The testimonies of London East India agency house merchants dominated the proceedings and their priorities influenced the conclusions of the committee.

Thus, on 26 March 1821, the Commons committee heard at length from Henry Blanshard, a London-based ship-owner and merchant who commanded a fleet of fourteen vessels. Blanshard strongly advocated the opening of the China trade, and stressed the importance of a port which could attract the produce of south-east Asia to supply the Chinese market. He recounted the rapid growth of Singapore, and pressed for its retention by the British.[80] Patrick MacLachlan, of the London agency house of Duncan & MacLachlan, emphasised the value of the port.[81] John Forbes Mitchell, of the London house of Smith, Inglis & Co., also threw his weight behind Singapore.[82] On 7 May 1821, Robert Rickards, of Rickards, Mackintosh, Law & Co., called for Singapore to be retained, citing the need to resist Dutch protectionism.[83] The Lords committee heard similar testimonies in favour of keeping Singapore, notably from William Fairlie, the prominent former Calcutta agency house merchant and partner in Fairlie, Bonham & Co.[84] Others spoke in defence of British merchants vulnerable to the effects of Dutch protectionism. These included Charles Grant, the venerable East India Company director, and John Gladstone, the Liverpool merchant.[85] But these were the exceptions. The vast majority of testimonies came from the London East India agency house merchants and their allies. The effect was to sear into the minds of British negotiators just how important Singapore and British trade in south-east Asia were to both the London and Indian agency houses and to British economic interests generally. The importance of the views of the merchants trading to the region was emphasised by Thomas Courtenay, a senior official at the India Board, in a lengthy memorandum written in March 1822 on the state of the negotiations between the British and Dutch.[86] The upshot was that the British eventually settled on a policy of delay and prevarication designed to impress upon the Dutch that a tacit acceptance that Singapore would remain British was an essential prerequisite for any resumption of negotiations. Only when the Dutch hinted that they were prepared to accept this in September 1823 were the negotiations re-opened.[87]

But the London agency houses also employed other means to press for the retention of Singapore and the defence of their interests in south-east Asia. They set up their own independent organisation, which actively colluded with the Calcutta agency houses to ensure that pressure upon the Company and British government would be brought to bear in India as well as in London. In 1822, the leading London agency houses formed their own separate pressure group to lobby in favour of retaining Singapore and resisting Dutch interference in British trade in south-east Asia. The East India Trade Committee's first Chair was John Begbie, a leading agency house merchant, and in September 1822 he wrote to John Palmer requesting that the latter mobilise his colleagues in the Calcutta mercantile community in a campaign supporting the East India Trade Committee's objectives.[88] Palmer obliged, and in April 1823 he set up the Society for the Protection of the East India Trade, a Calcutta-based pressure group which campaigned for the retention of Singapore and Dutch protectionism.[89] Towards the end of 1823, when it was clear that the Anglo-Dutch negotiations were about to resume, the East India Trade Committee stepped up its activities, lobbying the British negotiators for the retention of Singapore, a robust attack on heavy Dutch trade duties on Java, and also for the establishment of a new British port on the Cobourg Peninsula in northern Australia, to be called Port Essington. This port, together with Singapore, would thwart Dutch efforts to exclude British commerce from south-east Asia.[90] Nineteen London East India agency houses supported the plea, and a meeting was subsequently arranged with Bathurst at which these concerns were forcibly repeated.[91] While Begbie lobbied the politicians, George Larpent presented the same arguments to Thomas Courtenay, the India Board official.[92]

The appeal for a new port in the archipelago was rejected by the British negotiators, because it would almost certainly have scuppered any prospect of an agreement with the Dutch. But they took the agency house concerns about Dutch protectionism on Java very seriously indeed. In fact, George Canning, one of the principal negotiators, had been made aware of this particular problem by the agency houses and their allies through East India Company channels. In 1823 a group of British merchants in Java approached William Taylor Money, an East India Company director, recently 'out on rotation' from the directorate, about rumours that the Dutch authorities were planning to order the compulsory purchase, at fixed prices, by the Dutch government of all coffee grown by British merchants. Money took the matter up directly with George Canning in December 1823, just as the negotiations were resuming. Money widened the merchants' complaints into a more generalised critique of the whole philosophy which underpinned Dutch attitudes to the British and commerce in general.[93] Money himself had been a partner in a Bombay agency house before he retired to London and entered the directorate, and was a keen representative of the London East India agency house interest. He was particularly interested in commercial opportunities on Java. In 1818, in conjunction with John Palmer of Calcutta, he sponsored a commercial venture on the island launched by one Mr Miller.[94] Together with the activities of the East India Trade Committee, this approach to Canning ensured that he and the other British negotiators were well aware of the worries of the agency houses about Dutch activities in Java and south-east Asia. The treaty did not, however, ultimately prove to be the defence against the Dutch which merchants and politicians hoped it would prove.

The Singapore question and the activities of the London and Indian agency houses during the negotiations leading to the Anglo-Dutch treaty of 1824 showed the range of their political armoury, which encompassed influence within the internal machinery of the East India Company, recognised commercial expertise upon which politicians had to rely, and a new found confidence and ability to organise outside the confines of the Company. Both the East India Trade Committee in London, and the Society for the Protection of the East India Trade in Calcutta demonstrated that the older agency house interests were imbibing the same spirit of independence from the Company, and willingness to work outside its arcane institutions, that characterised the merchants of Liverpool and elsewhere. For the men of London and Calcutta this did not mean that a presence within the Company was to be scorned. Rather it was to be supplemented by the new tactics and strategies of independent political lobbying. The East India Trade Committee and the Society for the Protection of the East India Trade were to prove prototypes for much more effective and enduring political organisations, namely the Bengal Chamber of Commerce established in 1834, and the London East India and China Association founded two years later. In respect of the former, there was even an abortive attempt to set up a Chamber of Commerce in Calcutta in August 1825, led by John Palmer, the driving force behind the Society for the Protection of the East India Trade.[95] In London, one of the leading lights of the East India Trade Committee of the early 1820s, Sir George Hochepied Larpent, was to emerge as the key figure in the London East India and China Association of the 1830s. Larpent belonged to a younger generation of agency house men, with little or no direct personal experience of India, weak ties of loyalty to the Company, and with an eye open to the new opportunities offered by Britain's rapidly industrialising economy. All this inclined them to a bolder and more independent approach to promoting their interests, though they never quite renounced their links to the East India Company.

Thus, by the end of the 1820s the structured world of the East India Company, which for so long had accommodated the pursuit of private gain by merchants operating outside or on the fringes of the Company's privileges and monopolies, was beginning to disintegrate. The rebellious merchants of the provinces, with the blessing of the British state, had breached the Company's India monopoly and showed every inclination to demand yet more reform. In the process, Britain's economic relationship with India had been dramatically and irrevocably altered, as the latter became a market for British textiles, rather than a supplier of Indian ones. The sub-continent was increasingly perceived as a source of raw materials rather than manufactures. Globally, the Napoleonic Wars had established Britain as the dominant commercial and imperial power, a position underpinned by the nation's burgeoning industrial and financial strength. The political background in India to economic change was the continuing and remorseless conquest of the sub-continent by the East India Company, now more of a political and military entity than a commercial one. The Company's retreat from commercial operations in India had accelerated, and at home the organisation had not only lost its once dominant position in the financial world of the City of London, but it had also become heavily dependent upon the assistance of the British state. The London and Indian agency houses, which for so long had reconciled themselves to trading and operating politically under the umbrella of the Company's monopoly and political structures, had begun to break out of this cocoon, building new commercial relationships with provincial British industrialists desperate for Asian markets. In the process they found their own independent political voice, without yet entirely eschewing their hard-won influence within the Company. To describe all this as a revolution in Britain's commercial and political relationship with Asia would hardly be hyperbole; yet what was to follow in the early 1830s was to seem by comparison even more shocking and dramatic.

Five

CRISIS AND TRADE LIBERALISATION 1830–1834:
FINANCIAL CHAOS AND
THE END OF THE EAST INDIA COMPANY'S
COMMERCIAL ROLE AND PRIVILEGES

IF THE period 1813 to 1830 had witnessed fundamental changes in the nature of Britain's trade with the East India Company's possessions in Asia, what followed can be described as a blend of chaos and revolution. Between 1830 and 1834, all of the leading Calcutta agency houses were swept away in the worst financial crisis in living memory, bringing bankruptcy and destitution for many Europeans and Indians who had deposited their life savings in the houses. British India was plunged into deep economic depression and, following the demise of the Calcutta agency houses, new commercial organisations were established, mainly by the London agency houses, most of which survived the spread of the crisis to Britain. The crisis coincided with a new attack on the privileges of the East India Company, as its Charter fell due for reconsideration in 1833. From 1829, merchants and industrialists in the great provincial cities of Liverpool, Glasgow, Birmingham and Manchester resumed their assault on the Company's remaining privileges, particularly its surviving monopoly of the China trade. The new campaign came at a time of great political turmoil. The political debate which preceded the passage of the Great Reform Act in 1832 was accompanied by a wave of popular discontent. Many among the landed elite feared they might be witnessing the early stages of bloody revolution. Such was the background to this new debate about Britain's economic relationship with its Asian possessions.

A number of key questions about this turbulent period must be addressed. Firstly, what were the reasons for the great Calcutta financial crash of the early 1830s? Why did all of the Calcutta agency houses fail after enjoying such success and privilege for almost half a century? Secondly, what was the legacy of the crisis? What was the impact upon commercial and social relations between the British community in India and the Indian commercial elite? How were Anglo-Indian commercial organisations reconstructed in the wake of 1830–1834, and what was the role of the London East India agency houses in this process? Were the new structures which emerged stable and secure? Thirdly, was there any relationship between the crisis in India and the success of those who were pressing for further diminution of the East India Company's privileges? The Company not only lost its remaining monopoly of trade with China, it also ceased to operate as a commercial organisation, remaining essentially as an agency of colonial government in the wake of the Charter Act of 1833. What were the processes by which this new state of affairs was reached? What was the role of the new, emergent commercial organisations trading with India, in London, the British provinces and in India, in bringing about this termination of the commercial activities of what had once been a purely trading enterprise? Finally, surveying the system of British commerce with Asia which emerged from this traumatic period, and the new role of the East India Company as an agency of colonial governance in India and south-east Asia, what were the principal features of the new British commercial and political order in the east?

The events of the commercial crisis of the early 1830s were sudden, though there had been warning signs of impending trouble during the 1820s. There were a number of problems which manifested themselves in a variety of ways. Firstly, as shown, the opening of the India trade to newcomers from Britain brought new competitors for the traditional agency houses. In the late 1810s, gluts in the quantity of British manufactures in India, and the excessive supply of shipping in Indian ports hit the traditional agency houses hard. There was much concern about the general health of the Indian economy. Some commentators believed that the disruptive effects of opening the Indian trade extended beyond the period immediately following the implementation of the Act. In 1834, when the financial crisis in Bengal was at its height, James Silk Buckingham, a severe critic of the East India Company and campaigner against its monopoly, blamed the agency houses for failing to move into the new trade in importing British manufactures into India, choosing instead to leave this lucrative branch of commerce to the newly arrived merchants.[1] Looking back on the crisis from the late 1830s, the orientalist John Crawfurd, another campaigner against the Company, argued that it was the more gener-alised competition with the newly arrived merchants that was the problem. In addition to their involvement in the import of British goods, some of the new men competed with the older houses which previously had enjoyed exclusive involvement in the country trade and in other activities such as shipbuilding and plantation agriculture. As a result, the latter increasingly invested in highly speculative pursuits such as housebuilding and new crop ventures, which proved unreliable in the difficult climate of the 1820s.[2]

There was substance in the arguments of Buckingham and Crawfurd. Leading houses such as John Palmer & Co. ultimately turned their backs on the new import trade, in spite of some initial interest.[3] The doomed adventure by the same firm in salt production on Saugor Island also epitomised the foolish investment decisions cited by Crawfurd.[4] But there were sound reasons for the reluctance of the older houses to move into the import trade from Britain. The glut of goods and merchants caused by the 1813 Act demonstrated the fragility of the new import trade, and the decision by some agency houses to stick with the commercial lines they knew best, was understandable in the uncertain conditions of the time. Moreover, agency house investment had always been quite speculative and results had been uncertain and patchy. In any case, by 1820 there was some evidence of recovery from the impact of trade liberalisation as British and Indian merchants adjusted to a new state of commercial equilibrium. Britain's dominant global position, and its ability to redraw spheres of influence to suit the national and imperial interest, such as it did in south-east Asia, augured well for the fortunes of British commerce. This was one reason perhaps why the seriousness of the looming crisis of the 1820s was not recognised as quickly as it should have been.

The second development to hurt the agency houses was the outbreak of war between British India and Burma in 1824. As a result of its economic growth in the eighteenth century, and the emergence of a distinct cultural identity, the Burmese kingdom had been expanding its area of territorial domination under the Konbaung dynasty since the mid eighteenth century.[5] By the early decades of the nineteenth century, the Burmese began to encroach on the regions of Manipur and Assam, territories which brought them to the eastern borders of Britain's Indian empire.[6] The threat this seemed to pose to British interests made conflict inevitable. In 1823 a dispute over which side held jurisdiction over the island of Shapuri in the River Naaf on the Arakan border led to war in the following year.[7] The British had little comprehension of the difficulties of fighting in the climate and terrain of Burma, or the strength of the Burmese forces they faced. Consequently, it took until 1826 for the British to win. The cost of the war was huge. Estimated by one historian at £4.8 million it proved to be the sixth most expensive of the British imperial conflicts in the nineteenth century.[8] In order to finance this unexpected burden, the Indian government was forced to borrow, issuing in September 1824 a loan of Rs1 Crore (10 million; or about £1 million) at 4% per annum.[9] At first the effects of this promised to be manageable. Several years earlier the government had paid off a large sum arising from earlier loans, thereby flooding the commercial community in India with a large quantity of capital which needed to be invested. The new loan seemed to offer a convenient outlet for this surplus. But the unexpected duration and cost of the conflict swallowed it up by February 1825. A second loan at 5% had to be issued in May 1825, which turned a developing shortage of capital into a severe one.[10] Another Crore was even borrowed from the Nawab of Awadh to pay for troops and provisions.[11] The agency houses, which depended upon the deposits of investors in India to fund their commercial operations, now found that they had to pay much higher rates of interest to hold on to the funds of their depositors. By early 1825 they were paying 8 or 9% on deposits, to keep their constituents aboard.[12] Even when victory was achieved, the costs of a swollen army and the occupation of Lower Burma pushed the bill ever higher, sustaining the pressure on the agency houses. By the mid-1820s, the houses were registering their distress. In late May 1826 the six most important firms appealed to the Indian government for financial assistance, and receiving Rs20 lakhs in aid.[13] Continuing difficulties resulted in subsequent appeals for help in 1827, which were also met.[14] Ultimately however, these were to prove futile.

Difficulties in the British domestic market were a third major factor which contributed to the failure of the Calcutta agency houses. A sudden rise in the price of bullion in Britain in 1818 led to a progressive curtailment of bullion exports to Bengal. This in turn contributed to a fall in the amount of money in circulation in India, exacerbating the shortage of capital available for the increasing demands of government and the agency houses.[15] In addition, a major stock exchange panic in 1825 presaged a general downturn in the British economy, which curbed demand for imported Indian produce. By the late 1820s, this was felt most acutely in the falling value of Indian exports of indigo in Britain. The problem was compounded by the fact that the East India Company itself exported large quantities of indigo to Britain as a means of remitting home resources to meet the Company's domestic financial commitments in Britain. This compounded the problem of oversupply on the British market, and the price of indigo on the British market halved between 1821 and 1830.[16] The consequences for the indigo producers of Bengal and north-eastern India, and the Calcutta agency houses which had advanced money to them for so long, were devastating. The indigo trade had always been fraught with uncertainty and wild fluctuations. Production was vulnerable to the extremes of the Monsoon climate and the unpredictable shifts in the international market for the commodity. The agency houses had long advanced money to the indigo factory owners, in spite of recurring problems of default. By the 1820s, some prominent houses such as Palmer & Co. had resorted to taking whole or part ownership of the indigo factories of clients who were heavily indebted to the firm. By 1830, Palmer had a share in twenty-one factories of debtor clients, and actually took responsibility for running another twenty-two.[17] The problem was that with the collapse of the indigo market and prices, these assets rapidly lost their value. In this way, the instability of the British market compounded the problems caused by war in India.

Those accounts of the agency house crisis which stress the difficulties of war and the wider economic environment tend to depict the crisis of 1830–1834 as the result of factors exogenous to the agency houses themselves.

This is certainly the tone of the accounts offered by Tripathi and Peers. Tripathi locates the origin of the crisis firmly in the financial consequences of the First Burmese War and problems in the British economy, while Peers sees it as arising more from a general crisis in international trade.[18] Peers is much more critical of the leaders of the agency houses and the decisions they made during a period of great instability. Kling also emphasises the importance of the decline in the indigo trade as a factor which undercut the financial foundations of the houses.[19] An earlier historian of the crisis, Benjoy Chowdhury, cites all of these factors but lays particular emphasis upon the importance of Indian investment in the houses, and the increasing fragility of trust between the European and Indian communities during the 1820s. This suffered an especially grievous blow in 1826, with the failure of Mercer & Co., a British firm involved in the indigo trade, which had drawn heavily on Indian capital.[20] Other historians also point to a deterioration in Anglo-Indian commercial relations during this period. Bhattacharya identifies failure of Indian confidence as an important factor in the agency house failures of the early 1830s.[21] C.A. Bayly's study of north Indian society in the period 1770–1870 identifies a downturn during the 1820s in the wealth and confidence of elite groups in Bengal and elsewhere, resulting from the disbandment of India armies and the effects of more efficient and demanding British systems of revenue collection both in territories under their direct control, and those subject to indirect rule.[22] While these historians have certainly not absolved the agency houses of responsibility for their own fate, the tendency has been to see them primarily as victims of circumstance rather than as the architects of their own misfortune.

Nonetheless, contemporaries and historians have hinted at failures on the part of the leaders of the houses. Buckingham and Crawfurd's criticisms of their investment decision making in the post-1813 period have already been mentioned, and historians have added to these. Singh, for example, argues that it was the appetite of leading agency house partners for high living, which led them to overdraw their firms to fund excessively lavish lifestyles.[23] More recently, Peers and Bagchi have been blunter, blaming the failures of the houses on the sheer greed of individual agency house partners.[24] But while these judgements undoubtedly carry much truth, they lack an analytical edge. There has been too little examination of how the principles which governed the running of the agency houses contributed to their downfall.

Among the contemporary commentators and historians who have written about the downfall of the agency houses, several offer insights into the structural and managerial frailties of the agency houses. George Larpent, interviewed by a parliamentary Select Committee on Manufactures, Commerce and Shipping in June 1833, was well qualified to offer an opinion on the shortcomings of the Calcutta agency houses, which were in the throes of destruction, even as he spoke.[25] He had been a partner in the London agency house of Cockerell & Trail in January 1830 when its Calcutta 'sister' house of John Palmer & Co. had failed, partly because of decisions made by the London firm. Palmer & Co. was the first great agency house failure, and Larpent was well acquainted with the problems the Indian houses faced, and their flaws as commercial organisations. For Larpent, a simple basic error of principle lay at the heart of their commercial strategies and organisation. Larpent deplored the fact that the houses used the deposits of their constituents to fund their various investments in plantations, shipping and other activities. They were speculating with the monies of others, a state of affairs which encouraged imprudence and a lack of care on the part of the houses. It also meant that when the more ambitious schemes of investment failed, they could turn rapidly into banking crises, as those who had invested in the agency houses discovered that their savings had been lost in such dubious schemes. This was certainly the experience of John Palmer & Co., when it met its fate in January 1830.

Ironically, a factor in its demise was a decision taken by the firm's London sister house, in which Larpent was a partner. Late in 1829 the London firm, disillusioned with the poor performance and failed investments of their Indian sister house over a number of years, called in the very substantial debt owed to it by Palmer & Co.[26] The result was not only the failure of the Indian firm, but the consequent ruin of large numbers of Europeans and Indians who had invested their life savings in Palmer & Co. In turn this triggered a collapse in confidence in the security of the other houses, a factor which contributed to the failure of all of them by 1834. The sequence of events illustrated the dangers inherent in combining banking operations with highly speculative investments and commercial ventures. Larpent's point was that this blend of banking and bold, speculative entrepreneurship made not only the individual agency houses potentially unstable and prone to failure, but also the whole system of British finance in India, because the failure of an individual firm could precipitate a wider crisis of confidence among the European and Indian investors on whom the system depended.

In his evaluation of the failure of the agency houses written during the 1960s, the historian Benjoy Chowdhury echoed the sentiments of an anonymous contributor to *The Calcutta Courier* in 1834. Both identified a fundamental weakness in the operating methods of all of the agency houses, which severely impaired the quality of their management.[27] Few agency house partners saw their involvement in their respective firms as a permanent or even necessarily long term arrangement. Most yearned for the earliest possible return to Britain following the rapid accumulation of a personal fortune. Many aspired to a seat in the London partner house or even in the Court of Directors of the East India Company. All coveted a comfortable life of wealth and status in Britain. As a consequence, most agency house men felt little loyalty to their firms, their fellow partners or to the businesses for which they worked. As a result, the retirement or resignation of agency house partners was usually accompanied by heavy withdrawals of capital from the firms, in the form of the respective shares of the departing partners. Often such depletions of capital came at times of uncertainty for the agency house concerned, as it desperately sought new recruits to replace the retiring partner. But a more general result of this lack of commitment to the business was that fellow agency house partners frequently viewed each other as rivals rather than colleagues, as competitors in a race to claim the lion's share of the firm's resources, with the aim of repatriating this as a personal fortune. A feature of the agency houses which heightened this sense of mutual suspicion, and provided opportunities for agency house men to pursue their own interests at the expense of the firm, was the multiple lines of business in which they were involved. These included trade, banking, shipping and investment in various types of commodity production (indigo, sugar, salt). In practice, each partner tended to take responsibility for different lines of business, treating these as their personal fiefdoms from which they could amass their own personal fortune. Few individual partners had the time to supervise the operation of the business as a whole, a state of affairs which left the agency houses open to flagrant embezzlement and incited recurring conflicts within their managements.

These difficulties are evident in a recent study of John Palmer & Co., the firm whose failure in 1830 precipitated the wholesale collapse of the system.[28] In the 1820s, as the firm ran into increasing financial difficulties, so the partners manoeuvred to develop exit strategies which would allow them to survive with their personal fortunes intact. Two partners, John Studholme Brownrigg and Henry Hobhouse (John Palmer's son-in law) successfully escaped the firm in 1825 to new roles in the London firm of Cockerell & Trail, taking with them substantial amounts of capital at a time when the firm desperately needed all of its resources.[29] Bitter recriminations followed the failure of Palmer & Co., with Palmer and other partners accusing both Hobhouse and Brownrigg of illegally and secretly withdrawing funds from the firm in the early 1820s.[30] These claims were rejected, not least because the London firm did not wish for their new recruits to be disgraced. Following the failure of Palmers', one investor in the firm remarked bitterly:

> how industrially attentive the partners were to their own interests, and how they traded for their separate benefits, not at all taking into consideration that the moneys, goods and remittances abstracted from the concern ought to have been used for the good of the concern in general[31]

In spite of his protestations at the skullduggery of his former partners, John Palmer was almost equally guilty of putting his own needs before those of his firm. His vast family (twelve children and numerous other dependants) was accustomed to a high standard of living, and to maintain it

Palmer drew very heavily indeed on the profits of the house. So excessive had these become by the difficult years of the early 1820s, that the other partners imposed restrictions on his withdrawals, a decision which Palmer found bitterly humiliating.[32] But, in fact, the lack of effective, overarching management and surveillance in John Palmer & Co. had allowed other erroneous practices to flourish unchecked. The firm's shipping operations, which in most cases involved partnership between Palmer & Co. and individuals who jointly owned (and usually commanded) ships in the house's fleet, were subject to such outrageous frauds by the ships' captains, that one partner in the firm doubted that this line of business ever generated a profit.[33] Palmer himself was cavalier in his tolerance of debt, especially when he enjoyed close personal relations with the debtor concerned. This had long been a source of frustration for the London house, but it was only in the 1820s that a real effort was made to check Palmer's rashness in this field.[34] Graver still was the fact that the rivalries and jealousies between the partners had made them all blind to longstanding fraud in the cash handing procedures within the house itself, perpetrated by several of the firm's Indian clerks. Over a period of twenty years or so they stole Rs20 lakhs (about £200,000). The crime only came to light after the failure of the house, and fuelled anxieties about the solvency of the other agency houses.[35] Of course it is difficult to ascertain how widespread were the problems of internal management evident in the running of Palmer's house. Given the similarities in the organisation of the houses it is however reasonable to assume that the problems of partner disloyalty and bad debt were probably endemic. Certainly the revelations of Palmer & Co.'s mismanagement, and the fact that it was Palmer & Co.'s London sister house which had dealt the final blow, accelerated the general collapse in investor confidence in Calcutta and London. This contributed greatly to the subsequent failures of the other Calcutta firms, all of which had gone under by the end of 1834. It seems that the problems of Palmer & Co. were perceived to be general to all of the agency houses. There was widespread consternation at the failures of Alexander & Co. and Mackintosh & Co. in December 1832 and January 1833 respectively, and when Colvin & Co. closed their doors for the last time in April 1833, the general mood of despair made further failures inevitable.[36] Fergusson & Co, failed in December 1833, and Cruttendens just a month later.[37] The shock in London was intensified by several failures there also. In 1833 Rickards & Co. failed, and a year later Fairlie's, one of the most prominent of the London firms, shared the same fate.[38] Much to the City of London's relief however, the casualties stopped there, and mercantile houses in the imperial capital were able to regroup and develop new strategies to revive their Indian interests.

The London agency houses tried to learn from the crisis when they reconstructed their affairs in India. Cockerell & Trail, the London sister firm of Palmer & Co., the first Indian agency house to fail, pioneered a new form of mercantile firm in India which others copied. Cockerell & Trail had learned of the structural and managerial instabilities of Palmer & Co. at first hand from retiring partners such as Brownrigg and Hobhouse. They were determined that the new organisation set up to replace it would remain firmly under the control and direction of the London house, and would eschew all involvement in banking. It would restrict its operations to those lines of business which had become most important to the London firm, notably the export of British cotton manufactures. As early as June 1830, Richard Howe Cockerell, nephew of Sir Charles Cockerell, senior partner in Cockerell & Trail opened a new corresponding firm, Cockerell & Co. Its instructions were to refrain from banking and high risk speculation. It was significant that Howe Cockerell was assisted in establishing the new house by Thomas Speir, a merchant closely connected with cotton manufacturing in Glasgow, and who had been instrumental in organising credit for Cockerell & Trail in Glasgow.[39] Of course, as shown in the last chapter, many of the London houses had been cultivating links with the new generation of merchant firms set up by newcomers to India after the 1813 Charter Act. In the main they had refrained from banking, focussing instead upon either the import of British manufactures or the export of Indian commodities. Thus it was natural for the London houses either to expand their dealings with these, or to ensure that the new houses they set up were organised along similar lines, with much tighter direction from London.

Kling describes the emergence of this system in the early 1830s, as the new houses were steered towards specialisation either in the export or import trade into India, and were prohibited from financing their enterprise through banking the savings of East India Company employees, as did the older houses.[40] Instead, the exporting firms which flourished through making advances to indigo and other Indian producers, acquired the capital for this either by borrowing from Indian businessmen (*banians*), or from the importing houses, which held funds from the sales of British manufactures. Over time, many of these new houses moved into relatively new areas of commercial activity, notably the operational management of joint-stock companies on behalf of their shareholders.[41] Typical of the new type of firm was Carr, Tagore & Co., which combined the European expertise of former traditional agency house men, such as William Prinsep, and the capital and commercial ability of Dwarkanath Tagore, the eminent Bengali merchant and *zamindar*. Carr, Tagore and Co. was exceptional in that it engaged in banking through the Union Bank of Calcutta, an enterprise which was to fail in 1847 in a crisis reminiscent of the great crash of the early 1830s. It also came to act as managing agents for several joint stock companies, notably the Calcutta Steam Tug Association (set up in 1836).[42]

In spite of the severity of the crisis of the early 1830s, a substantial number of Europeans in Calcutta who had been involved in the failed houses responded with great resilience. William Prinsep, a senior partner in Palmer & Co., who went on to become a significant figure in Carr, Tagore & Co. has been mentioned, but there were others. Donald W. Gordon, an employee of Mackintosh & Co., was thrown out of work by that firm's failure in January 1833, but within the year had joined Prinsep at Carr, Tagore & Co.[43] Robert Jenkins, the ruined son-in-law of John Palmer, also set up new agency house in 1834 with William Ferguson, who had been in the failed firm of Fergusson & Co. They established a corresponding relationship with Fairlie, Clark & Co. of London.[44] Some of the bigger London financial firms could see promising opportunities in the vacuum created by the failure of the older agency houses. In September 1833, the American merchant Joshua Bates, a leading partner in Baring Brothers of London noted that he and his colleagues had been considering increasing the amount of capital invested in their Calcutta corresponding house, Gisborne & Co.:

> In the present depressed condition of the India trade by reason of the many failures we cannot fail to become receivers of a large portion of the goods from that country. It must be carried through and we shall soon feel the advantage of it[45]

A week later, a Mr Richards was sent out to Gisborne & Co. to supervise the expansion of its operations.[46]

But the great crisis also left scars and bitterness which would cause friction in subsequent years. Some of those who had survived the crash of the 1830s never forgot or forgave what they saw as the indifference (and in some cases outright treachery) of the London firms to their fate. The response of some London merchants was equally unforgiving in return. When William Prinsep visited London in summer 1834, he received an icy reception when he visited the offices of Cockerell & Larpent, and Sir Charles Cockerell simply refused to see him.[47] In turn, in spite of the rigorous controls imposed by the London houses, members of the newer houses asserted their right to a separate voice, as demonstrated by the prominence of their number among the firms who established the Calcutta Chamber of Commerce in 1834.[48] They were quite willing to speak out when they saw damaging policies being pressed by their London-based corresponding houses. But perhaps the most serious legacy of the crisis was its effect on the relationship between British and Indian businessmen. Relations between the old agency houses and the Indian business community had been quite close, not least because each of the firms used Indian intermediaries (*banians*) in their dealings with Indian businesses. Agency houses such as Palmer & Co. were famous for their intimate relations with Indian business, a reputation amply demonstrated in a concerted effort by a number of Indian businessmen to rescue the firm in the months following it failure in January 1830.[49] But Bagchi argues persuasively that the crisis, and the way in which it was dealt with under British colonial law, severely undermined Anglo-Indian trust. He contends that under the Insolvency legislation in force at the time, European creditors of the failed agency houses were dealt with much more fairly than their Indian counterparts, resulting in severe losses for the latter.[50] As a consequence, there was a tendency for Indians to be much more reluctant to enter with Europeans into the close commercial collaborative ventures which had existed under the old agency houses. Those who did so, such as Dwarkanath Tagore and Motilal Seal, took great care to ensure that they, unlike the victims of 1830 to 1834, were adequately protected by security on loans or other legal protection. But they were the exception. Bagchi's argument, that the crisis precipitated a trend towards the creation of separate European and Indian financial and mercantile spheres, is largely accurate.[51]

At the same time that the great financial crisis of Calcutta was unfolding, the latest round of discussions about the renewal of the East India Company's charter was getting under way in Britain. The debate was overshadowed by the dramatic political events leading to the introduction of the Great Reform Act in 1832, a period which saw several changes of government and much unrest in British cities. In respect of the new charter, key decisions were made very soon after discussions began in 1829, and the principles thereby established were largely upheld, although governments and their personnel changed as the Reform question moved towards its dramatic conclusion. Inevitably, the political focus on Reform produced delays in the execution of the new charter, but on the substantive questions its outcome was never really in doubt. Inevitably, the central issues were whether or not the Company's monopoly of trade with China would be renewed, and whether or not its power and institutions of government over India would be allowed to continue. Whether or not to allow Europeans to reside in and acquire property on Indian soil was another vexed question.

In respect of the China monopoly, the outcome was quickly agreed. The position of the Company in 1829 was even weaker than it had been in 1812/13. Part of the problem was the deteriorating state of the East India Company's finances from 1813 onwards. Bowen shows how during this period, following the opening of the India trade, the Company's trade with India rapidly declined, as private traders dominated the export of British textile manufactures, and demand for Indian textiles declined in Europe. In addition, the Company found it progressively difficult to increase the quantity of its exports of Indian goods to China, an essential requirement if the trade with China was to generate sufficient income to finance the huge purchases of Chinese tea which were so crucial for the Company's financial health.[52] Bowen estimates that after 1814, the Company's trade needed to generate £1 million in profits each year, in order for it to meet its heavy debts, charges and other obligations in Britain. But by the 1820s, profits from the China trade had peaked, and were increasingly offset by the growing losses in the Indian trade.[53] As a result, by the end of the decade, the Company had to import bullion from India and China into London in order to meet its domestic obligations. Doubts were also setting in about the efficacy and consequences of the China monopoly, which was increasingly being circumvented by American traders who purchased British manufactures through the agency of British-based merchant houses such as Barings, William Brown of Liverpool and Charles Everett.[54] There was a growing conviction that only through the introduction of free trade, under which British private traders would compete on equal terms with their American counterparts, would Britain's share of the lucrative Chinese market be preserved. Thus, there were some clear long term trends which fuelled the arguments of the anti-monopoly camp, and encouraged politicians to take an even more critical stance than they had done in 1812–1813.

But the role of the anti-monopoly interests in Britain in the final ending of the China monopoly should not be underestimated in this process. Victory for free trade was not a certainty in the absence of political will to make it so. The difficulties confronting governments over the Reform question, and the general political instability which that issue generated, might have resulted in compromises which were unsatisfactory for the free trade camp. The Company was still, after all, a formidable political presence in the City and Parliament, and governments in the period 1829–1832 had their minds on other issues. A concerted resistance by the Company, in the absence of a strong free trade lobby, might have preserved aspects of the remaining monopoly and other privileges. The importance of a sustained political campaign against the Company's privileges was all the greater, given the disruptive effects of the Reform debate on discussions about the East India Company. Select Committees of both houses were set up in February 1830 to consider the Company's affairs, but their deliberations were interrupted by the dissolution of Parliament in July 1830, and the emergence of a new government. The Commons Select Committee was reconstituted and resumed its proceedings in February 1831, only to be interrupted again by yet another dissolution in April 1831, and the political battle over the Reform question. Other problems caused further interruptions, and only in January 1832 was the committee finally able to complete its enquiries.[55] The political turmoil, and the lengthy parliamentary enquiries necessitated a rigorous and concerted effort by the opponents of the Company's privileges to ensure that the Company's still formidable political resources could not be deployed to thwart change.

The provincial merchants and manufacturers of Glasgow, Liverpool and Manchester and other cities proved to be even more formidable opponents of the Company than they had been in 1812–1813. The Liverpool East India Association, which was now a well-established and mature organisation, took the lead in organising the provincial interests to lobby government. In April 1829 it decided to send a deputation to meet government ministers and MPs in London to argue against the renewal of the Company's charter. It invited merchants from Glasgow to reconstitute their East India Association and join the deputation.[56] The Glasgow merchants and industrialists duly responded under the leadership of Kirkman Finlay, the prominent Glasgow industrialist and politician, re-establishing the organisation which had proven so effective in 1812/13.

Kumagai's recent PhD thesis provides the most comprehensive analysis of the provincial East India Associations during this period, especially their composition, strategies and tactics.[57] He shows in particular that the Glasgow association was dominated by the city's textile interests, while Liverpool's was composed of a wide range of the city's interests, with the association itself providing a unifying role for the city's mercantile community.[58] Both associations were led by men of high stature and wealth in their respective cities, and were well connected with MPs and senior politicians. They were also assiduous in their efforts to rally wider support in their localities, with Glasgow mobilising Scottish opinion and Liverpool promoting the cause in the towns of Lancashire, and in Manchester.[59] As a result, in April 1829 deputations from Glasgow, Liverpool, Manchester, Birmingham, Bristol and elsewhere converged on London, and brought their demands to the attention of the Duke of Wellington's government. A key figure was William Huskisson, then President of the Board of Trade and a Liverpool MP in close contact with the Liverpool East India Association.[60] On 6 May, deputations met to hammer out their demands, which included the opening of the China trade and an end to the strict restrictions on British residence in India. On the latter, the lobbyists wanted the right to own property in India, which they saw as essential to the economic development of the subcontinent. Three days later, these demands were presented by the deputations to the Duke of Wellington (the Prime Minister), Henry Gouldbourn (Chancellor of the Exchequer) and Lord Ellenborough (President of the Board of Control). The distressed state of the manufacturing districts was strongly emphasised, as it had been in 1812/13. Although the government made no immediate promises, the views expressed at the meeting were instrumental in Wellington's decision to set up a parliamentary Select Committee to consider the renewal of the Company's charter.[61] In fact, during the course of 1830 two Select Committees (one in the Commons and one in the Lords) considered the question of the East India Company, providing the free trade lobby with a platform from which they could persuade government of the need for change. It was an opportunity they did not shirk.

The strategies and tactics of the provincial East India Associations have been expertly analysed by Kumagai, who rightly identifies a number of key features, some of which were similar to the campaign of 1812–1813, and some which were strikingly new and different. As in the campaign against the India monopoly, they bombarded government and Parliament with petitions, almost 190 of these being sent by the various East India Associations and other bodies between February and July 1830 alone.[62] But it was when the Select Committees began to sit and interview traders, East India Company officials and 'experts' that the East India Associations and their allies demonstrated a degree of sophistication and aptitude for political manoeuvre which had not been evident in 1813. From the outset, leaders of the movement, such as Kirkman Finlay did their utmost to ensure that the Select Committees would receive convincing evidence on behalf of the anti-monopoly cause. To this end, every effort was made to ensure that the committees would call men sympathetic to the free trade cause, and that these witnesses would be briefed before being interviewed and debriefed afterwards, to ensure that as far as possible, consistent lines of argument would be impressed upon the minds of the committee members. It was an exercise in political choreography. From the various provincial deputations in London there emerged a small group of men, including Kirkman Finlay and James Cropper of Liverpool who orchestrated the putting forward of witnesses, carefully briefed them where necessary, and monitored the proceedings in an effort to ensure that later witnesses would deploy counter-arguments against points raised by Company interviewees. Of crucial significance, as Kumagai shows, were the strenuous efforts made to work closely with merchants based in London and others whose knowledge of India, China and the eastern trade could be used to best effect. The links between merchant houses in the City of London (including the London East India agency houses) and provincial manufacturers which had developed in the period since 1813, undoubtedly made this much easier, as personal connections had been established in some cases through business. It amounted to, as Kumagai suggests, an exercise in collaboration between provincial industrial interests and City 'gentlemanly capitalists'.[63]

Perhaps the most significant example of this was the relationship which emerged between the provincial campaigners and Barings Brothers, one of the richest and most influential merchant houses in the City, and one with important financial and commercial links with the USA, India and China. Barings had been heavily involved in procuring British manufactures for American merchants trading to China, a branch of their business which had grown dramatically in the 1820s. In the summer of 1828, Barings had undergone a major internal re-organisation, which saw Joshua Bates, Thomas Baring and Humphrey St John-Mildmay established as the managing partners in the house.[64] Their strategy for the future development of the business involved a general expansion of its activities in India and China, both on the firm's own account, and on behalf of its American clients.[65] Conscious of the growth of Liverpool's trade with Asia, and competition from such Liverpool merchants as William Brown in the American trade with China and India, Barings also set up its own subsidiary house in Liverpool in 1832.[66] It was clear to the partners that an end to the Company's China monopoly was in Barings' interest, as this would be a necessary pre-requisite for their own plans

for expanding the firm's activities in Asia. The Glasgow East India Association suggested to Kirkman Finlay in February 1830 that Joshua Bates could be
a useful ally. Their knowledge of him almost certainly arose from commercial
contacts with Barings enjoyed by Glasgow manufacturers.[67] Bates was arguably the most influential of a number of contacts in London suggested by the
Glasgow association.

But, in fact, Bates was called before the Select Committee even before the
free traders had the opportunity to recommend him. Bates appeared before
the Commons Select Committee on no less than three occasions in 1830; on
15 March, 30 March and on 3 June. He also appeared before the Lords Select
Committee on 10 June.[68] Bates argued that opening the trade to China would
result in a substantial expansion of British trade there, probably to the long
term detriment of Britain's American competitors in that market.[69] He also
argued that in the long term, an open private trade would deliver cheaper tea
to the British market.[70] This was powerful testimony from one of the most
highly respected men in the City of London, and Kirkman Finlay thought
that it was most important.[71] He believed that the impact of Bates' testimony
had been 'under-rated' by observers at the time.[72] The fact that Bates was not
a witness associated with the free trade campaign, only heightened the impact
of his comments. Although Bates was not called before the Select Committee
on the instigation of the free trade campaign, when James Cosmo Melvill,
Auditor to the Company and an expert on the Company's trade, challenged
some of Bates' estimated figures on Company and private trade freight costs,
Finlay took the trouble to contact Bates about Melvill's comments, so that
Bates was able to respond to them when he subsequently appeared before
the Select Committee on 3 June.[73] Bates was not entirely comfortable with
this approach, as he did not agree with all aspects of the demands of the
campaign. But nonetheless he acted on Finlay's information. There was also
a London-based lobby group, the 'Association for Colonisation to India and
Free Trade to China', set up in 1828, which liaised with the free trade movement, particularly the Liverpool East India Association.[74] In early March
1830 Finlay reported that members of the deputations 'have gone every day
into the City to look after evidence'.[75] Clearly, the links with London-based
interests was not only a new development, but one which greatly strengthened
the impact and credibility of the free trade case.

Among the new allies, one man in particular emerged as invaluable for
the free trade campaign. John Crawfurd, a Scot with a long personal history
in Asia, and with a growing intellectual reputation as an orientalist, became
an active friend of the free trade campaign in 1829. Edward Said's seminal
thesis on orientalist thought as an intellectual root of western imperialism
has become a central theme in modern thinking about empire, and in many
ways Crawfurd epitomised Said's notion of the influence of the orientalist
intellectual.[76] Not only did his writings, which spanned half a century, shape

western thinking about India, south-east Asia and China, but he was also an active political campaigner on a range of issues related to Britain's Asian empire. Born in 1783 on the island of Islay, Crawfurd trained as a medical practitioner before joining the East India Company in 1803. He served in northern India, before being transferred to Penang in 1808, where his rapidly gained mastery of the Malay language marked him out for more than just a medical career. He subsequently served as an administrator during the British occupation of Java between 1811 and 1816. In this time he amassed sufficient knowledge to write his *History of the Indian Archipelago* (1817), which established him as an orientalist 'expert' to compete with Thomas Stamford Raffles, his superior on Java, and bitter personal rival. In 1823 he succeeded Raffles as Governor of Singapore, and in the late 1820s led important political missions to Burma and Siam. These expeditions formed the basis for later publications, and the establishment of a formidable reputation as an expert on Asia. Disillusioned with Company rule and restrictive commercial practices, on his return to England in 1828 he threw himself into the campaign to strip away the remaining privileges of the East India Company.[77] Crawfurd used his reputation and knowledge of the east in various ways, publishing articles in favour of trade liberalisation, and even appearing before the Commons Select Committee in person. But he was also at the nerve centre of the London deputations, and he worked closely with Kirkman Finlay, Cropper and others to ensure that Select Committees received exactly the message the movement wanted them to hear. He advised a number of witnesses due to appear before the committees. For example, in late February he held a long interview with one Captain Coffin, a merchant familiar with the China trade who was due to appear before the Commons Select Committee. It is clear that Crawfurd carefully advised Coffin on what to say, and which points to make most forcefully.[78] This practice of coaching, of briefing witnesses before they were interviewed and debriefing them after in preparation for later testimonies, was a vital function provided by Crawfurd, which ensured that the Select Committees would be persuaded of the case. It proved to be extremely effective.

The fall of Wellington's administration, and its replacement in November 1830 by that of Earl Grey, proved to be a decisive development in respect of the question of the East India Company. By then, although the work of the first round of Select Committees had been interrupted by political events, certain key issues had been effectively decided, particularly the need to end the Company's China monopoly, and to allow residence and property ownership for British subjects in India. Grey, and his new President of the Board of Control, Charles Grant, made clear to the Chairs of the Company that these elements would form a central part of the new Charter Act.[79] Indeed, it was even hinted that the Company's role in administering India might be at an end, a possibility which caused much alarm within the directorate, but

one which seemed difficult to resist, given the unfavourable political climate
for the Company. However, Grey's government retreated from the threat of
ending the Company's role in governing India for several reasons. Firstly,
consideration of the replacement of the Company would have burdened
government and Parliament with an issue of enormous complexity, just at a
time when they were struggling to cope with the even more pressing matter
of parliamentary reform. The issues were much more politically sensitive
than just the question of how India was to be administered. The Court of
Directors exercised a great power of patronage, handing Company positions
to friends and allies. Replacing this would prove tricky, and there could be no
certainty about how the ending of patronage would be received by a political
class among whom numbered many who had either benefited from directors'
patronage in the past or expected to do so in the future. Secondly, the Select
Committees found, on the whole, that while the Company's administration
of India was not beyond criticism, it was the best option at the time. This
was due not only to an effective rearguard action by the Company's own
officials in their testimonies to the committees, but also to the fact that the
Company's governance of India was not in itself an issue which the free
trade lobby wished to challenge. Indeed, as Kumagai shows, one of the more
strident enemies of the Company, John Silk Buckingham, bitterly criticised
the Glasgow East India Association for its indifference to the question of
Indian government, complaining that 'they were for taking away the trading
character of the India Company only, and leaving them all the revenues,
patronage and political power which they possess'.[80] Thus, while from time
to time during the charter negotiation period, Grey, Grant and others might
hint darkly at the possibility of stripping the Company of its political role,
this mainly appears to have been a ploy to keep the directors compliant, when
occasionally one of their number showed an inclination towards resistance.
Thomas Babington Macauley, the Secretary of the Board of Control who
was to draw up the details of the 1833 Act, neatly summarised the prevailing
mood in government: 'But of all the substitutes for the Company which have
been hitherto suggested, not one has proved to be better than the Company,
and most of them could, I think, easily be worse'.[81]

Nonetheless, the relative quiescence of the Company and its directors in
the face of this prolonged assault on its power and privileges requires some
explanation. The fact was that defenders of the Company's privileges did little
or nothing to lobby in their defence and, as Philips shows, resignation and
fatalism seemed to characterise the response of the Company to attacks on its
China monopoly and other privileges.[82] The reason for this in part reflected
the deteriorating financial state of the Company in the 1820s. This made it
difficult to mount an effective defence against changes such as the end of the
China monopoly, which, given the threat of American competition, and the
apparent inability of the Company to expand trade with China, seemed to

be the best option to most disinterested observers. But in addition to these circumstances, which made reform difficult to argue against, there were also internal political reasons for the apparent inertia of the Company. The private trade interest had grown steadily stronger during the 1820s, increasing its representation in the directorate. The London East India agency houses in particular became a formidable grouping, and their developing links with British industry and interest in the export of British manufactures meant that they could see advantages in the end of the China monopoly.[83] Of course, as Philips shows, the agency house failures in Calcutta in the early 1830s, did impact upon the strength of the London agency houses within the directorate, allowing other interest groups (the City and 'Indian' interests) to reassert themselves, particularly through the election of new directors in the early 1830s.[84] However, the scale of the financial crisis in India made it more difficult than ever to argue that the Company's husbandry of the Indian economy had been competent, while the revival of the competing interest groups within the directorate made it difficult to achieve unity within the Company's leadership, as old rivalries re-emerged. Inertia and introspection were the inevitable consequence. Combined with the threat to the Company's governing role in India, and an assurance in January 1833 that the proprietors of the Company would be guaranteed an annual dividend of 10.5%, these factors muted any serious opposition to the reforms from East India House.

The Charter Act of 1833 was successfully steered through the Commons by Macaulay in the summer of that year, and he effectively defended the compromise enshrined in the bill of ending the Company's commercial life, whilst retaining its political, governing function. On the latter, Macaulay justified the continuance of Company governance of India on the grounds that the alternative of direct government from Whitehall would be subject to the destabilising influence of domestic party politics.[85] Residence and property rights in British India were granted by the Act, and much greater liberality permitted in respect of the movement of British subjects within the Company's territories. The Board of Control's power over the appointment of the Governor-General was reasserted, while the position itself was given greater authority. The directors' patronage was also preserved, but with the amendment that all directors would in future nominate four times the number of people needed to fill vacancies. The nominees would then be selected by competitive examination to fill the vacant places. It in many ways characterised the spirit of compromise which infused the Act.[86] The Act thereby terminated the Company's life as a commercial organisation and reinvented it as an agency of colonial government, one step removed from the British government in Whitehall. It was a logical and probably inevitable development, given the long-term deterioration in the Company's fortunes as a trading organisation, against a backdrop of imperial expansion in India. As Bowen aptly puts it, it was a rational final step from being an empire of business into being responsible for the business of empire.[87] Significantly, this meant that the Company's institutions for running itself and India would remain intact. Its bureaucracy and the expertise it offered would ensure that, as an organisation, its directors and officials would continue to exercise some influence over imperial policy in India. In fact, now that its commercial function had been abolished, the authority of Company men could recover to some degree, as the inefficiencies evident in the organisation's trading operations were now a thing of the past and no longer a target for the anger of those seeking to break down the Company's trading privileges. In this respect, it is an error to see the post 1833 Act period as one in which the Company was little more than an instrument of government from Whitehall, or an inevitable prelude to the oblivion which followed the Great Indian Rebellion of 1857. As will be seen, the Company could still exercise an important influence over policy in India and Asia, and it remained an important player in this field, almost until the end.

What major points of significance should be taken from this turbulent period in the history of the East India Company and British rule in India? First, it is clear that a decisive factor in bringing the Act of 1833 about had been the development since 1813 of new political and commercial links between those private trading organisations which had grown up under the aegis of the East India Company, the London East India agency houses, and the emergent industrial interests of provincial Britain. These had enabled the free trade movement of 1829–1833 to present a united campaign which encompassed both provincial industrial and metropolitan commercial financial interests in favour of reform. Moreover, the lead in organisational terms had come from the provincial organisations, the East India Associations of Glasgow and Liverpool. It was they who petitioned for change first and it was their leaders who orchestrated the campaign for reform. The London-based interests had largely followed where their peers from the provinces had led. This must be an important counter-argument to the 'gentlemanly capitalism' thesis of Cain and Hopkins, whose work tends to depict provincial industrial lobbies as outsiders, and downplays the effectiveness of their efforts to shape government colonial policy.[88] Cain and Hopkins are certainly correct that the long-term deterioration of the Company's financial position in trade, and the burgeoning costs of imperial rule and expansion in India increasingly persuaded British politicians to be open to change. But it would be an error to see this as making reform inevitable. Given the Company's (admittedly declining) importance in the financial centre of the City of London, and its significant representation in Parliament, changes which affected its interests and privileges required pressure from outside government to deliver reform. Without the formidable campaign mounted and led by the provincial interests and their metropolitan allies between 1829 and 1833, many of the Company's privileges, including the China monopoly, would probably have survived. After all, governments in this period were much more concerned by the question of parliamentary reform, and without an effective public campaign for change in respect of the Company, it is questionable whether politicians would have wanted to open a 'second front' against the Company at such an unstable and difficult time.

Secondly, Cain and Hopkins' notion that provincial manufacturers were not only political outsiders, but also detached from the more politically influential 'gentlemanly capitalists' of London, is refuted here.[89] The campaign had seen intense and effective political collaboration between provincial industrialists and leading City merchants, and this did not cease with the passage of the Charter Act of 1833. In fact, the uncertainties which followed the Act in respect of British policy in India and Asia ensured that the dialogue between 'gentlemanly capitalists' and manufacturers interested in Asian commerce would become louder and more intense. There remained so many questions to decide. How for example would the Company remit its Indian tax revenues to Britain to fund its dividends and other 'home charges' in Britain, now that it was no longer permitted to use trade as a channel for this? How would any new system impact upon the interests of non-Company traders? Moreover, the Calcutta financial crises of the early 1830s, and the need to reconstruct the commercial order there, provided another imperative for the maintenance of collaboration between industry and finance, and between province and capital. In fact, as will be seen, commercial interests located in Asia itself would also soon be drawn into what would become a trans-imperial network of British commercial interests in Asia.

Six

RE-ORDERING ANGLO-ASIAN COMMERCE AND POLITICS: 1833–1847

THE CHARTER ACT of 1833 certainly ushered in a new era in Anglo-Asian commerce and politics; but there remained much uncertainty about the future. In 1833 a number of issues remained unresolved, in spite of the debates of the previous three years and the hope that a new and more successful order could be established. It is worth outlining the issues which still needed to be resolved before addressing how the various interests connected with India sought to deal with them. First of all, it is important to understand that in 1833, the great financial crisis in Calcutta of the early 1830s had not yet run its course. Although the last of the great agency houses was not to fail until early in 1834, the scale and seriousness of the upheaval was beyond doubt a year earlier. This was clear even in London by then following the failures of several London East India agency firms. Some London East India houses had already begun to adjust to the aftermath of the crisis, by sending representatives to Calcutta either to set up new partner agency houses or to cultivate links with newer merchant firms established since 1813. But in 1833 it remained unclear how these new relationships between London and Calcutta commercial houses would operate. It was plain that the London houses wanted more control over the commercial operations the Calcutta firms would engage in, following the disastrous consequences arising from the combination of banking with speculative enterprise. No longer would banking be permitted as a legitimate line of activity for a partner firm answerable to a London East India agency house. The Calcutta houses would be strictly trading organisations. In addition, it became the practice for the London firms to take a directive role, instructing the Indian houses on commercial policy, usually through a partner in the Indian firm with close connections in London. These Indian firms tended to become more specialised during the 1830s, focussing either on the export trade in British manufactures to India or the import of Indian commodities to Britain. How these new relationships between London and Calcutta agency houses would develop over time remained to be seen.

There was a second set of issues which needed to be resolved. These concerned the direction of the political administration and economic development of India, now that the East India Company had retreated from commerce. In particular, the Company now needed to find new methods to remit to Britain the surplus revenues raised in India that were needed to pay the home charges. The methods adopted proved to be controversial and caused conflict with non-East India Company organisations trading with India. More generally, by the early 1830s the full impact of the commercial revolution of the previous twenty years had become clear. The once mighty Indian textile industry had been destroyed by competition from the mechanised British cotton manufacturers. The Indian economy, once a supplier of luxury textiles for the British and European markets, had become a market for British cotton manufactures. It was also emerging as a supplier of primary produce, notably opium, indigo, cotton, sugar and, from the 1840s, tea.[1] A problem for the Company was that the overall value of Indian exports had not risen sufficiently to meet its needs in the 1820s. The Company relied upon the export of Indian produce to Britain, and Chinese tea and other commodities acquired through the export of Indian goods to that market, to remit the funds to Britain needed to cover the home charges, the dividends, pensions and other costs of the Company in Britain. There were several difficulties, and the elimination of Indian textile exports to Britain was a particularly acute one. In addition, after 1813, the Company had to compete with private merchants who were now permitted to export Indian commodities to Britain on their own account. Because it relied upon its exports of Indian indigo to remit funds to Britain, the Company tended to continue with its exports even if the domestic British market was glutted. In the 1820s oversupply resulted from the increased exports of indigo by both the Company and the agency houses. The resulting collapse of indigo prices in Britain was certainly one factor in the demise of the agency houses in 1830–1834, but it was also very difficult for the Company, which by the end of the 1820s had to ship bullion to Britain to make ends meet.[2] As Bowen shows, this deepening financial difficulty helped persuade government that the Company's future was as an agency of imperial government rather than a commercial organisation.

Siddiqi has pointed to other reasons for the failure of Indian exports to meet expectations. He argues that previous analyses of the performance of opium, sugar, cotton and indigo exports from India in the early nineteenth century have paid too little attention to their value, in a context of rapidly changing terms of trade. Export performance in terms of value was severely undermined by a drain of gold from India by the Company as tribute, which exacerbated a decline in the value of the silver Rupee against gold-based currencies such as Sterling.[3] The result was that Indian exports generated insufficient income for the Indians who produced them or the British merchants who traded in them. Siddiqi contends that this was a contributory factor to the depression which beset the Indian economy in the second quarter of the nineteenth century, a phenomenon also identified by C.A. Bayly, who attributes the downturn to the demilitarisation of Indian society and the consequent suppression of consumption by Indian elites.[1] The central issue was how to develop the export potential of the Indian economy. This would be essential for the financial stability of Company rule, as well as for the continuing growth of British exports to India, not to mention the political stability of British colonial rule.

A third question which concerned non-Company interests connected with India was the future determination of British colonial economic policy in India and Asia. The London East India agency houses had long relied principally upon their power as stockholders in the Company to exercise influence over policy in India. Their influence reached a peak in the 1820s, when the houses and their allies commanded a significant presence in the Court of Directors.[5] But the failure of the Indian houses and its ramifications in London undermined their power in Leadenhall Street, whilst the success of the provincial anti-monopoly campaign had demonstrated that the Company's ability to exercise a decisive influence over the politicians was in sharp decline. The effectiveness of the campaign against the Company was not lost on merchants in London involved in trade with the east. The skillful co-ordination of the movement's lobbying activities across several cities, the recruitment of formidable experts like John Crawfurd, and the lead they gave to London interests in the campaign had left an indelible impression on mercantile leaders in the capital. Ominously, in contrast to the period following the 1813 Charter Act, the East India Associations of Liverpool and Glasgow did not disband once the objective of ending the Company's China monopoly had been achieved. Instead, they stepped up their efforts to shape government policy in India and Asia, shifting their attention to new issues. This was to have profound consequences for commercial politics in respect of Asia for decades after the Charter Act of 1833.

Finally, there was the question of the East India Company itself. The peculiar status created for it by the Charter Act left many issues to be resolved. Would the Company simply be absorbed into the bureaucracy of early nineteenth-century government? Or would the fact that it retained its own internal culture, its own system of education, training and promotion, added to its formidable expertise on Asian colonial affairs, enable it to maintain a significant influence over policy? Certainly the fact that it still had stockholders to whom dividends were due was a potential conflict of interest with the Company's role as an agency of colonial government. This continuing obligation helped sustain a spirit of independence in the Company's behaviour. Would the elimination of its failing commercial activities in fact strengthen it politically, removing as it did a chronic source of conflict with the British state? In these respects, the Charter Act of 1833 had taken both the East India Company and the British state into uncharted territory.

Even as the Charter Act was passing through Parliament in 1833, these questions occupied politicians, Company officials, provincial merchants and financiers in the City of London, particularly the London East India agency house partners with a vested interest in trade and empire in Asia. Perhaps unsurprisingly, it was one of the last who took the lead on the questions of developing the Indian economy and shaping the new structures of political influence in Asian colonial policy. By 1833, Sir George Hochepied Larpent was a fast rising partner in the firm of Cockerell & Trail, which was soon to become Cockerell & Larpent. He had already established his credentials as a political as well as a commercial operator. Although he had never visited India, this did not prevent him acquiring a formidable reputation in Anglo-Asian commercial politics. In the 1820s he had been a vigorous campaigner against the preferential duties enjoyed by West Indian sugar and rum over the produce of India and south-east Asia, and he published a major pamphlet on this question.[6] He had also been prominent in the East India Trade Committee, the body established in the early 1820s to influence the British negotiators who hammered out the Anglo-Dutch Treaty of 1824, which divided south-east Asia into respective British and Dutch spheres of influence, and preserved British possession of Singapore.[7] Of course as a senior partner of Cockerell & Trail he had also been implicated in the collapse of John Palmer & Co. in 1830, which was deliberately precipitated by the London house. As a result, Larpent emerged from the crisis of the early 1830s with a conviction that never again should commercial firms in India be permitted to engage in banking on their own account.[8] His firm were as good as their word, and did not permit their new sister house in Calcutta, R.H. Cockerell & Co., to engage in such activity. But this raised an important and troubling question: how to supply the capital necessary to develop the primary commodity production required to ensure the prosperity of colonial rule in India? After the demise of the traditional agency houses, European banking facilities in India were severely limited. In Calcutta, there were just two banks of note. The first was the Bank of Bengal which had been established in 1808. But this was heavily dependent on government backing and subject to a number of restrictions which limited its ability to lend, and therefore its capacity to promote Indian economic development.[9] The other was the unchartered Union Bank, set up by several agency house men and Dwarkanath Tagore in 1829. But the failure of the traditional houses, to which it had lent substantial sums, hit this bank hard. It was fortunate to survive the great crisis of the early 1830s. Though the Union Bank prospered later in the decade, its position looked shaky at the time of the passage of the Charter Act.[10] This limited provision in the Indian banking sector prompted Larpent to open a public debate on the question, even as the new East India Company Charter was completing its journey through Parliament.

On 1 November 1833, Larpent floated the idea of a British-based joint-stock central bank for India. He circulated it to senior figures in the City of London, initially approaching John Horsley Palmer, the former Governor of the Bank of England (1830–1833).[11] According to Larpent, what India desperately needed following the crisis of the early 1830s and the end of the Company's commercial activities was a massive injection of British capital. In addition to providing this, the bank would perform a range of functions, and would become pivotal for the economic success of the British empire in Asia. Firstly, it would supply loan capital for those who wished to develop the produce and manufactures of India, helping to strengthen India's emerging role as a supplier of primary produce. Secondly, it would 'oil the wheels' of international commerce by providing trade credits to merchants in India and Canton, thereby facilitating an expansion of the China trade. Thirdly, it would provide a medium through which the East India Company could in future remit its Indian revenues for payment of the home charges. There would be branches of the bank in all of the Indian presidencies, and together with the headquarters in London, these would enable it to become the centre of all currency exchange transactions. The sheer scale of such an organisation would require a huge capital to be raised in the City. Larpent initially envisaged £1 million, a figure he subsequently revised upwards to £5 million by 1836.[12] Larpent's proposal was circulated among the leading financiers and economic thinkers of the day, including Thomas Tooke the economist and expert on currency affairs, and Nathan Rothschild, the most influential financier of the time.[13] Initially, the idea was received with interest and approval. Tooke lucidly summarised the case for a bank:

> The establishment thereupon of a company or companies for the exclusive purpose of banking in India is a measure required by the soundest dictates of commercial policy, and it is now most urgently called for not only to avert the recurrence of evils which have resulted from the vicious system which has hitherto prevailed, but to fill the immense void of capital and credit occasioned by the recent failures, and to supply the funds which the opening of the China trade will render necessary to be provided against the purchases to be made of teas for shipment in Autumn of 1834[14]

Horsley Palmer was warier. He feared, correctly as it turned out, that many of the London East India agency houses would regard such a bank as an overbearing competitor, and he concluded that it might be best to confine its operations mainly to remitting Company funds to meet the home charges.[15]

Larpent's ideas were influenced by a new strand of thinking and developments in the field of international banking. The 1830s and 1840s saw the establishment of a number of banks dedicated to the development of trade with the colonies. These included the Bank of Australasia, chartered in 1835, and the Colonial Bank (the West Indies and British Guiana) in 1836.[16] The colonial banks, as they became known, were predominantly concerned with the financing of trade, although initially it was contemplated that they might engage in direct investment in the colonies.[17] These banks became sufficiently prominent in the 1830s for the Treasury to introduce special measures to regulate their operations.[18] What was striking about Larpent's plan is its sheer ambition. He contemplated an institution which would be more than an exchange bank with operations limited to currency transactions and providing trade credits. It would engage in direct investment in the productive capacity of the colony, as well as enabling the Indian government to meet its obligations to its British creditors. In this respect, Larpent envisaged an organisation of much greater wealth, significance and economic power than the other colonial banks of the time, which, as Geoffrey Jones shows, were primarily concerned with financing trade.[19]

The political context in which Larpent developed his ideas had important consequences for their outcome. As shown, far from closing down their operations in the wake of their success in 1833, the East India Associations of Liverpool and Glasgow, and the Manchester Chamber of Commerce continued to lobby on a range of issues. For example, throughout the early 1830s they complained to the British government about Dutch protectionist policies in south-east Asia, which they regarded as contrary to the letter and spirit of the 1824 Treaty of London.[20] By 1836, Larpent and a group of merchants involved in trade with India, south-east Asia and China concluded that representation within the Company's institutions were no longer sufficient to defend their interests. In that year, over a hundred merchants and firms in London subscribed to a new organisation: the London East India and China Association (London EICA). They elected Larpent as their first Chairman when it held its inaugural meeting in March at the Jerusalem Coffee House in the City.[21] Two of the most prominent financial houses in the City of London, Barings and Barclay Brothers signed up to the new organisation, indicating the extent to which it was seen as an important channel of political influence.[22] From the outset, the new organisation threw in its lot with the Liverpool and Glasgow East India associations. John Stikeman, the first secretary of the London EICA, informed Liverpool and Glasgow of this intention on 31 March.[23] The formation of the London EICA was a milestone in the development of Anglo-Asian commercial politics. It represented the formal establishment of a common front between merchants in London and the provinces to defend and promote common interests. While London and the provinces had worked together before on an *ad hoc* basis, as in the campaign against the China monopoly in the early 1830s, the creation of the London EICA marked the consolidation of that working relationship within a more formal network of collaboration. It was the culmination of over a decade of flourishing commercial links between London agency houses and the industrialists of northern Britain, together with a realisation on the part of the London men that the East India Company was no longer the centre of power and political influence that it had once been. This reinforces the point made at the end of the last chapter, that Cain and Hopkins' assertion that the 'gentlemanly capitalists' of the City and the industrialists of provincial Britain remained politically distant from each other, does not hold from the 1830s in respect of commercial interests linked with India.[24]

At almost the same time that the London EICA was founded, George Larpent's plans for an Indian central bank became public. A prospectus for the bank was published in May 1836, signed by thirty-two London merchants and sixty-three merchants and industrialists from eight provincial cities, especially Manchester and Liverpool.[25] These included firms such as John Gladstone & Co. and Rathbones & Co. of Liverpool, and Barings in London. In respect of the latter, Thomas Baring MP was made a director of the new bank.[26] Clearly Larpent had been working hard to drum up support all over the country in preparation for the launch of the proposal. The bank was to have a capital of £5 million, and the plan was that it would engage in exchange banking, loans to producers in India, and of course control the remittance of East India Company revenues to meet the home charges. It was clear that the bank would very quickly become the most important institution of imperial economic management in British Asia. The almost simultaneous foundation of the London EICA and the launch of the new bank could not have been a coincidence, and indicates the scale of Larpent's ambition. What Larpent envisaged was the creation of a new central bank for India which would quickly come to dominate the channelling of investment to British imperial possessions in Asia, and also control the remittance of Company funds to meet the home charges. Such a bank would be an extremely wealthy and influential organisation, and its senior officials among the most powerful men in the British Empire. Taken in the round, the leading position in the new bank, combined with the chairmanship of the London EICA, would have elevated Larpent to a position of enormous wealth and political influence, on a par with eminent families such as the Barings and the Rothschilds. Here was a strategy to establish Larpent as a major player in the City and the world of colonial politics, one which would have made him, to use Cain and Hopkins' typology, probably the most powerful 'gentlemanly capitalist' of his day. It would also affect the regional balance of political influence in Britain in respect of colonial economic policy in Asia, re-asserting the traditional dominance over policy formation which had formerly been enjoyed by the merchants and financiers of London through the agency of the East India Company, but which had been lost with the emergence of the Glasgow and Liverpool East India Associations.

Historians have found the abortive Indian bank scheme of 1836 hard to evaluate. Geoffrey Jones has asserted that most of the colonial banks which emerged during this period were concerned with the financing of trade, rather than direct investment in productive enterprises such as plantation agriculture.[27] Yet it is clear from Larpent's thinking and the prospectus, that the 1836 scheme was much more ambitious. Even more controversially, Baster, the first historian of the colonial banks, dismissed it as a 'stalking horse' a bogus scheme which was intended to elicit commercial and political resistance, and once it had been rejected, to dissuade others who might wish to float serious colonial bank schemes for India.[28] It is a view shared by some other historians, notably Kling.[29] This conviction was based on claims made by an important contemporary of Larpent's, Robert Montgomery Martin. Martin was the driving force behind several later Indian bank schemes, the first of which was mooted in 1840. Martin claimed that it was the London East India agency houses in collaboration with the provincial East India associations, led particularly by Sir George Larpent, who used their influence within the East India Company, and with senior politicians, to block not only Martin's scheme for a 'Bank of Asia' in 1840, but also several subsequent schemes in the early 1840s.[30] Martin argued, and Baster accepted his view, that Larpent's earlier advocacy of an Indian bank in 1836 had been a ploy to discourage serious proposals for such an institution. It was an interpretation of events which portrayed the London houses as essentially conservative organisations, opposed to real reform in the system of India commerce and finance.

But the more one considers the careful planning and discussions of the idea in Larpent's personal correspondence between 1833 and 1836, and the strenuous efforts he made in order to persuade so many merchants to sign up for the prospectus in 1836, the less credible seems the 'stalking horse' explanation. Nowhere in Larpent's correspondence is there evidence to suggest that the bank scheme was anything other than a serious proposal to which he was wholly committed. Furthermore, to attempt to deceive so many prominent London merchants about the scheme would have been the height of folly, especially in light of Larpent's aspiration to be leader of the Indian commercial lobby, as demonstrated by his chairmanship of the London EICA. F.H.H. King, Robert Montgomery Martin's biographer, also casts doubt on this analysis, leaning towards the view that the 1836 scheme was in fact a bona fide attempt to create a colonial bank for India.[31] In view of these considerations, there can be little doubt that the 1836 scheme was a serious and honest project. Why then did it fail, and why did Larpent and the London East India agency houses subsequently set themselves against fresh efforts to establish a bank?

The reasons for the failure of the scheme lay in the responses of provincial merchants in Glasgow and Liverpool, and sections of the mercantile communities of London and Calcutta. The reaction by the Glasgow East India Association was swift and negative. On 20 July 1836 the bank directors approached the India Board and the East India Company Court of Directors with details of the scheme, and both of these bodies requested the opinions of the Bank of Bengal and the Indian government, before offering any view of their own.[32] But the Glasgow East India Association was already preparing a devastating public response in opposition to the proposal. The reasons for their opposition was set out in a pamphlet published in autumn 1836, in response to a pamphlet from the economist J.R. McCulloch which supported the scheme.[33] In simple terms, Glasgow saw the bank as a thinly veiled attempt to reassert the dominance of London in a different form:

> ... the effect in India of so large a capital and such a vast influence supported by such a privilege, would be to absorb all existing competition, and to prevent in future the forming of any other bank, while its effects in England would probably be to benefit London to the detriment of the outports.[34]

In early July 1836, the Glasgow East India Association had set up a sub-committee to consider the bank scheme, on which Thomas Speir came to occupy a key position. Ironically Speir, a Glasgow manufacturer, enjoyed a close link with Larpent's firm, Cockerell & Larpent. It had been he who had gone with the delegation to Calcutta in 1830 to set up the firm of Cockerell & Co. following the demise of John Palmer's house. Speir's brother subsequently joined Cockerell & Co. in Calcutta, and was well placed to excite opposition to the bank there as well.[35] Thomas Speir seems to have gained intelligence of Larpent's plans, enabling him to organise early resistance to the plan. Using the network of provincial contacts built up during the Charter debate of the early 1830s, the Glasgow East India Association stimulated resistance to the plan in Liverpool and Manchester. A major problem for the promoters of the bank was the fact that the government, who would have the final say on whether or not to grant a charter to the Bank, were awaiting the advice of the Indian government and the Bengal Bank on the matter. This hiatus allowed the anti-bank campaign to gather momentum. Throughout the summer there ensued a pamphlet war between the two sides, and an ongoing debate in the press. John Crawfurd was persuaded to support the bank.[36] But crucially, as Horsley Palmer had predicted, there emerged an opposition faction in London amongst the London East India agency houses. They saw the bank as a potential competitor in the fields of commission and exchange business. William Allen, editor of the *Asiatic Journal*, took up the anti-bank cause in collusion with the Glasgow East India Association.[37] It was opposed by *Alexanders East India Magazine*, the *Asiatic Journal*'s principal rival in the capital.[38] But, crucially, in London opinion swung towards the anti-bank faction during the course of the summer. When Stikeman, secretary to the London EICA, received a petition against the bank scheme from the Glasgow East India Association, he circulated it amongst the membership, and found that a majority of members supported Glasgow's opposition to the bank. Stikeman noted that:

> ... it accords with the views of this association, and has been submitted to the perusal of the Chairman [Larpent][39]

One can only imagine Larpent's humiliation at this sharp rebuff to his leadership. Very soon, supporters of the bank began to drop off, as the opposition campaign gathered momentum.[40] An attempt in late August by the bank scheme's supporters to rally support in India amongst the Calcutta correspondents of the London East India agency houses and the Indian administration, also badly misfired.[41] Unfortunately for the supporters of the scheme, the Indian administration had already agreed in principle to an expansion of the capital and activities of the Bank of Bengal, and the London scheme was seen as an unwelcome and meddling intrusion. The Governor-General, Lord Auckland, described the London bank as a 'swaggering interloper', while Henry Thoby Prinsep, Secretary to the Bengal government dismissed it as a 'wild scheme of the exchange'.[42] Prinsep in particular was concerned about the Indian government handing over such a crucial economic function to a group of people in London over whom it would have no control. This negative response was bolstered by advice Auckland received from a Mr Fullarton, who had long experience of banking in India. In a lengthy report which was sent to London as well as Auckland, Fullarton argued that Bengal financial institutions were more than capable of meeting the needs of India, and that a London bank would simply lack the local knowledge needed to make prudent investment decisions.[43] He also stressed that India was too backward and undeveloped for such a sophisticated institution.

The appeal to the Calcutta agency houses did not elicit the desired response either. In February 1837 the *Bengal Hurkaru* published a letter from the solicitors to the London bank to those amongst the bank's shareholders who were members of London East India agency houses, urging them to persuade their Indian sister firms to support the bank scheme.[44] The letter and the proposal became a major issue of debate in the newly established Bengal Chamber of Commerce in the following month. Ultimately, the chamber voted against the scheme, following careful consideration of it by one of its sub-committees.[45] The Calcutta firms, like the London East India agency house opponents of the bank, saw it as a threat to their own businesses, mainly because of the bank's probable involvement in exchange operations and the negotiation of bills of exchange. These were areas of business in which the houses themselves were engaged. Besides, there was still a simmering resentment in Calcutta at the way in which the old Calcutta houses had been allowed to founder. William Prinsep, formerly of Palmer & Co., which had been deserted by Larpent's own house in 1830, was an opponent in the Bengal Chamber of Commerce, and it was no doubt significant that Henry Prinsep, the savage critic of the bank in the Bengal administration, was his brother.

It is not surprising then that support for the bank scheme ebbed away during the autumn of 1836. By January 1837, the bank was a fading scheme, which was finally killed by Auckland's negative response early in that year. But it was surely dead long before then, probably from the time that Larpent realised that he could not carry the scheme in the London EICA. In January 1837, Stikeman hinted to the Glasgow East India Association that informal pressure within the London EICA had curbed the initial enthusiasm for the bank scheme in the capital.[46] Herein probably lies the true reason behind Larpent's trenchant opposition to later bank schemes. The episode taught Larpent a bitter lesson. If he aspired to lead the East Indian mercantile community, and build his influence over British colonial policy in Asia on the national stage, he had not only to abandon the notion of a powerful London-based bank for India, but also clearly establish himself and the other London firms as a bulwark against the establishment of such an organisation. This was necessary if Larpent was to command the support of the industrialists and merchants of provincial Britain, and the revived firms of Calcutta. Thus he opposed later attempts to establish a major Indian central bank, such as that by Robert Montgomery Martin in 1840. Larpent's new opposition to an Indian bank was thus intended to revive his influence, not only with his commercial friends and allies in the provinces, but also in London. Instead of Larpent succeeding in becoming an eminent 'gentlemanly capitalist' who had reasserted the political and commercial dominance of the capital in the face of the challenge from Britain's emergent industrial centres, he had become a leader of a cosmopolitan movement which not only spoke for commercial interests across Britain, but also for mercantile communities in Asia.

This alliance of provincial and metropolitan merchants, working both within and without the structures of the East India Company, proved a formidable obstacle to those who sought to revive the notion of a new Anglo-Indian bank. The first such attempt, led by Martin and Sir Gore Ouseley in February 1840, was rejected outright in just two months by the East India Company and the India Board.[47] The Board of Trade advised the bank organisers that it had been the plan for the bank to engage in the issue of currency and dealing in international bills of exchange (the remittance business) which had particularly incited resistance, an objection which came from the London East India agency houses which were deeply involved in this line of business. Martin and William Jardine tried to go half way towards meeting this advice when they submitted a second proposal in July 1840, omitting currency issue from the range of services the bank would offer, but retaining involvement in remittance. Under advice from the London houses and their provincial allies the Company first stalled and then ensured rejection by the India Board in April 1842.[48] A third project was launched in June 1842, with Martin again playing a leading role. This time although the bank was intended to play some part in dealing in international bills of exchange, the scale would be much more limited, as its initial capital would only be £250,000. Interestingly, the Indian government were largely placated by the limited size of the bank's operations, regarding it as posing no significant threat to existing Indian institutions.[49] This time it was the Board of Control, led by the Treasury which scuppered the plan. The principal objection was that India was simply too backward, and so incapable of rapid development, which meant that such a bank would merely excite a destabilising speculation in the City which could have serious consequences.[50] None other than Sir George Larpent had assisted Treasury officials and politicians to this judgement, writing to Gladstone about the limited potential of India in June 1843.[51] He believed that India's future was as a primary producing economy, and that the colony was incapable of developing a competitive manufacturing sector, not least because of the success of British manufactures in the Indian market. As such the scope for profitable investment was always likely to be limited, and returns disappointing.[52] By 1844, it seemed that the prospects for new Anglo-Indian financial institutions to promote investment and trade in Asia were bleak indeed; opposed as they were by this alliance of provincial industrialists, merchants and London-based gentlemanly capitalists. In effect, the latter configuration of interests was protecting the existing commercial status quo by blocking the emergence of powerful new competitors in the commercial relationship with India and Asia. One consequence was to preserve what remained of the political influence of the East India Company, which also feared the arrival of large new financial institutions, the establishment of which might bring into question the rationale for its own continued existence.

This political relationship between the London East India agency houses and the commercial and industrial men of the provincial cities became steadily closer during the later 1830s and 1840s, principally through the flourishing co-operation between the London EICA and the Glasgow and Liverpool East India Associations. A range of issues drew them closer together, and produced close collaboration, especially in their efforts to change aspects of British colonial policy in Asia. For example, sugar imported into Britain from the West Indies paid lower duties than Indian sugar, a particular source of grievance in view of the need to expand the latter's export potential. The London EICA and the Glasgow and Liverpool East India Associations co-operated in a campaign to equalise duties, and they were successful in 1836.[53] This was followed in 1841 with a second successful assault on West Indian privilege, this time against the unequal duties imposed upon West Indian and Indian tobacco and spirits.[54] London and the provinces also consistently lobbied against the imposition by the Dutch of heavy duties on British imports into Java, though with less success.[55] They were also quick to offer a collective response when Anglo-Chinese relations began to deteriorate at the end of 1830s, urging government to protect access to the Chinese market.[56] Together with their allies in Glasgow, Liverpool and elsewhere, the London EICA sought to roll back the last remaining barriers to freer commerce with Asia, and in this sense they were continuing the process of liberalisation of commerce which the Charter Acts of 1813 and 1833 had promoted.

The later 1830s saw a new development which was to strengthen this emergent British network of commercial organisations interested in colonial economic policy in Asia. Following the Charter Act of 1833 and the retreat of the East India Company from commerce, merchants and businessmen across the empire in India and south-east Asia saw the need to organise themselves politically in order to defend their interests. In part this reflected the same reasons which had motivated merchants in London. The Company's actions in the great crisis of 1830–1834, and uncertainties about what kind of organisation it would become as an organ of government, free of commercial responsibilities, prompted merchants in the Indian presidencies and elsewhere in Asia to establish their own Chambers of Commerce. The Calcutta Chamber (re-formed several years later as the Bengal Chamber), set up in 1834, was in many ways a response to the uncertainties of the new era ushered in by the failure of the traditional agency houses, and the need to ensure that the new order would be stable. But it was also in part a result of the fact that the East India Company's administration had, in the end and at the behest of the Court of Directors, abandoned all efforts to prop up the failing houses in the early 1830s, impressing upon the Calcutta merchants the need to be active defenders of their own interests.[57] The Calcutta Chamber's constitution committed it to a number of functions, including the gathering and dissemination of commercial information, but most notably to 'use every means in its power for the removal of evils and the promotion of the common good; to communicate with Authorities and individual parties thereupon'.[58] Canton followed suit in the same year, setting up its own chamber. The Bombay Chamber, set up in September 1836, represented the Indian (especially the Parsi) community as well as the European, and it quickly pressed for substantial improvements in the road networks connecting the city to its hinterland.[59] Almost simultaneously, John Alves Arbuthnot, a leading Madras merchant, led the movement to set up a Chamber in that city, which also came into being in September 1836.[60] In December 1836, it asked the London EICA to lobby the government in London to ensure that Madras would be included as one of the qualifying ports under the new sugar bill, which equalised duties on East and West India sugar.[61] This quickly became a familiar pattern: a Chamber of Commerce in a distant Asian port, enlisting the help of East India Associations in Britain (especially in London) to protect their commercial interests. A network thereby developed which provided mutual political support and the commercial intelligence necessary to present convincing arguments and to improve business performance.

In the Straits Settlements of the Western Malay Peninsula, the pressure to create new commercial representative bodies was particularly acute. To save money in 1829 the East India Company had reformed the system of government in the Straits, ending the Presidency status enjoyed by Penang since 1805, and consolidating the administrations of the three settlements of Penang, Malacca and Singapore into one single Straits government. This paved the way for a reduction in the number of major administrative posts from nineteen to just eight, which represented an alarming reduction in the status of the Straits Settlements, and a clear signal of their subordination to the Company's government in India.[62] Neither of these developments was welcome to the mercantile communities of the Straits Settlements, who feared that their interests would command a low priority in Calcutta and the Court of Directors in London. As mentioned, the Dutch were also operating protectionist policies against the import of British manufactures and other commodities into their south-east Asian possessions, which particularly hurt the commerce of Singapore. If these developments were not worrying enough, an eruption of piracy in the seas around the Straits Settlements in the mid-1830s threatened to undermine British trade still further. But it was the planned solution to the problem mooted by the East India Company's government in India which stirred traders in the Straits into action. In 1836, to meet the costs of patrolling the Malay Straits against pirates, the Company proposed the introduction of customs duties at Penang and Singapore, which had hitherto been centres of free trade.[63] Chambers of Commerce were set up at both ports early in 1837, and they began immediately to lobby against the policy.[64] Significantly, the Singapore Chamber turned to the London EICA and the Glasgow East India Association to represent them before Parliament and the British government, both of which successfully lobbied the East India Company and the government against the proposed duties.[65] It was the first in a succession of issues on which the Straits Chambers would turn for assistance to the British East India and China Associations.

From the late 1830s, the rise of this trans-imperial network of Anglo-Asian mercantile interest groups had a profound effect upon the balance of power between the East India Associations in Britain. Whilst in the early and mid-1830s London had followed where Liverpool and Glasgow had led, the rise of these Asian organisations tilted matters back in the favour of London. This was because the London EICA's position in the capital, its proximity to Parliament and government, as well as the financial centre of the City, made it the logical ally to whom the Asian chambers would turn.[66] Thus, in 1837 the Chambers of Commerce of Calcutta, Madras, Bombay and Singapore were all fulsome in their praise of the London EICA's role in securing the equalisation of East and West Indian sugar duties, and in representing their respective interests to the British government.[67] The opposition which London interests had encountered in Calcutta in 1836, when the first plan for an Anglo-Indian bank was mooted quickly gave way to a reassertion of London's leadership. the London EICA's geographical advantages, and its residual connections with the East India Company's administrative machine in London, also enabled it to gain some ascendancy over its provincial counterparts, who came to see the London EICA as key to securing allies in Parliament and government. In March 1839, the secretary of the Glasgow East India Association described the London EICA thus to Stikeman, the secretary of the London association:

> Being at headquarters – the fountain of all information and also possessing the advantage of near and personal access to public men and public documents, you enjoy that which qualify you to be the head and guide of similar organisations[68]

Indeed on several occasions, Glasgow and the other provincial associations openly deferred to the London EICA's leadership. For example, when in November 1840 the London EICA and the Glasgow East India Association were approached by the Penang Chamber of Commerce for support in protesting to the British government against Dutch aggression in Sumatra, the Glasgow men indicated that they would follow the London EICA's advice on how best to proceed.[69] Similarly, when resisting the Indian bank schemes in 1843, the Glasgow association again took its lead from the London EICA.[70] In this way, in spite of the defeat of the 1836 bank scheme, the London-based interests began to assert their leadership in Asian commercial affairs. But this recovery was based on persuasion and careful collaboration with commercial groups in the British provinces, and it gave due cognisance to their interests: hence the solid front against a London-based Indian bank which was maintained in the early 1840s. There was no separation of provincial industrial and London financial interests here, as depicted by Cain and Hopkins.

  This new political context for Anglo-Asian commerce provides the background for a number of initiatives, designed to solve the central problem of increasing India's export of primary produce. These addressed not only the production of commodities, but also the facilitation of their export. Thus the late 1830s saw such key developments as the growth of steam shipping in the trade between Britain and ports in India and Asia. There were several abortive efforts in the late 1830s to establish a shipping company serving the Britain to India route, including the East India Steam Navigation Company, first proposed in 1836, and an initiative in 1838 headed by Timothy Curtis, Governor of the Bank of England. Both of these foundered because of the opposition of the East India Company, which was trying to develop its own service via a route from Bombay to Suez. This demonstrated that the Company was not a toothless puppet of government, because both of these failed initiatives enjoyed some government support. Eventually the Peninsular and Oriental Company was formed in April 1840, and East India Company objections were overcome, in part because of the appointment of Sir George Larpent as P&O's first Chairman between 1840 and 1842. By the end of the 1840s P&O had developed services to India, Singapore and China, following its successful takeover of the mail services to Asia in the early 1840s.[71]

The London East India agency houses in general, and Larpent in particular, were also involved in another major initiative of the late 1830s and 1840s. During the 1830s, the East India Company had been experimenting in the cultivation of tea in its gardens in Assam, north-eastern India, but, true to the terms of the 1833 Charter Act, its intention was to sell these to a private company to develop large-scale production. As in the field of steam shipping, the London East India agency houses took a leading role in exploiting this opportunity. On 12 February 1839, a committee met in Great Winchester Street, London to discuss the possibility of establishing a company to purchase the East India Company's tea gardens in Assam, and no fewer than six of the leading East India houses signed a letter to the Court of Directors expressing an interest in a company, including Palmer, Mackillop & Co., Cockerell, Larpent & Co., Crawford, Colvin & Co. and others.[72] When a delegation from the committee met the Court of Directors just two days later, they were led by none other than Sir George Larpent, who was able to report that the Court of Directors offered no opposition to the formation of what became the Assam Company.[73] In spite of some initial resistance to the plan from the Indian government, by the time of the new Assam Co.'s Annual General Meeting on 7 May 1841, Larpent was the Chair of the directors, and was able to report that acquisition of the Assam plantations had been completed.[74] In 1842/3 80,000 pounds of tea had been produced, rising by 1845/6 to just under 195,000 pounds.[75] While this was a long way from dominating the market, the Assam Co. had established India as a producer of a commodity which had previously been the exclusive preserve of the Chinese. The presence of London East India agents such as Larpent on the board of the Assam Co. was highly significant, indicating the leading role these organisations still played in the development of India. Interestingly, some of the other shareholders subsequently became East India Company directors, indicating that in spite of the non-commercial nature of that organisation after 1833, leading commercial men and politicians interested in India affairs still sought office within it. For example, Ross Donnelly Mangles MP, a former East India Company servant, became a shareholder in the Assam Co. in 1841/2, at about the same time that he became MP for Guildford.[76] In 1847 he became a director of the East India Company, rising to become its Chairman in 1857. John Harvey Astell was a director of the Assam Company throughout the 1840s, and became a director of the East India Company in 1851, occupying a director's seat in both organisations throughout the 1850s. Such was the web of personal business and political

roles which meant that the East India Company was not merely an administrative appendage of government.

Another major area of Indian economic development in which the
London firms became involved was railway development. But here they
found that provincial suspicions of London interests remained strong. The
'railway mania' of the 1840s, which affected Britain, inevitably spilled over
into speculative projects in the colonies.[77] By 1844 two railway projects had
emerged. Promoters of the East Indian Railway wanted a line which would
ultimately connect Calcutta with Delhi, while the Great Indian Peninsular
Railway was intended to connect Bombay with first the cotton growing interior, and finally Delhi itself. The projects were initially the inspiration of two
committed railway enthusiasts: Macdonald Stephenson and John Chapman.
The former, after some time in India undertaking research in the early
1840s, argued for a railway network which would connect the three Indian
presidencies.[78] On Stephenson's return to Britain in 1844, in spite of initial
scepticism at his proposals, the London East India agency houses, through
George Larpent, became interested in the idea of a smaller project which
would connect Calcutta with the interior of northern India, possibly being
extended as far west as Delhi, if it proved successful.[79] A committee of interested London merchants and others was set up with a view to creating an East
Indian Railway Company (EIRC) to take the idea forward, and in 1845 such
a company was formed.[80] Chapman was also busy, producing in 1844 his own
proposal for a railway from Bombay eastward across India.[81] Like Stephenson,
Chapman first approached London-based interests, including the East India
Company, the London EICA and a selection of 'English Railroad capitalists'.[82] Chapman's plan also found its way to Larpent in the summer of 1844,
but though he expressed enthusiasm for the project he was not prepared to
take it up. Larpent agreed to forward it to his contacts in the Board of Trade
and the East India Company for views and to drum up support from other
sources.[83] Larpent's preference for the East India railway scheme probably
reflected his own firm's interests which were centred on Calcutta and the
eastern half of the sub-continent. By early 1845, Chapman had resorted
to drumming up support in the provincial cities, especially Liverpool and
Manchester. The attraction for these cities was that western India promised
to be important for the supply of raw cotton, and the railway would improve
the efficiency of transport of the commodity to Bombay, for shipment to
Lancashire.[84] By June of that year, a company had been formed to create the
Great Indian Peninsular Railway (GIPR).

Although these two companies were not competing directly for the right
to construct the same line, circumstances over the next two years served to
set them and their supporters against each other. Key problems faced by both
organisations were the heavy capital costs involved in the projects and the
lengthy period of time before returns from the railways would furnish divi-

dends for shareholders. Both of these were likely to be severe deterrents for any potential investors. It was believed by the promoters of both companies, that the British government needed to guarantee a minimum dividend to shareholders in order to persuade them that the risk of their capital would be minimal and the return on it both prompt and attractive. For over two years, the promoters of the EIRC haggled over this question with the Court of Directors of the East India Company and the Board of Control. The promoters initially wanted either a lump sum of £30,000 from the government, repayable once the line became profitable, or a government undertaking to pay for dividends to shareholders before the line generated profits. The promoters' hopes rose briefly early in the negotiations when the Court of Directors proposed a 4% guarantee for 99 years.[85] But the Board of Control quickly vetoed this because of the cost and the fact that the GIPR, and other developing railway schemes for other regions in India, would inevitably want similar terms. Not until July 1847 was a tentative agreement reached with the EIRC that government would guarantee a dividend of 5% for 25 years.[86] The plan was that a line from Calcutta to Delhi would be built, at an estimated cost of no more than £3 million. Ominously, however, in August before the contract was sealed, the government insisted that the promoters raise £100,000 towards meeting these huge expenses, and this sum was to be paid into the East India Company's treasury.[87] The reasons for this lay in the deteriorating state of the economy and the state's finances, and the likelihood that other Indian railway companies would want similar terms[88]. A bad harvest in 1846, a drain of gold to pay for imports of corn, and a general downturn in confidence in the money market, all converged to make government insist upon a large deposit from the EIRC promoters and shareholders. The developing pessimism in the City was such that the company was unable even to raise the £100,000 by the due date, and were compelled to plead for several extensions of the time limit.[89]

Nonetheless, the promoters of the GIPR were deeply anxious about the implications of the deepening economic gloom and the apparent initial success of the EIRC in their negotiations with the East India Company and the British government. So much so, that during 1846 and 1847, Indian and British provincial industrialists and merchants were enlisted to lobby the British government to support the project. Chapman went to Bombay in 1845/6 and won the support of the Bombay Chamber of Commerce and officials in government there.[90] The Liverpool East India Association was approached in November 1846, and pledged its support to the project.[91] In summer 1847, the Manchester and Glasgow Chambers of Commerce both lobbied the government, and in September the prominent Liberal MP John Bright threw his weight behind the GIPR.[92] But the response of the Board of Control gave the promoters cause for concern. When the GIPR put its plans to the East India Company Court of Directors in June/July 1847 they received a favourable response, which promised similar terms to those pledged to the EIRC. But the Board of Control overruled this recommendation.[93] W. Leach, the Board of Control official dealing with the application, refused Chapman's request for an interview to discuss the reasons for the Board's refusal to grant similar terms, and indeed even to process the application.[94] One colleague of Chapman's in the project identified Leach as 'our great opponent' and correctly cited government concern about making too many financial commitments as the reason behind the opposition.[95] Chapman suspected Leach of a preference for 'the Bengal line and his friend Larpent's interests', a suspicion which he voiced on a number of occasions.[96] In a context of limited government finance and competing railway interests, Chapman suspected that the London-based interests would receive favourable treatment.[97] He and the other promoters resolved to see John Cam Hobhouse, the President of the Board of Control, and to maintain the stream of provincial overtures to government until the Board changed its mind.[98] Further evidence of rivalry between the railway companies emerged when the EIRC argued publicly that their line would be just as beneficial for the cotton interests in Britain as the GIPR. Supporters of the GIPR contested this claim in the newspapers.[99] Hobhouse, however, deterred by the deteriorating state of the economy and the government finances, refused to be moved, even by the intensity of the provincial petitions in favour of the GIPR. In September 1847 he signalled to Bright that no early decision on the Bombay line should be expected as long as the crisis in the money market continued to deepen.[100] The question of government support and recognition of the EIRC and the GIPR would not be resolved until after the looming commercial crisis of 1847/8 had run its course, and for the time being the Indian railway projects revived old rivalries between London and the provinces which had, for the most part been contained through the co-operation between the East India Associations.

In general, the period from the 1833 Charter to 1847 saw considerable growth in the trade of British India, but this masked certain problems and instabilities. The value of imports into India rose from Rs42 million in 1834 to Rs102 million in 1847, while the value of exports rose from Rs79 million to over Rs133 million in the same period.[101] As numerous historians have observed, this was a period in which India completed its transition from being an exporter of manufactured commodities to becoming a supplier of primary produce.[102] The principal exporter to India in this period was of course Britain, which furnished goods worth Rs28 million (about 67% of Indian imports) in 1834, rising to Rs35 million in 1838 (also about 67%).[103] British cotton manufactures made up about a third of British exports to India during this period.[104] Britain also constituted a large market for Indian exports, receiving 41.2% of Indian exports by value in 1834–1835 and 39.5% in 1837–1838.[105] In respect of imports from India, commodities such as indigo continued to be very important, fluctuating considerably in value, but accounting for between

15% and 30% of India's total exports by value during this period.[106] Raw cotton made up about 15–20% of India's exports, a significant commodity for the British cotton industry, which was becoming increasingly concerned about its heavy dependence upon supplies from the USA.[107] The growth in Britain's trade with India and Asia was of course reflected in shipping arrivals from, and departures to, Asian ports. London's inward shipping from India and elsewhere in Asia rose from 323 ships (131, 600 tons) in 1836 to 581 (251,000 tons) in 1846.[108] Particularly striking however, was the growth of Liverpool's trade with Asian ports, arrivals rising from 126 (43,500 tons) in 1836 to 211 (86,900 tons) in 1846.[109] Liverpool had by then established itself as the second major trading port with Asia, and its shipping arrivals and departures were greater than the combined totals for all other British ports outside London.[110] The construction of the Albert Dock, which specialised in the Asian trade, during the 1840s in many ways came to symbolise the arrival of Liverpool and the provinces as major players in the trade with Asia.[111] But equally important to British imperial trade in Asia more generally was India's large export trade to China, the receipts of which facilitated the purchase of tea, silks and other Chinese commodities in high demand in Britain.[112] In 1834–1835, China received 36.6% of Indian exports by value, and 37.8% in 1837–1838.[113] Opium had long been the single most important article in this Indian export trade to China, a fact which explains the willingness of the British to go to war to protect access to the Chinese market during the first Opium War of 1839–1842, and their insistence upon access to that market as a condition of the peace which followed, reinforced by the acquisition of Hong Kong.

But this apparently positive scenario of continuing growth in imperial trade was deceptive. The 1830s and early1840s have been identified as decades of stagnation in the Indian economy, in which exports suffered severe and destabilising fluctuations in demand, with damaging consequences for north Indian society in particular.[114] The continuing economic impact of British imperial rule certainly contributed to these difficulties. Asiya Siddiqi argues that the first half of the nineteenth century saw a steady outflow of gold from India to Britain, establishing the Rupee as a silver-based currency, the value of which against gold-based Sterling fell during the period, and for the rest of the century. The terms of trade for Indian exports therefore deteriorated, furnishing Britain with cheaper primary produce to fuel its industrial revolution, and suppressing earnings and living standards in India.[115] The situation was compounded by the domestic British costs of empire. The East India Company still had to remit to Britain its surplus revenues in order to service the home charges, and by the mid-1830s it had developed three methods of repatriating funds. The first and most important was the sale by the Company in London of bills payable in India to British traders wishing to import Indian and Asian produce. The sterling receipts filled the coffers of the Company and enabled it to meet the home charges, while the traders received a safe and convenient channel by which they could convert their resources into rupees with which to purchase Indian commodities. Thus importers of Indian produce had ready access to the Rupee, a factor which increased the supply of Indian imports and helped keep their prices down. This method was the principal one by which the Company effected remittances.[116] Between 1835/6 and 1846/7, Rupee bills on India raised between £1.5 million and £3 million for the Company annually. The second method involved the Company authorities at Canton in China receiving Spanish Dollars from traders exporting opium and other goods from India to China, in return for bills payable in India. These dollars would then be issued by the Company in Canton to other British private traders purchasing Chinese tea and other goods, in return for bills payable to the Company in London. This second, rather more convoluted method remitted between about £400,000 and £1 million per year between 1834/5 and 1839, when the first Opium War curtailed the practice.[117]

The third and most controversial method was known as the 'hypothecation system'. This involved firms in India buying Indian commodities from producers and merchants by paying for them with bills drawn on (that is, payable by) the London East India agency houses. The recipients of these bills would then sell them to the East India Company, which would transmit them to London for payment by the London houses. Thus were Company funds remitted by 'hypothecating' bills against commodities exported from India to Britain.[118] Between £200,000 and £1.3 million was remitted annually in this way between 1834/5 and 1846/7.[119] But this third method was the subject of much disagreement within the British mercantile community. On the one hand, it certainly brought a great deal of business to the London East India agency houses, and placed them in a position of some political influence in relation to the East India Company and the British government. On the other the Company's purchases of hypothecated bills could vary unpredictably from year to year, depending upon their financial needs. In a year when the Company wished to remit large sums through hypothecation, this meant that it would buy large amount of bills in India, encouraging speculators in India to buy larger amounts of Indian produce than the domestic market could absorb. This exacerbated the problem of the falling price of Indian goods in Britain and ultimately undermined the interests of the London houses and merchants engaged in importing Indian goods. It also resulted in violent swings in the exchange rate between Sterling and the Rupee, yet another factor which rendered the Indian trade unpredictable.[120] These concerns eventually turned the London agency houses against the system, but it was a measure of the East India Company's enduring political influence that until the late 1840s it successfully defeated attempts by the London and Provincial East India Associations to compel them to use only the sale of Rupee bills in

London.[121] Thus the overall condition of Anglo-Asian trade in this period, though showing increasing volumes and values, was complex, unpredictable and unstable. The problems became evident in the great commercial crisis of 1847/8.

The decade and a half after the end of the East India Company monopoly had thus been one of reconstruction in terms of economic relations between Britain and Asia. The period also saw political realignment among the commercial interest groups which shaped colonial policy in India, south-east Asia and China. These included the East India Company itself, the London East India agency houses and other London-based City financial groups, the merchants and manufacturers of provincial Britain, and the new wave of merchant firms and their Chambers of Commerce in Calcutta, Bombay, Singapore and elsewhere. In terms of commercial change, there had been the emergence of a new wave of merchant firms in Calcutta to replace the failed traditional agency houses. Many of these new houses were at first subject to much closer direction by their sister houses in London, which were eager to prevent a recurrence of the calamity of the early 1830s. As a result, the older practice of allowing the Calcutta firms a free hand in determining their activities was abandoned, especially in the field of banking. This meant that the new generation of firms were very different in terms of the range and practice of their commercial activities. The impact of the crisis had also left a deep legacy of suspicion between the European and Indian commercial communities which was never really overcome. But there were also those among the new houses who fiercely resisted what they saw as the overbearing dictates of the London firms, a view fuelled by a suspicion that London had been either responsible for the crisis of the early 1830s, or at least unsupportive of their Calcutta allies during it. As a result, the new houses came to exercise greater independence in their commercial dealings and they found their own voice in the Calcutta Chamber of Commerce, an initiative which was quickly copied by merchants all over the east.

Trading activity itself also underwent major changes. The merchants of provincial Britain became major players in the Asian trade, particularly those based in Liverpool. Furthermore the East India Company's new methods for remitting funds had a major impact upon the practice of trade in India and Britain, creating speculative markets for bills in London and India which served to make exchange rates and trade much more unpredictable. In addition, the end of the Company's commercial activities had opened new initiatives to develop the Indian economy, by better transport through steam shipping and railway construction schemes, and the development of new commodities such as Indian tea. There had also been efforts to strengthen the financial system in India, notably through reform of such institutions as the Bank of Bengal, and the emergence of new banks such as the Union Bank in Calcutta, and efforts to establish new banking organisations in Bombay,

Madras and elsewhere.[122] The Banks of Bombay and Madras were thus established in 1840 and 1843 respectively.[123]

But of course not all initiatives to enhance Indian economic development succeeded. Some, like the abortive attempts to establish a central bank for India in 1836, 1840, 1842 and 1844, failed to create new institutions, in spite of support from leading men in the City of London and a willingness to cede concessions in the face of resistance. This highlights the importance of the new political landscape created in the wake of the Charter Act of 1833. The pivotal moment came in 1836, when Sir George Larpent, an archetypal aspiring 'gentlemanly capitalist' in Cain and Hopkins' terms, led the first Bank of India project. Larpent clearly saw the bank as an enterprise which would bring him huge wealth and political influence, his appetite for which was demonstrated in his leading roles in the London EICA, P&O, the East India Railway Company and the Assam Company. But the fact that the 1836 scheme was abandoned so rapidly by Larpent and his allies, and that they subsequently led the resistance against any similar initiatives, was the result of a new distribution of influence and power in Asian affairs. It was the provincial merchants and manufacturers, mobilised by the Glasgow and Liverpool East India Associations, together with a faction amongst the London East India Agency houses, suspicious East India Company officials and hostile Calcutta merchants, who forced a dramatic *volte face* on this issue. It signified that any new policy likely to affect commercial affairs in India and Asia would have to carry the support of this new trans-imperial network of interests, or at least the larger portion of it. Cain and Hopkins' account of a dominant 'gentlemanly capitalist' elite, aloof from 'outsider' provincial manufacturers and able to use their connections in the political and social elite to get their own way, does not accurately represent the constellation of interests which shaped events in the 1830s and 1840s. This is not to reject their interpretation entirely. The concept of the gentlemanly capitalist certainly fits the career of Larpent, whose ambitions were political as well as material, and it is certainly the case that there was a distinct City interest at work in the field of Asian economic policy, embodied in the London EICA and constituting an alliance of London mercantile and financial interests. Moreover, it does seem that by the early 1840s the London EICA's access to Parliament and government gave it a prominent leading position within this wider network of commercial pressure groups, a point readily acknowledged by the Glasgow East India Association's leaders. It was also the case that conflicts between provincial industrial and London mercantile/financial aspirations did re-emerge from time to time as shown in respect of the 1836 bank scheme and the rivalry between the Great Indian Peninsular Railway and the East Indian Railway companies in the mid-1840s. Nonetheless, the keynotes were collaboration and the sharing of information, which drew together not just business interests across Britain, but also with the periphery of the eastern empire. From the later 1840s London was to become more dominant in this network, but even then the notion of provincial 'outsiders' being ignored or outflanked by 'insider' City gentlemanly capitalists probably masks the subtleties and complexities of imperial commercial politics, at least in Asian affairs.

The position of the East India Company in this new 'order' also requires some comment. Most histories of the Company downplay the importance of the post-1833 period, regarding it as one in which the organisation was reduced merely to administering state policy. This tends to overlook the fact that this was still a company with shareholders to pay and one which continued to possess structures (the Courts of Directors and Proprietors) which could be used as a channel for representing commercial and political interests. Moreover, its employees, both in London and India, could still lay claim to a high degree of expertise on Asian affairs, which demanded consideration in any debate on policy. Thus, the arguments for rejection of the 1836 bank scheme put forward by senior Bengal administrators was an important factor in the defeat of that initiative, and indeed of subsequent efforts to establish similar organisations in the 1840s. As mentioned, in 1836 the Governor-General Lord Auckland had used Fullarton's report on Indian banking to rebut the scheme.[124] Fullarton's basic contention was that India was too backward for a major joint-stock bank, which would be suitable 'to more advanced stages of civilisation'.[125] In simple terms, Fullarton contended that India's existing banking system was adequate for the country's needs. This argument was used by the Board of Control and the Court of Directors when they rejected the 1840 Bank of Asia scheme concocted by Robert Montgomery Martin.[126] Larpent cited Fullarton's paper directly when resisting the East India Bank project in 1843, and C.E. Trevelyan, the Treasury minister who eventually vetoed the plan, was clearly persuaded that, as Fullarton had argued, India was simply too uncivilised for a major bank of this nature.[127] In this way, the Company's command of 'knowledge' of the east continued decisively to influence government policy. The Company's successful resistance to attacks on the 'hypothecation system', at least until the end of the 1840s has also been noted. Furthermore, in all of the debates about economic policy in Asia, be it banking, the development of tea production, the means of remittance to service the home charges or the construction of Indian railways the Court of Directors was listened to carefully by government. Senior directors were, after all, frequently influential figures in the City or even MPs. Indeed, the retreat of the Company from commercial activities in 1833, and the end of the criticisms which its former role had brought upon it, arguably raised government estimation of the impartiality and competence of the Company and its personnel. It had become virtually, after all, part of the state machinery of imperial governance. All of this meant that its ability to influence policy remained more potent than most historians acknowledge.

By the mid-1840s, then, the features of a new commercial and political order in the determination of British policy in Asia were evident. It was characterised by the ability of a plurality of interests based in London (including the East India Company), the British provinces and in Asia itself to shape imperial policy in that region. After a period in which the provincial manufacturers and merchants had made the running, as exemplified by the success of the Glasgow and Liverpool East India Associations in the Charter Act negotiations, London had reasserted itself. There seemed every reason to believe that this constellation of forces would lead the future economic development of India and Asia and would determine future imperial policy. But, as will be seen, fundamental weaknesses in the British financial system and in Asian commerce would once again plunge the Indian empire into crisis, and usher in yet another phase of commercial and political change.

Seven

CRISIS, THE RESURGENCE OF LONDON AND THE END OF THE EAST INDIA COMPANY: 1847–1860

IN THE mid-1840s countries all over Europe were plunged into severe turmoil. Poor harvests and a general downturn in international trade, which was exacerbated by financial panics which spread rapidly across the continent, created the worst political and economic crisis since the end of the Napoleonic Wars. Abortive revolutions in Germany and France in 1848 revived memories of 1789 and 1830. Even Britain, the world's leading economic and imperial power, was rocked by the severity of the depression. Bankruptcies, rising unemployment, poverty, famine in Ireland, Chartist agitation and the rise of the anti-Corn Law league buffeted the political establishment. The Repeal of the Corn Laws by Robert Peel's Tory administration split the party and ushered in decades of Whig/Liberal political and intellectual dominance. The crisis reached its peak in 1847/8 when a wave of failures and bankruptcies swept through Britain's major cities, hitting the City of London particularly hard. The Irish famine and a succession of poor harvests bankrupted a number of corn merchants in the summer of 1847, particularly in Liverpool.[1] Excessive speculation in railway construction in the early 1840s also contributed to the crash. The full severity of the crisis became apparent in September 1847 when the London merchant firm of Messrs Gower, Nephews & Co. failed, to be followed by scores of failures in London, Liverpool, Glasgow, Manchester and elsewhere throughout the autumn.[2]

All sections of trade and industry suffered, but large numbers of firms involved in trade with Asia, particularly among the London East India agency houses and similar businesses in provincial cities such as Liverpool, were destroyed by the crisis. The failures were not confined to Britain. Most of the Calcutta firms connected to failing houses in London and elsewhere were also brought down. Morier Evans, writing only a year after the crisis erupted, listed the monthly failures, which included some of the most eminent names in the Asian trade. Reid, Irving & Co. went under in October, to be quickly followed by Cockerell, Larpent & Co., and the demise of the latter brought the career of Sir George Larpent to an end.[3] In total twenty London East India agency houses failed, and this was mirrored in Calcutta, were numerous Indian firms went under, including Cockerell & Co. and Carr, Tagore & Co.[4] The crisis was to have profound consequences for Anglo-Indian commerce, and it radically altered the balance of power within the network of British and imperial commercial communities which controlled it. Of course the crisis was not primarily caused by the Asian trade, and it claimed victims across the full spectrum of commerce and industry. Nonetheless, its consequences for Britain's eastern trade were very severe indeed. To what extent was this due to the weaknesses in Anglo-Asian trade alluded to in the previous chapter? Why was the crisis of 1847/8 so disastrous for this branch of commerce?

Both contemporaries and historians have identified a number of factors which contributed to this cull of firms engaged in the Asian trade in London, Calcutta, Liverpool and elsewhere. Tripathi argues that the commercial practices by which the London agency houses and their sister firms in India exported Britain manufactures to India and imported Indian goods into Britain, made the both the British and Calcutta houses extremely vulnerable to a major economic downturn. These firms were at the heart of an elaborate system for providing credit, which enabled British manufacturers to export their wares and British merchants in India to export Indian produce to Britain and Europe. The London East India agency houses facilitated the export of British manufactures to India and Asia by making advances in bills of exchange to manufacturers for up to 40% or 66% of the value of goods consigned to India. Once they reached India, they were sold by a Calcutta merchant (the consignee).[5] The Calcutta consignee paid for the British manufactures by sending to Britain bills payable at six months sight, but Tripathi notes that the bill of lading of the manufactures would frequently be used by the Calcutta trader as security to borrow funds from the Indian partner firm of the London house. These loans were frequently renewed on the dubious grounds that the Calcutta trader needed more time to realise his returns.[6] Generally, the Indian partner firms were well placed to make large profits in Calcutta. The agency house failures of the early 1830s had left Calcutta and eastern India short of both capital and sources of credit to oil the wheels of trade. The new Indian partner firms of the London agency houses stepped into the breach, advancing funds to purchasers and producers of such commodities as indigo, usually in exchange for bills payable in London. These bills were then remitted to Britain, enabling the Indian firm to settle debts it owed to the London house. This was a lucrative business, since the Indian firms, like their London partners, made substantial profits on commissions, interest on advances and other charges. Traders of limited means especially depended on the services of the Indian houses, which provided funds to buy Indian commodities and often arranged for their export. The goods would be received by the house together with bills for the commodities from the trader. The Indian house would send the goods to the London house for sale, together with the bills, which were payable to the London house, usually at ten months sight.

But these arrangements led to problems. In due course, many Indian houses were tempted into heavy speculations on their own account in Indian commodities, paying for them with bills drawn on the London house, also at ten months sight. But the instability of the British market for such commodities as indigo, and the long term deterioration of Indian commodity prices in Britain, meant that the sales frequently failed to meet expectations. Under these circumstances, one might expect the London houses to curb bill drafts upon them for goods unlikely to produce a healthy profit on sale in Britain. But Tripathi notes that generous credit services available in the City made the London firms complacent. It was easy for them to raise money quickly to meet bills drawn upon them. Many were tempted into a web of debt, rather than risk destabilising relations with their Indian partner firms by refusing to have bills drawn upon them by the latter. The prevailing arrangements for trade and credit made it easy for the London houses to choose this course. The Indian house would send the bills of exchange and the Indian goods, the London house having ten months before it had to pay the former. But the Indian house would send the bill of lading for the goods to the London house by the overland mail, and this usually reached London within 6–8 weeks. The bill of lading could be then be used by the London house to raise money in Lombard Street immediately, thus ensuring that it had funds readily to hand some eight months before it would have to honour the bill upon them. In the meantime, the Calcutta house and other private merchants continued their speculative purchases of Indian commodities, issuing further bills on the London houses and repeating the dispatch of bills of lading to assuage the London houses' need for funds. The outcome was that the debts owed by the Calcutta houses to the London houses began to mount, especially during the 1840s, when indigo prices fell and trade in general suffered from global turbulence.

Why were agency houses in London firms and similar firms in Liverpool so willing to engage in what was essentially 'overtrading', the creation of bills to generate funds becoming almost an end in itself? The unpredictable and violently fluctuating nature of the Indian trade was itself a factor which encouraged British agency houses to tolerate the speculative activities of their Calcutta correspondents. There was always the hope that an upturn in trading conditions would generate higher prices and profits in the import trade, allowing the ultimate settlement of debts. In addition, the East India Company's practice of bill hypothecation as a secondary means of remittance of its revenues to meet the home charges created a general climate of speculative activity, with the Company's intermittent purchases of such bills, frequently with little regard for actual market conditions in Britain for these hypothecated exports. While the London East India agency houses came to oppose bill hypothecation because of the unpredictability of the East India Company's purchases and its destabilising effects on the Asian trade, for a long time they were more ambivalent than the merchants of provincial Britain, who were consistent and strident in their opposition to the practice. The reason for this was shrewdly identified by one member of the Glasgow East India Association in 1835:

> One of the conditions of the East India Company's advances on Eastern produce is that it be consigned to London. This causes an unequal distribution of the trade in favour of the Metropolis. If the advances in a season be £1,200,000, the sales amount of the hypothecated produce may amount to £2,000,000 of which half but for the reason stated, find its way to the various outports. To the influential class of merchants who act as agents, and having a commission on the business, but no interest in the profit and loss, it is obviously a very desirable object to have such an extension of business, requiring almost no advance of capital of their own. Ship-owners, dock proprietors, brokers and various other classes, are similarly interested in the maintenance of practice which thus operates in their favour, but adversely to the general interests of Eastern commerce.[7]

In this respect, the London East India agency houses had a vested interest in the system, and the speculative activity it generated in the export of Indian goods. Ultimately, the London firms joined their provincial counterparts in blaming the hypothecation system for the instability of the Asian trade which contributed to the crash of 1847/8. But Tripathi rejects the notion that the failures of that disastrous year can be solely laid at the door of this practice, and he cites the problems of excessive speculation, overtrading and the lack of regulation of commercial practice as far more important reasons for the crisis.[8] Many contemporary observers expressed similar suspicions, most notably the prominent Liverpool merchant, and later Chair of the Liverpool East India and China Association (Liverpool EICA, it was now designated the China as well as the India association), Charles Turner.[9]

However, there can be little doubt that hypothecation did encourage reckless behaviour by merchants in both India and Britain. Furthermore, as the crisis of 1830–1834 had demonstrated, operating complex credit and trading transactions across the globe, in a business culture free of external regulation and dependent upon personal trust, was fraught with peril. Distance and deceit prevented adequate scrutiny by the London houses of the affairs of their Indian sister firms, despite all the efforts made during the early 1830s. The failure of Cockerell & Larpent in London exposed the staggering amount of accumulated debt owed to the firm by Cockerell & Co. of Calcutta. It also revealed that the London house had been deceived about the assets of the Indian firm and its ability to cover that debt. At a meeting of the creditors of Cockerell & Larpent on 18 October 1847 it emerged that Cockerell & Co. owed £774,118, of which £339,118 was in the process of being remitted to the London firm.[10] This did not initially cause undue alarm, as accounts from the Calcutta firm for the year ending 30 April 1846 had suggested that its total assets amounted to £895,300, adequately covering its debt to the London firm. But when a Mr Martin arrived in Calcutta to confirm the accuracy of the accounts, he discovered that Cockerell & Co.'s assets were only worth £511,800.[11] The difference was attributed to sudden recent heavy losses in indigo, and high local interest rates which post-dated the 1846 accounts. But there was a suspicion that the Calcutta house had deliberately misrepresented its true position.

Cockerell & Co. went under in January 1848. Certainly in its review of the failures in Calcutta in November 1848, the *Bankers Magazine* claimed that Cockerell & Larpent had been secretly informed by a partner in Cockerell & Co. several years before the crisis that the Calcutta firm was 'rotten'. But the London firm ignored this warning.[12] The review recounted similar stories of overspeculation by houses in Calcutta and Britain, and the unreliability of information exchanged between the two mercantile communities. As a result, failures in London triggered failures in Calcutta via the chain of unpaid debt. Church, Lake & Co. fell because of the collapsing price of Indian produce in London. Colville, Gilmore & Co. met its end because of the failure of Barclay Brothers in London; Ewing, Aird & Andersons because of the bankruptcy of Gower, Nephews & Co., also of London. Smith, Cowell & Co. collapsed due to the failure of Messrs Samuel Phillips of London, and Murrays of Liverpool.[13]

There were other factors which contributed to this chain reaction of bankruptcies. Heavy investments in sugar plantations on the island of Mauritius proved ill-conceived because of the high costs of labour and freight, and the Sugar Duties Act of 1846, which ended the preferential terms enjoyed by sugar imported into Britain from the British colonies.[14] At least four of the failing London houses had plantations on Mauritius worth a total of £1.5 million.[15] But once again, it was a tale of miscalculation and over-optimism. Larpent admitted that his own plantations on Mauritius were losing heavily as early as 1844–1845, before the Sugar Duties Act due to his own underestimation of costs.[16] It was reported that Reid, Irving & Co. were guilty of similar errors in respect of their Mauritius plantations.[17] In all, the failures of 1847/8 were largely due to imprudent speculation and dubious commercial practice in both Britain and Asia.

The shock of the failures of 1847 was compounded by public exposure of the catalogue of errors which caused the crisis. Doubt was cast on a number of important initiatives in Asian commerce and economic development. The end of Sir George Larpent's political career was certainly a bombshell. Here was a man whose political and business links, and his position as an MP for Nottingham, placed him in the highest echelons of politics and society. Morier Evans regarded Larpent as a potential future Governor of the Bank of England, and noted his ambition to sit as an MP for the City of London.[18] Certainly Hobhouse, President of the Board of Control believed Larpent's ruin would kill the East Indian Railway Company project, since as chair of that company he had been its main driving force. He asked Henry Tucker, then Chair of the East India Company 'whether that scheme can possibly go on after Larpent's failure,' adding that 'it seems absurd to send out the dispatch to India if it cannot'.[19]

A similar crisis of confidence beset the Assam Company. The AGM in May 1848 debated whether or not the Company should persist with its existing tea plantations, a reflection of growing pessimism among the shareholders in London. While this was not a direct consequence of the financial crisis of 1847, the situation could not have been helped by the Company losing Larpent as its chairman.[20] In fact, both the East Indian Railway Company (EIRC) and the Assam Company survived the loss of their Chairman, and went on to become successful enterprises. But the crisis left a gaping hole in the City of London's Asian contingent. The question was by whom and how this would be filled. The provincial British cities had also felt the brunt of the crisis, with failures in Liverpool, Glasgow and elsewhere. In Glasgow, a decision was made late in 1847 to subsume the Glasgow East India Association into the city's Chamber of Commerce, a move which seems to have partly reflected the impact of the crisis on that city.[21] While both the London EICA and the Liverpool EICA continued, the crisis had ruined prominent merchants who had filled senior positions on the executive committees of these organisations. There were, however, enough survivors to ensure continuity. Among the committee for London in 1850 were men such as William Lyall, Richard Durant, Archibald Hastie MP, William James Thompson and William Dallas, who had all occupied seats on the committee in the early 1840s.[22] Nonetheless, the collapse of the London East India agency houses had wrought changes which would fundamentally alter the balance of commercial political power between London and the British provinces, and between the East India Company and commercial interest groups in Asia.

Although trade and economic initiatives in Asia suffered in the short run from the crisis, recovery came quite swiftly within a few years. The more stable economic conditions which prevailed in Britain in the 1850s ensured that Britain's trade with Asia grew steadily and impressively during that decade. Trends in the values of exports from and imports into India demonstrated the speed and scale of the recovery. Exports from India to the world fell from about Rs170 million in 1845 to Rs133 million in 1847, but then recovered to Rs181 million by 1850, and reached Rs329 million in 1860.[23] Imports into India fell from Rs107 million in 1844 to Rs83 million in 1848, but recovered to Rs115 million in 1850 and Rs235 million by 1860.[24] Rothermund demonstrates that inflation in food prices in India in the 1850s ensured that the recovery in this period did not translate into prosperity for the majority of Indians, a fact which undoubtedly contributed to the Great Rebellion of 1857. But it is clear that British trade with her premier imperial possession recovered swiftly.[25] In particular, exports of British cotton goods to India showed a spectacular recovery. Exports to India of British yarn and twist rose in value from Rs11.3 million in 1850–1851 to Rs20.5 million in 1860–1861; while exports of piece goods rose in the same period from Rs33.7 million to Rs96.5 million.[26] While India enjoyed a trade surplus with the world at large, a substantial deficit in its trade with Britain became an enduring feature of the nineteenth century. Nonetheless, Indian economic development was helped by the fruition in the 1850s of the great railway schemes.

In spite of Hobhouse's fears that the crisis of 1847 would destroy the East Indian Railway Scheme, it proved more durable than he feared. In response to Larpent's demise, others stepped into the breach. Indeed, the late 1840s produced a solution to the issue which had stalled discussions only a few years earlier: the question of a government guarantee of dividends to shareholders. The promoters of both the EIRC and the Great Indian Peninsular Railway Company (GIPRC) had argued that the scale of investment required, and the lengthy period before profitable returns could be expected from the railways, necessitated some kind of government guarantee of a minimum dividend for shareholders for a period. This had led to rivalry between the two railway companies, especially in the fevered financial climate leading to the crisis of 1847/8. But the swift recovery which occurred after 1848 ensured that there were ample resources for both projects. The situation was assisted by an agreement in 1849 on the terms of a government guarantee to the EIRC, which were soon afterwards also applied to the GIPRC and the other Indian railway companies. A jubilant John Chapman attributed the success of the GIPR to the appeals of northern manufacturers who wanted to increase supplies of cotton from India.[27] Under the terms of the agreements with the Indian railway companies, the East India Company received capital from the EIRC, and in return gave a 99-year guarantee of 5% interest on it, to help it meet obligations to its shareholders. The intention was that as railway receipts grew, they would be used to fund dividends to shareholders and to repay to the East India Company any sums it had previously spent on guaranteed interest.[28] The result was that during the 1850s, railway construction gathered pace, with almost 3,000 miles completed by 1860.[29] This expanding network boosted Indian exports of such raw materials as raw cotton. By 1858, India supplied about 133 million pounds of raw cotton to Britain, or 13% of British imports of the commodity. But this rose to 392.7 million pounds in 1860 (75% of British raw cotton imports) and 615 million pounds by 1866, as the British were forced to turn to India as the American Civil War reduced supplies from that quarter.[30] As well as assisting this expansion, India's railway network, together with the development of the telegraph and the steam ship, drew India and Britain's Asian colonies into an emergent global system of trade and production.

In spite of the survival of the London and Liverpool East India Associations, the recovery of the 1850s also brought major changes in the commercial and political structures of Britain's Asian trade. The most significant of these came in the field of Asian banking. Earlier attempts to establish large new banks, especially ones dealing in the exchange business, had been thwarted since the mid-1830s by the concerted resistance of the East India Company, the London East India agency houses and the provincial industrialists and merchants. But after 1848 the political landscape had changed in several important ways. First, the demise of twenty East India Agency houses had removed one of the principal barriers against new institutional initiatives in finance. Moreover, the nature of their failure signalled the need for new arrangements in the conduct of trade and financial relations with the Asian colonies. The perception was that large new joint-stock banks could offer a degree of security which their opponents had demonstrably failed to provide. Secondly, the mid-1840s had significantly changed the outlook of senior politicians in respect of Asian economic affairs. A legacy of that decade was the consolidation of ideas around free trade and *laissez faire* as the new orthodoxy in economic thinking. This new intellectual climate was not congenial to residual institutions from the era of monopoly such as the East India Company. The Conservative Party, bitterly divided over free trade and the Corn Laws, was for the time being a spent force ideologically, opening the way for prolonged liberal intellectual hegemony. Many of the younger generation of Liberal politicians were enthusiastic acolytes of the new economic thinking. Some had seen at first hand the debacle of 1847/8, and welcomed the case for change.

Among these, James Wilson was perhaps the most influential. A lifelong supporter of *laissez faire*, Wilson had founded *The Economist* in 1843 to promote his ideas. By the late 1840s he was a fast rising star in the Liberal firmament, becoming an MP in 1847, a secretary at the Board of Control in 1848, Financial Secretary at the Treasury from 1852 to 1858, Vice President at the Board of Trade in 1859, and ultimately financial member of the Council of India.[31] Significantly, Wilson sat on the House of Commons Select Committee on Commercial Distress in 1848, investigating in detail the causes and consequences of the great crisis of the previous year. Another important figure was Sir Charles Wood, who was Chancellor of the Exchequer from 1846 to 1852 in Lord Russell's administration. He, like Wilson, was a firm supporter of free trade and *laissez faire*, and these convictions informed his tenure as President of the Board of Control from 1852 to 1858.[32] A third figure was Robert Lowe, a young Liberal lawyer, recently returned from Australia where he had made his fortune. A leader writer for *The Times* in 1851, he became

MP for Kidderminster, and was appointed to a secretary-ship in the Board of Control at the end of 1852, where he played a leading role in shaping the Charter Act of 1853. Lowe's Australian career had pitted him against strong vested interests in that colony, and he brought with him a conviction that administrative reform of the old colonial establishment was long overdue.[33] Significantly, among the Liberals in Parliament were a set of voluble and energetic radicals, led by Richard Cobden and John Bright, who not only zealously espoused the ideology of *laissez faire* and free trade, but who regularly criticised the East India Company for its warlike and imperialist policies and its dilatory management of the Indian economy. Although the precarious position of the Aberdeen ministry in Parliament meant that even reform-minded ministers like Wilson and Wood had to tread carefully, it is clear that they were receptive to the overtures of the free trade, anti-Company lobby in the Liberal ranks. There is, for example, evidence that Wood's enthusiastic promotion of railway construction and other public works in India was at least partly motivated by this vociferous radical faction.[34]

The ferocious hostility of this lobby towards the East India Company was evident in several areas other than Asian banking in the early 1850s. Cobden campaigned fiercely against what he saw as the expansionist tendencies of the Company, which were demonstrated in the second Anglo-Burmese War of 1851–1853.[35] But the new antipathy towards the Company was perhaps most strident in the parliamentary debates, and on the two Select Committees which considered the renewal of the East India Company's Charter in 1852. As a result, the Charter Act of 1853 ended the patronage of the Court of Directors in the appointment of Indian civil servants, replacing it with a system of competitive examinations. The number of directors was reduced from twenty-four to eighteen, and the authority and status of the Board of Control was enhanced, underlining its primacy over the Company's institutions. Moreover, the new Charter would remain in force, not for twenty years as had been the custom, but 'until parliament shall otherwise provide', leaving open the possibility of a peremptory end of Company rule in India. The Act was followed by a separate Government of India Act in 1854, which reformed the Governor-General's Council, and set up a separate Legislative Council to advise the Indian government. These reforms reflected a growing conviction in Parliament and government that the Company and its governing structures were obsolete and inadequate.[36]

Thus the East India Company, and those who had opposed new initiatives in colonial banking during the 1830s and 1840s, faced a more hostile set of political leaders than had previously been the case. The first issue to arise concerned the Oriental Bank, an organisation originally established in Bombay in 1842 as the Bank of Western India. Like the promoters of the abortive bank projects of the 1840s, the Oriental Bank aspired to engage in exchange banking, not just between Britain and India, but across Asia. To this end it established branches in Ceylon, Singapore and Hong Kong, but it was refused a charter by the East India Company, and during the 1840s was excluded from exchange business with Britain. But in 1851, it acquired the struggling Bank of Ceylon, which had been set up in 1841 by a Royal Charter which gave it permission to engage in exchange and remittance business anywhere to the east of the Cape of Good Hope, though not directly with Britain.[37] The Oriental Bank acquired the Bank of Ceylon to provide a pretext to apply for a Charter of its own, on the grounds that the Bank of Ceylon had previously enjoyed this status. In 1851, the British government granted it a charter, and it became the Oriental Banking Corporation. But the decision itself caused controversy, because under Act 47 George III c.68 (1807) the granting of Royal Charters to Indian banks was the prerogative of the India Board in consultation with the East India Company. The problem was that the British Treasury had granted the Charter without consulting the India Board.[38] In fact, legal advisers to the government ruled that the Treasury had acted within its rights, even in allowing the Oriental Bank to engage in exchange banking and remittance. It transpired that in law, there was no requirement for the Company or the India board to be consulted.[39] But to forestall a major row within government, James Wilson at the Treasury, assured the India Board that any further bank charter applications would be subject to the decision of the India Board and the Company. Their permission would be essential if a bank wished to issue its own notes within the territories governed by the East India Company. The Company was satisfied by this reassurance, but its twenty-year defence against the establishment of a chartered exchange bank which would be allowed to deal in remittances, had been breached. The way was now open for other new bank proposals to come forward, and these would be far more difficult to rebuff. The Oriental Banking Corporation now held a monopoly of exchange banking and this ran contrary to the competitive, *laissez faire* spirit of the time.

In fact two major new bank schemes became public at the time the Oriental Bank's charter was being so hotly debated within government. The first of these was the Chartered Bank of India, Australia and China, which applied for a charter in October 1852. Significantly some of the promoters and directors came from the ranks of the London East India agency houses, notably Peter Bell, of the East India agency house of Scott, Bell & Co., which had failed in the crisis of 1847/8. Others included William Cook of Messrs Cook, Sons & Co. of St Paul's Churchyard, London, W.S. Lindsay of W.S Lindsay & Co., another East India firm, located in Austin Friars near the Bank of England, an enclave for such firms, and T.A. Mitchell, an MP and a member of Messrs Sampson, Mitchell & Co., of 9 Broad Street, again in the heart of the City. Another promoter, Joseph Morrison, belonged to Messrs James Morrison & Co., Australian merchants, of Philpot Lane.[40] Clearly a faction within the City now felt able to break ranks and promote a major new London-based joint stock exchange bank, in spite of the ferocious resistance encountered by their predecessors just a few years earlier. The second proposed bank, the 'Bank of Asia', was also backed by men long connected with India. These included T.W. Henderson, formerly of Remington & Co. in Calcutta and connected with Jardine, Matheson & Co. in China, R.L. Leckie from Leckie & Co. of Bombay, and J. Fraser of the Singapore house of Maclaine, Fraser & Co.[11] Another supporter, John Entwistle, was a member of the executive committee of the London EICA in 1852.[12] Ambitions to reconstruct commercial and financial relations with Asia through the agency of new, large joint-stock banks had been revived with a vengeance in the wake of 1847/8. How would they fare in the new political climate?

The old forces of resistance were certainly not dead and they quickly moved into action. The East India Company was first to attack. In November 1852, James Cosmo Melvill, Secretary to the Company, spelt out its objections to the Board of Control. He repeated the old line that India simply had enough banks already, and that new ones would destabilise rather than improve the Indian financial system. He claimed that exchange banking had been forbidden by the Company in the case of existing chartered banks, an assertion which was strictly incorrect in light of the success of the Oriental Bank in securing a Charter just a year earlier. But Melvill was familiar with the controversy raging around this, and probably thought it politically expedient to remind the Board, and through them the Treasury, of the questionable decision in that case. He emphasised the potentially destabilising effects charted exchange banks might have on the Company's arrangements for remitting funds to meet the home charges. Finally, Melvill launched an attack on the joint stock principle behind the new banking schemes, arguing that:

> It needs no argument to prove that the bank which proposes to issue notes and at the same time to engage in business of a speculative character requires every check which can be placed upon its proceedings, with a view of ensuring the security of its customers – and to allow to the partners in such a scheme the privilege of limited liability would, in the Court's opinion, be tantamount to removing the main check against improper and reckless management.[13]

In passing this on to the Treasury, Cumming Bruce of the Board of Control stressed the Board's concurrence with these views, and repeated objections offered and supported by both the Company and the Board in respect of the Bank of Asia in 1840.[14] Other familiar opponents of Indian banks soon entered the debate about the new schemes. In July 1853 nine City of London merchant firms signed a long petition opposing the banks. These were East India agency house survivors of the debacle of 1847/8, and included Palmer, Mackillop & Co., Gregson & Co., Forbes, Forbes & Co. and Alexander, Fletcher & Co. Significantly, all of these firms were associated with the London EICA.[45] Among their number was also Baring Brothers. The objections they offered were also familiar: they repeated the lack of a need for new banks in India, and warned that the creation of more banks would lead to overtrading, and a destabilisation of Indian government finances. They warned that the success of the Oriental Bank in securing a charter was 'a great evil'. They also attacked the joint stock principle as likely to lead to irresponsible behaviour, and finally they complained that the banks would offer unfair competition in a field of commerce traditionally left to the East India houses. Evidence soon emerged that the old connections between London and provincial merchants were at work. Two days later the Manchester Chamber of Commerce and the Manchester Commercial Association penned an almost identical letter to the East India Company.[46] In September the Liverpool EICA registered similar objections to those of the Company and the Board of Control.[47] As in the 1840s, a vigorous opposition was being offered by a pragmatic alliance of the Company, London East India agency houses, and provincial merchants and industrialists with interests in the Indian trade. It probably expected to succeed once more.

But times had changed. After much discussion between the Treasury, the India Board and the East India Company Court of Directors during the course of 1853, the two new banks were granted their charters. They were permitted to engage in exchange banking, subject to the rule that they could only issue notes within the territories subject to the East India Company's authority with its express permission.[48] The alliance between the Company, London East India merchants and provincial merchants and industrialists had been defeated at last on the banking question. The debates over the issue within government reveal how the political and intellectual climate in respect of Britain's Asian empire had changed since the early 1840s. The argument offered by James Wilson, recently appointed as Financial Secretary to the Treasury in 1853, became the basis for the government case for granting the charters. He contended that as the Oriental Bank had been granted its charter two years earlier, any denial of similar status to the new bank schemes would be to allow it a monopoly over banking in Asia.[49] While this was certainly an important consideration in the decision, Wilson had other reasons for supporting the charters. In June 1853, as the debate over the new bank charters intensified in Whitehall, Wilson circulated a lengthy memorandum on Indian banking to, among others, Sir Charles Wood, President of the Board of Control. In this, Wilson considered the new bank schemes in the wider context of the development of Indian commerce since the great Calcutta financial crisis of the early 1830s. He noted that the London and Calcutta agency houses had been the most strident opponents of banking reform since the 1830s, on the grounds that such organisations were unnecessary and would interfere with their own business activities. But, in fact, Wilson noted that in the absence of large exchange banks, their conduct in the management of trade and the provision of credits facilities had been disastrous, and had been largely responsible for the financial crises of the early 1830s and 1847/8. Wilson had been on the Select Committee of the Commons which had investigated the commercial distress of the late 1840s, and he was particularly scathing about the dubious practices among the London and Calcutta agency houses which had led to the latter debacle:

> I remember being then, as all members of the committee were, struck with the extraordinary state of things in Calcutta which led to the great overtrading and ultimate ruin of those houses. In the absence of established and well accredited means of conducting the exchanges a system had arisen exactly similar in its nature to that known at home by the term 'accommodation bills', was introduced. Houses in Calcutta drew upon their own houses in London, and the houses in London to cover themselves drew upon their houses in Indian or the India houses drew new sets of bills, and with the proceeds of such bills, purchased other bills upon other houses (of a similar character) and transmitted them to the houses in London to pay former bills of their own drawing. And thus an enormous amount of cross bills became current, representing no transactions, and what was even worse, drawn without any regard to the state of the exchanges whether profitable or ever so much the reverse under the dire necessity at all hazards to meet their engagements.[50]

Under these circumstances, the failures of 1847/8 had been unavoidable. But Wilson was convinced that had there been bona fide joint-stock exchange banks in existence, 'these practices could never have obtained a footing'.[51] Moreover, Wilson reviewed recent trends in British trade with Asia, and trade within the region itself, and concluded that these required new strategies and institutions to protect British imperial economic interests in Asia. The discovery of gold in Australia at the end of the 1840s presaged a large and rapid expansion of Australian trade with India and China, as rising Australian population and wealth created greater demand for tea, coffee, sugar and rice. Wilson envisaged a new period of growth in the intra-Asian trade, which would bring prosperity to Britain's Asian empire, but which would also require careful management if the financial disasters of the first half of the century were to be avoided. The mooted new exchange banks, together with the Oriental Bank, could provide the inter-colonial financial structures necessary to facilitate this projected growth in Asian and imperial trade, and place it on a stable footing.[52] Thus Wilson envisaged that the banks would provide a new institutional framework for the conduct and promotion of imperial commercial activity in Asia. It would supersede the unreliable structures based around the agency houses and the East India Company, created during the long period of the Company's retreat from privilege and commerce. Implicit in Wilson's analysis was a belief that the East India Company had outlived its value even as an agency for the governance of India, and that the future prosperity and stability of the British Empire in Asia

required the emergence of new large scale and joint-stock financial institutions to oversee and finance the Asian trade. It was, in effect, an attack upon
that constellation of interests (East India Company, agency houses in India,
China and London and provincial merchants and industrialists) which had
led in this field in the first half of the century. In this respect, the decision by
the British government to grant the bank charters represented a much larger
shift in state policy towards India than it perhaps seemed at the time, and it
presaged the far–reaching reforms which were implemented in the wake of
the Great Indian Rebellion in 1857/8. Wilson's June 1853 paper on Indian
banking demonstrates just how rapidly government was coming round to the
view that major reform in respect of the British Empire in Asia was long
overdue, and why the rebellion prompted such a radical response by government and Parliament.

But the East India Company, and the associations which represented the
London East India and the provincial interests, continued to try to frustrate
these new competitors. In 1855 the Company adamantly refused to comply
with overtures from the Bank of Asia to relax its prohibition on the issuing of
notes by exchange banks in the Company's territories, even though the bank
tried to elicit the support of the Treasury.[53] The Bank of Asia even tried to
persuade the government to allow it to relinquish its recently charter in favour
of a new one which would embody a merger with a rising Indian bank, the
Bombay-based Mercantile Bank of India, London and China, which was
itself seeking a charter to confirm its status and secure limited liability.[54]
The Bank of Asia management clearly hoped that the merger would enable
it to engage in the full range of banking activities within the Company's
territories, since Mercantile already enjoyed this right. But this was refused
by the Treasury, in part because the Bank of Asia had not yet implemented
its existing charter, or even begun to function as a bank.[55] The refusal was
a victory for the Company and its allies, and in fact the Bank of Asia was
subsequently dissolved, demonstrating that a charter was not an immediate
guarantee of commercial success. But Mercantile went on to petition for
and receive its own charter in July 1857, thereafter establishing itself as yet
another London-based joint stock exchange bank, now called Chartered
Mercantile Bank of India, London and China, which would compete with
the old East India agency houses.[56]

The 1850s therefore saw major changes in the commercial landscape, with
the emergence of new joint-stock exchange banks challenging the surviving
agency houses in the finance and conduct of the trade with Asia. These
changes in commercial structure and practice were mirrored by political
changes. Mention has already been made of the absorption of the Glasgow
East India Association into the Glasgow Chamber of Commerce, and this
was a sign that those merchants in the city involved in the Asian trade felt
that their interests were best defended as part of a larger body representing

the whole body of Glasgow's mercantile and industrial class. In Liverpool there were also significant changes. In the late 1840s a Liverpool-based Italian merchant, Leone Levi, began to campaign for the establishment of a Liverpool Chamber of Commerce which could speak for the entire mercantile community of the city. Levi lamented divisions within the Liverpool community, notably between West and East India traders, which had served to hamper the ability of the city to present a united voice in matters of state policy towards trade and empire. He believed that a Chamber of Commerce could remedy this problem. Moreover, Levi believed that the Chamber could act as a catalyst for the establishment in Liverpool of new banks and finance houses which could diminish the dependence of the city's merchants on the financial services provided by the City of London, especially in such activities as bill negotiation.[57] The Chamber was duly established in 1850, and the Liverpool EICA found itself having to work alongside the new organisation, though it retained a separate existence throughout the 1850s. In 1849 it sent three representatives to sit on a committee of the various trade associations in the city which were conferring on the question of a Chamber of Commerce, but it did not choose to subsume itself within that organisation at the time.[58] However, the London EICA worked with the Chamber on Asian questions, and the two organisations lobbied the government in respect of the East India Company's Charter Act of 1853.[59] Increasingly, though, the Chamber took the lead on Asian questions. For example, following the Indian Rebellion in 1857, and the dissolution of East India Company rule in India, there was a major question of how Liverpool's interest in the Asian trade should be defended under the new arrangements. The central issue was whether or not to maintain the Liverpool Office in London, an institution which had represented Liverpool merchants involved in trade with India since the 1830s. The question arose because of the death of the secretary of the office. Significantly, it was the Liverpool Chamber which agreed to maintain it, and to appoint Thomas Baines as its new secretary.[60] Also in 1858 the Chamber set up a special committee to review the new arrangements for governing India, following the end of Company rule. This was a role which formerly would have been undertaken by the Liverpool EICA.[61] The Chamber rapidly became the voice of Liverpool on Asian questions, and while the Liverpool EICA soldiered on, it ceased to function entirely in the mid-1870s, leaving the Chamber as the sole mouthpiece on Asian affairs. The London EICA disappeared from the scene even sooner, with no annual reports apparently being published after 1856, though there is some evidence that they may have staggered on into the 1860s, as their help was solicited by the Straits interests as late as 1864.[62] The end of the East India Company seems to have triggered the demise of this important pressure group representing commercial interest groups connected with Asia.

But an even more dramatic example of this remoulding of the political landscape in Asian commercial politics was evident in south-east Asia. The commercial communities of the Straits Settlements of Penang, Malacca and Singapore had been at loggerheads with the East India Company since the late 1820s. At that time, Penang had lost its presidency status and the administration of the Straits Settlements had been severely pared back as the Company sought to make economies.[63] The Charter Act of 1833 ended the Company's direct engagement in the China trade from India, an aspect of the organisation's activities which had ensured that the Straits of Malacca, the waterway through which this trade was conducted, was of premium concern. In truth, the Company was no longer so interested in the fate of the British communities in south-east Asia. It was a loss of status which was as acutely felt by the business communities in the Straits, as it was by the officials who found themselves effectively demoted by their superiors in London and Calcutta. A vague suspicion that the Company regarded the Straits as a backwater of marginal importance was given substance in the mid-1830s, when a problem of Malay piracy necessitated decisive action by the authorities. While the Company arranged for maritime policing and military operations to combat the problem, it took the view that the Straits communities themselves should pay for this, and in late 1835 it announced the imposition of planned duties on trade at the Straits ports.[64] But the Straits Settlements, especially Singapore, had always resisted the introduction of trade duties, taking the view that their success was largely attributable to the free trade regime which attracted traders from all over the region and the world. For merchants in the Straits, the proposal merely confirmed the indifference of the Company to their needs and interests, and they launched a campaign in 1836 which resulted in the creation of Chambers of Commerce at Singapore and Penang, the establishment of collaborative links with the East India Associations of London, Glasgow and Liverpool, and the retreat of the Company from its proposed tariffs.[65] Other issues inflamed the relationship between the Straits merchants and the Company. In the late 1830s, the Company's administration in Bengal sought to impose regulations which would limit the leasing of land to cultivators to just twenty years, a period insufficient for cultivators of crops such as pepper and sugar to be sure of a good return on their investments.[66] Once again this was defeated by 1840, mainly due to the Singapore and Penang Chambers securing the help of the London EICA and John Crawfurd in London.[67] Throughout this period, the Straits merchants also complained incessantly to the Company and to the British government about Dutch protectionism in south-east Asia, but to no avail. While the Company could not be blamed for the refusal of the British state to act on the issue, it helped foster the general impression in the Straits that it was indifferent to the needs of the British communities there.

Matters came to a head in the mid-1850s, when the Company in India embarked on yet another ill-conceived plan for the Straits. In 1855 it announced that the Indian Rupee would replace the Spanish Dollar as the official currency of the Straits Settlements. It ordered that all revenues would have to be paid in Rupees, a stipulation which meant that a high proportion of mercantile transactions would also have to be in that currency. The Company's intention seems to have been to strengthen commercial ties between India and south-east Asia by creating what would have been in effect a 'Rupee zone'. It would also have made the collection of revenues in the Straits cheaper, removing exchange costs. But the Company entirely misjudged the response of the Malay and Chinese traders in south-east Asia, who quickly made it clear to the British merchants in the Straits that they were deeply unhappy at the impending demise of the Dollar, which had been the currency of trade for centuries. The fear was that the imposition of the Rupee would result in a collapse of Chinese and Malay commerce with the Straits Settlements. The Singapore Chamber took the lead, lobbying the British government and Parliament both directly and through the London EICA.[68] Once again, the Company beat a hasty retreat, and the plan was dropped in March 1857.[69]

But the Straits merchants had had enough. In 1858, just when the Great Indian Rebellion was at its height, John Crawfurd, that doughty defender of Straits interests, at the behest of merchants in Penang and Singapore, published a lengthy memorandum which castigated the Company for decades of indifference and misrule in the Straits. He called for the Straits Settlements to be removed from the authority of the Company and the India Board, and granted Crown Colony status, thereby placing it under the wing of the Colonial Office.[70] It was supported by a petition to Parliament from the European inhabitants of Singapore, which set out the reasons for their longstanding hostility to Company rule in no uncertain terms:

> Ignorant, apparently, of the many circumstances in which the Straits Settlements differ so widely from Continental India, the Supreme Government has almost invariably treated them from an exclusively Indian point of view, and shown a systematic disregard to the wants and wishes of their inhabitants, however earnestly and perseveringly made known. And only by appeals to the Imperial Government and Parliament, have needful improvements desired by the inhabitants of the Straits Settlements, been brought about. Or redress obtained for injustice inflicted on them by the Government of the East India Company.[71]

The call was timely because, following the suppression of the rebellion, Company rule in India was ended, and deliberations were set in motion which resulted in the Straits Settlements securing Crown Colony status in the 1860s. As early as 1860, this independence from Company rule brought positive changes. The Oriental Bank, which had a branch at Singapore, had been pressing for some time to be allowed to engage in the full range of banking activities there, including the issue of notes, a request which had been refused by the Company.[72] After the end of Company rule in India, the Oriental Bank resumed its efforts, this time with the support of the mercantile community at Singapore.[73] Some fifty-three merchants and firms on the island supported the call.[74] After initially resisting the request on the advice of the Government of India, Charles Wood, the Secretary of State for India ruled that the power to issue notes should in future be subject to the rule of whatever legislative body was established for the Straits Settlements, following the granting of Crown Colony status.[75] In practice, the Straits Settlements had established conditions for banking which set it apart from India. The Chartered Mercantile Bank of India, London and China was granted the same privileges soon after, and following further efforts in 1861 it won the right to establish a branch at issue notes at Penang, establishing beyond doubt that the banks in the Straits would now be free of the restrictions on banking which still applied in India.[76] This paved the way for the emergence of a very different commercial environment for British business in south-east Asia, and emphatically signalled its divorce from British India. It also necessitated the emergence of new strategies of political representation for Straits merchants. Their connections with the East India Associations in Britain were withering as the latter were wound up or absorbed into larger organisations such as the Chambers of Commerce; though the London EICA did assist in lobbying the Colonial Office in 1864, in respect of the financial arrangements for the transfer of the Straits Settlements to that department.[77] Thus in January 1868, a group of merchants and individuals in London who had links with south-east Asia formed the Straits Settlements Association, with none other than the elderly John Crawfurd as their President.[78] This body aimed to lobby government directly on Straits affairs, rather than through other organisations in London or the provinces. In this way the Straits men had broken away from the trans-imperial network which had emerged in the 1830s. This signalled the fragmentation of that network as economic change in London, and declining government sympathy with the old institutions of the Company and the London East India agency houses, led to the break up of what had once been a formidable political alliance.

From 1856 the events which ultimately led to the demise of the East India Company's government of India gathered momentum. The Treaty of Nanking with China of 1842, which opened British trade with the five 'treaty ports', had never placed the opium trade on a satisfactory basis, because the trade remained illegal. In late 1856, the seizure of the ship *Arrow* by the Chinese authorities, on the grounds that it was heavily involved in opium smuggling, triggered the second Opium War of 1856–1860, which ended in British victory and the opening still further of the Chinese market. Wong argues persuasively that it was the importance of opium revenues to the British administration in India which was instrumental in prompting the severity of the British response.[79] Other historians, notably Barber, stress the importance of the Indian export of opium to China in offsetting India's trade deficit with Britain and enabling the Company to meet the home charges.[80] But the main point was that the war itself was controversial in Britain and called into question yet again, and especially among radical anti-imperialists, the morality of the East India Company's regime in Asia. Ominously, however, in May 1857, the revolt of Indian Sepoys at Meerut in India triggered a much more serious conflict in India, which threatened the very existence of the British Indian empire. The events of the Great India Rebellion are too complex and controversial to be dealt with here. Suffice to say that the horrors of the war, its cost and the urgent necessity for fundamental reform in British government in India, all sounded the death knell of the Company's administration. The Government of India Act of 1858, passed in August of that year, ended East India Company rule in India. All East India Company assets, political engagements such as treaties, and control of the Indian civil service, passed directly to the Crown. The Board of Control was dissolved, and the office of President transformed in to position of Secretary of State for India, carrying Cabinet rank and effectively embodying direct British government control over the former territories of the Company. A Legislative Council of 'experts' on Indian affairs was set up to advise the Secretary of State. The Governor-General and his Council in India would in future be appointed by, and be formally answerable directly to, the Secretary of State. The Company itself remained in existence until its dissolution in 1874, with the Court of Directors meeting occasionally to distribute its dividends. It was an ignominious end for what had once been the mightiest commercial organisation in the world.

Of course the creation of this new regime in India has been scrutinised by historians. As well as creating a new political administration, the government had to address more fundamental operational questions, especially in respect of Indian finances. Throughout the 1850s, in spite of the apparent robustness of British rule and trade with India, there were growing worries about the Company's aggressive tendencies towards its neighbours. The Second Burmese War of 1851–1853 had resulted in the expansion of British rule into parts of that country, which drew criticism from such prominent anti-imperialists as Richard Cobden. Moreover the expense had resulted in mounting budget deficits for the India government, and these deficits became much greater in the wake of the Great Rebellion of 1857.[81] This meant that a major priority for the new administration was to regularise Indian finances and reduce the deficits as quickly as possible. To this end, Charles Wood, appointed Secretary of State for India in 1859, persuaded James Wilson to take up the post of Financial Member of the Council of India. In a long memorandum on the Indian financial system, Wilson made clear his intention to overhaul the administrative system of revenue collection and finance, and to assert direct personal control over financial decisions.[82] While Wilson died soon after his arrival in India in 1860, the spirit of his policies were continued, with the balancing of the Indian budget becoming a major priority. This proved controversial in a number of respects, not least following the introduction in 1859 of high tariffs on the import of British manufactures into India (especially British cotton goods). It sparked off an energetic campaign against the tariffs by the Manchester Chamber of Commerce and related organisations.[83] The tariffs were in fact repealed in 1862, though the extent to which the Manchester lobby brought this about has been questioned by Cain and Hopkins, who argue that the improving state of Indian finances by 1862 made such a change likely even without pressure from the Lancashire manufacturing interest.[84] But, more generally, Cain and Hopkins see the political and financial reforms following the rebellion as creating an environment in which the export of capital to India, for the construction of railways, investment in agriculture and a range of other activities, could flourish. Direct control of Indian affairs by the British state, coupled with the financial reforms, helped create a climate of confidence which encouraged investment in India and the development of its economy. Accompanied by the rise of the new exchange banks, and the subsequent emergence of new banking organisations in Asia such as the National Bank of India (1870s) and the Hong Kong and Shanghai Bank (1865), these changes created a new political and financial order which allowed faster progress in the development of the Indian economy. But the principal beneficiaries and drivers of this new phase of Indian development tended to be the investors, banks and other financial institutions of the City of London, the 'gentlemanly capitalists' who occupy centre stage in Cain and Hopkins' interpretation of British imperialism. While provincial manufacturers and merchants also gained from the growth of the later nineteenth century, they remained peripheral in the determination of policy and the benefits which arose from it.[85]

This interpretation of post-1858 development is certainly persuasive. The disintegration of the network of political organisations (the East India and China Associations and Chambers of Commerce in Asia) in the 1850s seemed to operate against the interests of the British provinces, who found themselves on the losing side of the debate about the exchange banks during that decade. The absorption of the Glasgow EICA into the Glasgow Chamber of Commerce in 1848, the gradual supersession of the Liverpool EICA by that city's Chamber of Commerce during the 1850s and 1860s, the disappearance of the London EICA at the end of the 1850s, and the separatist strategies of the Straits merchants, all contributed to the fracturing of important collaborative links between Liverpool, Glasgow, Manchester, the imperial periphery and London in the sphere of colonial economic policy making in Asia. The process was accelerated by the drift of many successful mercantile firms to London, usually by the initial establishment of branches in the City, followed in due course by a wholesale relocation of the business. Thus houses such as

Ogilvy & Gillanders and Harrisons & Crosfield followed this path. A similar trend was also evident in respect of British commerce with Latin America.[86] This facilitated the resurgence of London as the premier centre for the determination of Asian policy, and the main beneficiary of Indian development, a position which it had enjoyed at the beginning of the nineteenth century.

But there is a case for suggesting that understanding of colonial economic development in Asia and the determination of policy in that region during the later nineteenth century would benefit from new research on the relationships between City interests, and the commercial communities in the British provinces and at the imperial periphery. The provincial Chambers of Commerce continued to try to shape policy towards India and Asia. A few examples in respect of Liverpool and Manchester illustrate the point. From the late 1860s, Liverpool, Huddersfield and a number of other provincial towns campaigned for the representation of the British manufacturing export interest within the governing structures for India.[87] In 1876, a director of the Manchester Chamber of Commerce was duly appointed to the Legislative Council for India.[88] The British government also regularly consulted the Liverpool Chamber of Commerce on trade with Asia. In 1872 the Secretary of State for India asked for the Chamber to furnish him with intelligence about the India trade.[89] Then in 1883 the Board of Trade requested the Liverpool Chamber provide it with trade statistics on shipping and cargoes which had passed through the Suez Canal two years earlier.[90] Indeed, there is evidence that part of the trans-imperial network of commercial pressure groups which had operated in the 1840s had been revived by the 1870s. In 1871, at the request of the Bombay Chamber of Commerce, the Liverpool Chamber petitioned Parliament for the establishment of a Select Committee to investigate taxation and expenditure in India.[91] The Liverpool Chamber was also very active in campaigning for the development of a trade route into China through Burma, lobbying Parliament on this no fewer than eight times between 1858 and 1869, and continuing to press this cause up to the end of the nineteenth century.[92] Indeed during the period leading to the invasion of Burma in 1885, Wallace Brothers, the City of London-based finance house which owned the Bombay-Burma Trading Corporation, whose logging activities were threatened by the Burmese government, orchestrated links between the Rangoon Chamber of Commerce and the British Chambers of Commerce (including those of London, Liverpool, Manchester and Glasgow), mobilising them to press for tough government action. This was undoubtedly a crucial factor in the British decision to go to war in 1885.[93]

The contention here is not that British imperial policy in Asia was determined by an equal partnership of British provincial, colonial and City of London-based interests. Cain and Hopkins' argument for London, gentlemanly-capitalist dominance of imperial policy remains convincing in substance. It seems likely, however, that they may have underestimated the ability of interests outside London to exert influence over policy, and the willingness of the London gentlemanly capitalists to recruit them as allies in their efforts to shape policy. In this respect, there may well be scope for a new interpretation of British colonial policy in Asia (and possibly elsewhere in the empire) in the later nineteenth and twentieth century. While this would probably acknowledge the leadership of City gentlemanly capitalists, it would place them within a context of fluid trans-imperial networks of interest groups, which allowed influence over the determination of policy to those non-City men who have hitherto been defined as 'outsiders' in the Cain and Hopkins thesis. The 1850s may have seen a shift of economic power and political influence in favour of the City in relation to provincial Britain and its industry, and the commercial communities in colonial Asia, but it should not be overstated. Further research may well reveal that a more complex model of the 'gentlemanly capitalist' thesis is needed, one which accords a larger role for economic interest groups in provincial Britain and on the imperial periphery.

Eight

CONCLUSION: THE DECLINE OF THE EAST INDIA COMPANY AND THE EVOLUTION OF BRITISH COMMERCIAL AND POLITICAL INTERESTS IN ASIA, 1793–1860

THE GREAT INDIAN REBELLION of 1857 and the termination of East India Company rule over India just a year later thus ushered in a new phase of British imperialism in Asia. The end of the Company's regime meant that, at last, the British state had to accept unequivocal responsibility for the governance of former Company possessions. Consequently, new governing institutions were established in Asia which were directly answerable to government and Parliament in London, through the Secretary of State for India and the India Office. These changes went hand-in-hand with a new culture of governance, created by the trauma of the Rebellion. Military reforms resulted in a shift away from Hindustan as the main recruiting ground for the Indian army towards the Punjab and other regions from which troops were perceived to have shown greater loyalty to the British. The policy of undermining Indian law, culture and involvement in the machinery of government, which had been applied under the last few decades of Company rule, was abruptly reversed. An initiative was launched to recruit educated Indians into the lower ranks of the Indian Civil Service. The Straits Settlements, which for so long had complained about their poor status under Company rule, were eventually granted Crown Colony status and placed under the jurisdiction of the Colonial Office. Perhaps the most telling changes were the economic consequences of the new arrangements. The new regime, underpinned as it was by the state, restored the confidence of British business, encouraging a flood of capital into India, in railways and plantation agriculture. The financiers and investors of the City of London were major beneficiaries of this process, and, according to Cain and Hopkins, probably the main determinants of later economic policy.

But the long road to direct rule by the British state and the prolonged demise of the East India Company had exercised profound effects upon the development of British commerce in Asia, and this shaped the politics of the emerging capitalist system in Britain and its empire in a number of important ways. For the historian, a number of key questions need to be addressed in respect of this extended period of transition. What was the legacy of this period for the nature of commercial politics in Britain and across the empire? How did the long period of conflict and co-existence with the East India Company shape the organisations, aspirations and attitudes of merchants, industrialists and financiers in British and Asian colonial cities? How did the various groups of interests fare during this period? How was their development shaped by the complex unravelling of Company rule? What was the legacy of the Company's slow death for the development of commercial politics in Britain and the Asian empire? Moreover, what light does this throw upon the accuracy of such historical interpretations of empire as the 'gentlemanly capitalism' thesis? What new insights into the workings of the British Empire does this episode offer? The best way to explore these issues is to consider in turn the fortunes of key players in the story: the London East India interests (principally the London East India agency houses), the provincial mercantile and industrial interests in the UK (particularly in key cities such as Liverpool, Manchester and Glasgow), the varied commercial communities in Asia itself and lastly the East India Company. Finally, some conclusions may be drawn from these sectional narratives in respect of the gentlemanly capitalism thesis and the question of how imperial policy was determined.

Let us first consider those London-based financial and mercantile interests who emerged from the East India Company during the period. These were principally the East India agency houses set up in London by retiring partners in the Indian agency houses, organisations which flourished as a result of permission from the East India Company to engage in the intra-Asian country trade, banking, shipping and investment in plantation agriculture. Frequently using the deposited savings of Company servants and soldiers, the Indian firms developed a close relationship with the Company, working within the confines of its monopoly and restrictions, with varying degrees of friction. The London houses were set up to deal with the London end of the Indian houses' business. Activities included agency and other financial services for the constituents (clients) of the Indian houses who frequently were employees of the Company, handling the sales of imports of indigo and Indian piece goods via the 'privilege trade' which allowed a limited amount of private commerce between Britain and India, and managing the British end of the personal and business affairs of the Indian houses and their partners. These London firms, from the last decades of the eighteenth century, invested heavily in East Indian stock and became a major interest group within the

East India Company in their own right. They enjoyed growing representation in the Courts of Proprietors and Directors. The relationship between the London East India agency houses and the East India Company from the outset was deeply ambivalent, and to some extent remained so throughout the period. On the one hand, their desire to engage in trade between India and Britain on a large scale set them squarely against the Company's monopoly and privileged position. But, on the other hand, their position as Company stockholders, and the dependence of their business activities on the goodwill of the Company and the custom of its employees, made the cultivation of good relations with the Company's hierarchy essential. This made it very difficult for the London houses to challenge the Company's privileges consistently. Nonetheless, they took a robust line in the campaign for a relaxation of the India monopoly leading to the Charter Act of 1793, and thereafter in an effort to maximise private channels of commerce within the Company's 'regulated monopoly'. But it was a painful experience, for which leaders such as David Scott paid a high price in incurring the hostility of major factions within the Company hierarchy. In fact, many London agency house men were wary of the consequences of a complete opening of the India trade, especially to the provinces, a reservation made abundantly clear when, in 1812, some of their number supported restriction to the port of London of any 'liberalised' import trade from India. While the houses were critical of the Company's monopoly, they did not initially cherish the notion of competition with provincial outport merchants. For this reason theirs was quite a passive role in the agitation which led to the opening of the India trade in the 1813 Charter Act; and they were content to allow the British provincial merchants and industrialists to take the lead.

The opening of the India trade, however, brought fundamental changes in the commercial activities of the houses, which in the long run had major political repercussions. The houses increasingly became involved as commission agents arranging and financing the export of British manufactures (principally cotton goods). As a result, whereas during the 1812/13 agitation they had remained aloof from the provincial campaign against monopoly, during the campaign against the China monopoly of 1829–1830 there was much more collusion with the provinces, especially in the Select Committee investigations of the period. It is fair to say, however, that once again their involvement in the East India Company's internal structures as stockholders muted their voice in this later agitation, a tendency perhaps exacerbated by the fact that their influence within the Courts of Proprietors and Directors had grown significantly during the 1820s. Once again it was the provincial lobbyists, especially the East India and China Associations of Liverpool and Glasgow, which made the running. Indeed, for much of the early 1830s the leadership of non-Company opinion on Asian commerce and colonial policy seemed to reside in the provinces. No doubt the great financial collapse of that period in Calcutta contributed to this, as it hit the London houses hard, both financially and in terms of their influence within the Company, as elections to the directorate saw other interest groups gaining at the expense of the houses. Perhaps the clearest acknowledgement of this deference to the provinces came in 1836, when the London East India agency houses and others formed the London East India and China Association (London EICA), an organisation which copied the forms and methods of the Glasgow and Liverpool EICAs. The London EICA quickly made contact with its provincial counterparts within days of its formation. Within the year provincial dominance was asserted once again, when Glasgow, with allies amongst the London East India agency houses, successfully led the resistance against Larpent's scheme for a Central Bank for India. In the process, the campaign effectively set up an alliance of London and provincial interests, together with the East India Company, which stymied several similar initiatives in the 1840s.

But, as the 1830s wore on, the London agency houses, through the London EICA and their enduring presence within the East India Company's structures of power, began to assert themselves within this new alliance of interests. They were assisted by a number of factors. Firstly, the London houses enjoyed close links with commercial groups throughout Asia, connections which were strengthened by the establishment of new Indian houses in Calcutta in the wake of the crisis of the early 1830s. Many of these were initially subject to much closer direction and control by the London firms. Secondly, the emergence of political organisations representing these colonial commercial groups, in the form of Chambers of Commerce for Bengal, Bombay, Madras, Singapore and elsewhere, tended to strengthen the hand of the London EICA, since the London agency houses enjoyed especially strong links with these communities. This made the London EICA the first British pressure group to which the Asian Chambers of Commerce usually turned, though strong links were also fostered with the provincial EICAs. Thirdly, the London agency houses were pivotal in the whole conduct of trade with India and Asia. They provided the credit and overseas contacts which were necessary for the export of manufactures, and they also controlled much of the import trade from India. As such, they were the fulcrum for the whole apparatus of trade, and they commanded intelligence about shipping, commodity prices, exchange rates, bill discount rates, all of which dictated the course of trade. This control of information placed them at an advantage over their provincial counterparts and allies. Finally, of course, the geographical privileges of the gentlemanly capitalists, namely their proximity in London to key centres of power in Parliament, Whitehall and Leadenhall Street, also enabled the London houses to lead campaigns on a variety of issues, as well as take advantage of new opportunities which arose. For example, several of the London houses, including George Larpent's, were very well placed to promote with the Company and the government such initiatives as the Assam Company and the East Indian Railway Company. The result was that by the eve of the great crisis of 1847/8 the London houses and their pressure group, the London EICA, could be said to have become leaders of the alliance of non-Company interests involved in Asia. Within their ranks there were also individuals like Larpent who clearly nurtured ambitions for political power through commerce. Such men embodied the gentlemanly capitalist aspirations described by Cain and Hopkins. But the key point is that they were heavily dependent upon the support and co-operation of both the provincial mercantile and industrial groups and those on the periphery of empire. In no way were those in the provinces and at the periphery outsiders; rather they approximated to equals in this trans-imperial political and commercial network. London was merely *primus inter pares.*

The great crash of the late 1840s upset what had looked to be a stable configuration of forces in the field of Asian commerce. But the most severe impact was upon the London firms. The annihilation of twenty of the leading London East India agency houses, together with their sister houses in Calcutta, was a devastating blow from which they never truly recovered. The crisis not only destroyed key leaders and aspirant gentlemen capitalists such as Sir George Larpent, but it also completely discredited the system of international commerce which they had controlled for so long. Perhaps more seriously, it obliterated their reputation for financial sagacity. It therefore undermined their ability, in concert with the Company and the provinces, to block major new initiatives in the field of exchange banking. Indeed, parliamentary investigations into the causes of the crisis imbued leading politicians like James Wilson with an urgent desire for reform of the institutional framework which governed the Asian trade. Thus the 1850s saw the establishment of a number of joint-stock exchange banks such as the Oriental Banking Corporation, the Chartered Bank of India, Australia and China and the Chartered Mercantile Bank of India, London and China; and these new corporate financial organisations usurped the older partnership-based London East India agency houses as the main players in the financing of trade with Asia. This metamorphosis of Asian commerce and financial interests in London was completed in the wake of the major reforms in the system of Indian government in 1858. The establishment of direct rule by the British state stimulated investment in Indian railways and the Indian economy generally in the later nineteenth century, giving rise to a politically influential class of investors in the south of England, and a range of merchant banks and other mercantile/financial organisations engaged in this lucrative export of capital to India and Asia. It was in this period after the 1850s that the dominance of London gentlemanly capitalists in colonial policy towards Indian economic affairs and development became most pronounced.

What of the fortunes of mercantile and industrial interests in provincial

Britain during this period? It is clear that they were major players in the prolonged struggle against the East India Company and its privileges. Indeed, it is the view here that the battle with the Company was very important in the formation of provincial industrial political consciousness and organisation. This is most apparent if one compares the provincial agitations against East India Company privileges in the campaigns leading to the successive Charter Acts of 1793, 1813 and 1833. In 1793, provincial merchants and manufacturers certainly lobbied for concessions in the Indian trade, especially access to the Indian market. But there was no co-ordination between the main cities, and no clearly articulated common aims, a weakness which largely nullified the effectiveness of their efforts. In contrast, by 1812/13 the commercial elites of Glasgow, Manchester and provincial outports such as Liverpool and Bristol, fortified by a further twenty years of economic development and scrutiny of the way the Company handled its affairs, had a much better measure of the task in hand. They realised fully the need to present a common front in favour of free trade with India, and to this end they created formal political organisations (the East India and China Associations) to unify opinion in their respective cities. Moreover, these pressure groups communicated with each other to orchestrate their efforts, culminating in a unified provincial delegation to London which agitated forcefully and effectively for change. Twenty years on this common front was replicated in the debates leading to the Charter Act of 1833. But this time provincial leaders had built links with London merchant firms and leading commentators on Asian affairs such as John Crawfurd. In addition, by now the spokesmen and leaders of the provincial lobby groups had a much more confident grasp of the complexities of the Asian trade, and of the arcane machinery of the East India Company. Their responses to questioning by the various parliamentary Select Committees which shaped the Charter Act of 1833 were carefully choreographed and they managed to ensure that their case was expertly presented. Without question they outmatched the defenders of monopoly with ease.

Crucially, whereas in 1813 most of the provincial East India Associations were wound up following the passage of the Charter Act, after 1833 they all remained in active existence. They moved on to lobby on a wide range of other issues, including Dutch protectionism in south-east Asia, the equalisation of duties on East and West India sugar, and what was seen as Chinese aggression towards British trade. In this they were joined firstly by the newly created London EICA and later by the Chambers of Commerce representing mercantile communities in a number of Asian cities. Throughout this period, the provincial lobbyists were motivated by a determination never again to be subject to the dominance of London. This was most passionately and clearly articulated in the opposition they offered to a series of London-based schemes for major joint-stock Indian banks. The prospect of a large and wealthy London-based joint-stock financial institution was seen as little more than the effective revival of the East India Company in a new guise. Of course, as shown in chapter six, the advantages enjoyed by the London-based interests meant that by the 1840s they had established themselves as *de facto* leaders of what had become a trans-imperial alliance of commercial pressure groups. But the provincial organisations remained doggedly vigilant of what they saw as a tendency among the London men towards overbearing hegemony. This was displayed in the mid-1840s during the rivalry between the London agency house-backed East Indian Railway Company and the provincially supported Great Indian Peninsular Railway Company, when provincial suspicions resurfaced in the face of what they saw as favouritism among politicians and East India Company officials towards the former company.

The crisis of 1847/8 hit the Asian commercial interests in the provincial cities hard, though perhaps not as severely as those in London. Nonetheless the political ramifications were far reaching. The Glasgow East India Association was absorbed into the Glasgow Chamber of Commerce. While the Liverpool association avoided this fate at first, it found itself eclipsed by the city's new Chamber of Commerce which soon became the principal mouthpiece for the city. More significant, however, were the changes occurring in London, which saw first the diminution of the influence of the London agency houses and The London EICA, and their alliance with the provincial and imperial pressure groups. This was most evident on the question of the new exchange banks. By the late 1850s, however, the close alliance between London, the provinces and the periphery was disintegrating, as the decline of the London EICA, the rise of the new joint-stock exchange banks and the growing independence of the Straits interests, all took their toll. This undoubtedly represented a reduction of political influence for the provinces, though it remains to be proven that the active Chambers of Commerce for cities such as Liverpool, Manchester and Glasgow were ineffective in their efforts later in the century to shape imperial policy in Asia.

Commercial communities in Asia had also come of age during this period. At the beginning of the nineteenth century, the agency houses and non-East India Company free merchants were, as seen, highly complex businesses. They did their utmost to protect and promote their interests by seeking to influence the Company administration in India. In the main Indian presidencies for the first three decades of the century, these efforts were *ad hoc* and informal in character. They usually involved spontaneous organisation to meet the exigencies of specific issues, usually under the leadership of a prominent figure in the local merchant community. For example, John Palmer frequently performed this role in Calcutta. Where the object was the lobbying of the Company authorities in London, or the British government, India-based British merchants generally sought the co-operation of the London East India agency houses, which enjoyed close links with Indian sister firms. Indeed, it is fair to say that in the realm of wider imperial politics, and indeed on many issues concerning India, British commercial interests in Asia generally looked to their allies in London to take the lead. It in part reflected the large degree to which they were connected commercially to the London firms, and in some cases by kinship and aspiration. The life-long ambition of most agency house partners was, as seen, to join a successful London agency house. It seemed natural, therefore, to look to these London connections for political leadership and direction. As has been established, the growing interest of the London houses in new lines of business, particularly in the export of British manufactures to India, meant that this loyalty on the part of the traditional Indian agency houses was not reciprocated, a fact which the Indian firms were slow to recognise. Moreover, even among the new merchants who arrived in India after the liberalisation of the India trade in 1813, there was a tendency to look to London for direction. This reflected the speed with which many London agency houses moved into the newly developed export trade in British manufactures, especially cotton goods, to Asia, and the growing reliance of the new merchants in India upon the London firms.

However, the great crisis of 1830–1833 began to change the political as well as the commercial habits of British business in Asia. The period of course saw the wholesale liquidation of the oldest and best-established Calcutta agency houses. Initially, in Bengal at least, these changes suggested an intensified dependence of some British businesses on their London correspondents, as the latter moved to set up new firms in Calcutta which were directly under their control. Certainly co-operation between London and India-based British mercantile firms remained a priority, since they needed to continue to work and trade in partnership to take full advantage of the newly liberalised commerce between Britain and China. But, in spite of these factors promoting greater direction from London, in the wake of the crisis of the early 1830s, the Anglo-Indian commercial communities sought their own distinctive political identity. They increasingly supported new commercial initiatives of their own without reference to their London or British partner firms. Behind this new spirit of independence lay a general suspicion that the London agency houses, together with the Company and the government in the capital, had not supported the Indian houses in their moment of dire need during the crisis of 1830–1834. When one considers the ruthlessness with which Paxton, Cockerell & Trail undercut the foundations of John Palmer & Co. in 1830, triggering the crisis which led to its demise, it is clear that this suspicion had some foundation. An important expression of the feelings of bitterness and mistrust was the establishment of the Calcutta Chamber of Commerce in 1834, the first such body created for the formal expression of collective political objectives by the Calcutta mercantile community. Within a year or so, similar chambers had also been established in Bombay and Madras, to be joined by the end of the decade by Canton, Penang and Singapore. In Calcutta, early in 1837, the re-constituted Bengal Chamber of

Commerce became the main voice for Indian opposition to George Larpent's scheme for a Bank of India. The defeat of this scheme must have been a source of glee to those seeking revenge for perceived betrayals by London men during the crash of the early 1830s.

Of course these bodies did not work in isolation, and they frequently turned to similar organisations in Britain and within the empire to lobby for common interests. By the mid-1830s the Asian Chambers of Commerce worked regularly as partners with their British counterparts, forging alliances around common interests, such as opposition to Dutch protectionism in south-east Asia, and a campaign to open the Chinese market. In this respect, they also became drawn into the trans-imperial commercial and political network which sought to shape British imperial policy in Asia. It should be noted that these Asian organisations also provided a platform, albeit indirectly in some cases, for Indian, Chinese or other indigenous mercantile groups to lobby for the protection of their interests. As this network began to fragment in the 1850s, some of these Asian interest groups began to adopt a more autonomous political strategy, particularly the merchants in the Straits Settlements.

This tendency also reflected a much greater degree of entrepreneurial independence among some Anglo-Asian mercantile communities. A number of British businessmen in the east, in some cases with Indian partners, branched out into new ventures in the 1830s, taking full advantage of the final retreat of the Company from commerce, and of the vacuum left by the demise of the older agency houses. These initiatives took many forms, but two examples from Bombay perhaps underline the newly found confidence of these men. The banking organisations which became in the 1850s the Oriental Banking Corporation, and the Mercantile Bank of India, London and China were originally established in Bombay, and then relocated to London as joint stock companies. In respect of these two exchange banks, it was initiatives launched at the periphery which helped to change radically the complexion of Anglo-Asian commercial interests in the City during the 1850s, a process of transformation which strengthened the hand of London-based 'gentlemanly capitalists' in relation to the industrial and mercantile interests of provincial Britain. Commercial interests at the edge of empire were not passive spectators of structural changes in the City and the British economy in terms of relations with Asia. They had a substantial impact upon the direction of that change. Of course, these Anglo-Asian commercial groups and organisations did not divorce themselves from collaboration with their counterparts in provincial and metropolitan Britain even after the disruption of the well defined trans-imperial network which had emerged in the 1830s and 1840s. But there is a real need systematically to trace these connections, particularly through the network of imperial Chambers of Commerce which flourished later in the century. This may well show that the determination of imperial policy in India and Asia was, as in the first half of the century, a complex interaction of interests, in which the City of London was perhaps the senior partner, but did not work in isolation.

What of the East India Company? Clearly this was an organisation in retreat throughout the period, surrendering not only its monopolies of trade with India and China, but also losing by the 1820s its pre-eminent position as one of the main pillars of the London stock market. Little wonder then that earlier histories of the Company have tended to treat the Charter Act of 1833 as the date which signifies the end of the Company as an organisation able to exercise real influence in the determination of colonial policy in India and Asia. But this underestimates the residual influence which the Company still enjoyed until the early 1850s. Paradoxically, the trans-imperial network of organisations representing provincial British industrialists and merchants, London East India agency houses and mercantile firms in Asia, which played a major role in ending the Company's privileges in 1813 and 1833, helped bolster the Company's standing in both commercial and political affairs. The reality was that this network worked very closely with the Company in a number of areas. The controversial system of bill hypothecation, though opposed by many in the British provinces, was built upon intimate commercial relationships between the Company and the finance houses in London and Asia which tied the latter into the continued existence of the Company. Even the most trenchant critics of the Company in Liverpool, Glasgow and Manchester aligned themselves with the Company when it came to resisting the bank schemes of the late 1830s and 1840s. Moreover, the Company's formidable bureaucratic machine continued to enjoy all the advantages which the daily operational running of empire provided. It still occupied a leading position in respect of gathering intelligence on Asian political and commercial affairs, and leading Company intellectuals such as John Stuart Mill remained powerful advocates of Company rule in India right up to the end in 1858. All new commercial initiatives, be they proposals for new banks, the establishment of railway companies or the development of Indian tea production, had to be presented initially to the Company's Court of Directors. While the Court did not always prevail on such questions, it still got its way on some occasions.

Probably at least as important as the end of its commercial activities in the decline of the Company was the great economic crisis of the late 1840s. This destroyed most of the London East India agency houses whose trade in bills of exchange was inextricably linked with the Company system for meeting the home charges. The crisis also opened the way for the rise of new joint-stock companies, particularly the exchange banks, whose fortunes were not so closely intertwined with the Company's financial arrangements. Also, the political consequences of the crisis of the 1840s did not serve the Company well, facilitating as they did the ascendancy of Liberal politicians whose *laissez faire* ideological leanings disposed them against it. Even more crucially, the enquiries into the causes of the great crash of 1847/8 were damning in their assessment of the whole conduct of trade and finance with India, and the Company in particular was singled out for savage criticism. One result of this was the end of the Directors' patronage under the Charter Act of 1853, and another was the introduction of competitive examinations for the recruitment of staff. The fact that the Act was not bound to remain in force for twenty years, as were the earlier Charter Acts, signalled that the Company's days were numbered.

But there also remains the perennial question of the nature of the East India Company. Bowen has provided an excellent overview of the historical debate about what kind of organisation it was, and the reasons for and nature of its metamorphosis from trading company to agency of imperial rule.[1] At one extreme are those who see in the Company a prototype for the great multi-national corporations of the twentieth century, a view posited by Chaudhuri and Robins.[2] At the other are Furber and Phillips, who regard the Company as little more than an organisational umbrella, under which other commercial interests flourished in pursuit of their own interests.[3] While Bowen is right to be a little sceptical of these rather reductionist perceptions of the Company, two important points should be made. Firstly, there can be little doubt that it did become an incubator for the development of new business enterprises in Asia, particularly in shipping and in the development of the Indian and later the London East India agency houses. These latter organisations grew up within the protection of the Company's monopoly, became a presence within its councils, and never entirely broke free of it, in spite of challenging many of its privileges. Paradoxically, it was also probably an important reason for the survival of the Company until the mid-nineteenth century, as these powerful emergent new commercial groups had much to lose in terms of privileged access to power and commercial opportunities if the Company were wound up. Secondly, the powerful position of the Company in the City and in the political world of London in the late eighteenth and early nine-teenth centuries, which slowed the organisation's death, also encouraged the rise of political organisation amongst commercial groups outside London, as it became clear to merchants and industrialists in Glasgow, Manchester and Liverpool that only aggressive, disciplined and co-ordinated lobbying could hope to persuade the British state to end the Company's privileges. Thus the entrenched position of the Company played a crucial role in the political education and maturation of those sections of industrial Britain concerned with the Asian trade. If the East India and China Associations of Glasgow and Liverpool were pearls of industrial and provincial commercial political organisations, the Company was the grit in the oysters which produced them.

The longevity of the Company, with the fluidity of Anglo-Asian commerce and politics during its long period of decline, offers numerous insights in respect of some of the wider debates about the nature of the British Empire, and the reasons for its expansion during the nineteenth century. A recurring theme in this book has of course been its implications for the debate about Cain and Hopkins' thesis, which identifies the 'gentlemanly capitalists' of London as the prime movers behind the growth of empire and the determination of imperial policy. It is a thesis which has attracted many criticisms, some of which are echoed here. Perhaps the most comprehensive of these was also one of the earliest: the resounding rebuttal by Martin Daunton of Cain and Hopkins' depiction of the division of finance and industry in Britain, and the relegation of the latter to the position of political outsiders.[4] Certainly the present study shows, as Daunton contended, that there were comprehensive and robust business relations between provincial industrialists and London financiers and merchants, particularly in the export of British manufactures.[5] Indeed, it goes rather further than Daunton in demonstrating that the provinces were not only active political collaborators with City gentlemanly capitalists and business organisations in Asia, but were also much more active and effective on the national political stage than even he suggests. Daunton's defence of industrial political influence largely focuses upon their dominant role in local politics, and an assertion of the growing dominance of their *laissez faire* ideas in a new orthodoxy in favour of a limited state committed to free trade.[6] But when one examines the provincial agitations leading to the Charter Acts of 1813 and 1833, and the emergence of the East India Associations with their networks linking London with provincial industry, and both with British business in Asia, it becomes clear that industry was a consistent and well-organised national force in the determination of imperial policy in Asia, whose collaboration was actively sought by gentlemanly capitalists in the City. It does seem that the end of the Company in the 1850s, the emergence of the new exchange banks, and the growth of British investment in India mainly by investors in south-east England, resulted in a tilt in favour of the gentlemanly capitalists. But this is not to concede that industry lost its voice in this arena. This remains an under-researched area, which might in due course reveal that the support of industrialists was as actively pursued by gentlemanly capitalists in the second half of the nineteenth century as it was in the first. As Green has persuasively argued, the democratisation of British politics from the 1860s meant that it was increasingly important for gentlemanly capitalists to build coalitions of support for cherished objectives: a trend which made collaboration with industrial elites, Chambers of Commerce and other shapers of popular opinion, more compelling.[7]

Another target for the critics of Cain and Hopkins has been the notion of the City as a source of political influence. The argument offered by Howe is that the City was not a unified entity in respect of what it wanted from the British state and in the field of imperial policy.[8] This was most vividly illustrated in the lack of a clear consensus within the City on such key questions as that of free trade versus protectionism in the 1850s.[9] Daunton also makes this point for the later nineteenth century.[10] It is certainly the case that serious divisions occured within the City, even among financiers and merchants engaged in the same geographical branch of commerce. The bitter divisions among the London East India agency houses over Larpent's Bank of India Scheme in 1836, and to a lesser extent in the subsequent bank initiatives of the early 1840s, are vivid examples of such internal squabbles. As has been seen, these also encouraged City factions to seek allies in the provinces, undermining further the notion of City versus industry separatism. But notwithstanding these real divisions, in the case of India and Asia the City did manage, on the whole, to offer a consistent voice on a wide range of issues. Moreover, divisions were in part overcome by the efforts of prominent individuals, whose greater wealth and energy equipped them to take the lead. Sir George Larpent in many ways embodied the concept of the aspirant gentlemanly capitalist, commanding formidable wealth, with an interest in every new initiative, including a bank, a railway, a shipping line and a tea company. This was combined with a leading role in political campaigns through his position as Chair of the London East India and China Association. Even after his ruin, other figures emerged, ensuring that by the 1860s the City was indeed the loudest voice in debates about the future of Britain's Asian empire. In this respect, the gentlemanly capitalists of the City did establish themselves as senior partners among the commercial groups interested in this sphere during the second half of the nineteenth century.

To conclude, the main challenge offered here in respect of the gentlemanly capitalist thesis concerns the evolution of the *modus operandi* of its protagonists, and their relations with other interest groups such as industry and British business interests in Asia. It is the contention of this study that far from City financial interests and provincial industry being separate entities with little commercial or political collaboration between them, the very opposite principle was at work in respect of the East India Company's empire. In fact, the slow death of the East India Company, and the fierce battle to, first, undermine its privileges, and later to shape imperial policy, proved to be the unifying factor which brought together London merchants, provincial industrialists and merchants at the edge of empire. This political and commercial alliance reached its zenith in the 1830s and 1840s, only for the crisis of 1847/8 to restructure radically Asian commerce, especially in the City of London, and cause the disintegration of what had been a formidable trans-imperial commercial and political network. The extent to which aspects of it were revived later in the century remains open for further research. Another factor concerns the importance of linkages between commercial interests in Britain, particularly in the City, and those in India and Asia. Darwin has stressed that this remains a field of limited study so far, and he cites the term 'imperial bridgehead' as a useful concept which needs to be explored in respect of how gentlemanly capitalists gathered intelligence of developments at the imperial periphery, and how issues of informal versus formal empire were resolved.[11] It is clear that, in respect of British imperial strategy in Asia during the first half of the nineteenth century, these interests on the periphery worked closely and systematically with their British counterparts to shape policy. A trans-imperial network, consisting of a range of British economic interests and varied Anglo-Asian commercial communities in the east, emerged to influence the British government on Asian political and economic questions. It was a network which shared intelligence and orchestrated political lobbying campaigns directed at the British state on a very wide range of issues. It raises the question of whether similar networks arose in other geographical theatres of British imperial expansion and policy development. Perhaps here lies an important clue for historians seeking new answers to old questions about the relationship between business and the British Empire.

NOTES

One: Introduction

1   See, for an overview of these developments: P. Lawson, *The East India Company: A History* (London, Longman 1993).

2   N. Robins, *The Corporation that Changed the World: How the East India Company Shaped the Modern Multinational* (London, Pluto Press 2006) p165.

3   C.H. Philips, *The East India Company 1784–1834* (Manchester, Manchester University Press 1961).

4   H. Mui and L.H. Mui, *The Management of Monopoly. A Study of the East India Company's Conduct of its Tea Trade, 1784–1833* (Vancouver, University of British Columbia Press 1984).

5   H.V. Bowen, *The Business of Empire: The East India Company and Imperial Britain, 1756–1833* (Cambridge, Cambridge University Press 2006).

6   Lawson, *The East India Company: A History* pp159–162.

7   Robins, *The Corporation that Changed the World* pp155–167.

8   Their work has been developed over a number of years. The most important publications include: P.J. Cain and A.G. Hopkins, 'The Political Economy of British Expansion Overseas 1750 to 1914' *Economic History Review* 33:4 (1980) pp463–490; P.J. Cain and A. G. Hopkins, 'Gentlemanly Capitalism and British Expansion Overseas I: The Old Colonial System 1688–1850' *Economic History Review* 39:4 (1986) pp501–525; P.J. Cain and A.G. Hopkins, *British Imperialism 1688–2000* (Edinburgh, Pearson 2001).

9   Bowen, *The Business of Empire* p31 and p37.

10   Ibid., p40.

11   Cain and Hopkins, *British Imperialism* p84.

12   Ibid., pp278–284.

13   Ibid., pp51–53.

14   W.D. Rubinstein, *Capitalism, Culture & Decline in Britain 1750–1990* (London, Routledge 1993) pp143–145.

15   Cain and Hopkins, *British Imperialism* p52.

16   I. Nish, 'British Mercantile Co-operation in the Indo-China Trade from the End of the East India Company's Trading Monopoly' *Journal of Southeast Asian History* 3:2 (1962) pp74–91.

17   B.B. Kling, *Partner in Empire: Dwarkanath Tagore and the Age of Enterprise in India* (Los Angeles, University of California 1976).

18   Probably the best account of the crisis is still D. Morier Evans, *The Commercial Crisis 1847–1848* (London, Letts, Son and Steer 1849).

Two: Origens

1   For a particularly useful overview of this early period of the Company's history see K.N. Chaudhuri, *The English East India Company: The Study of an Early Joint Stock Company, 1600–1640* (Reprint, London, Routledge 1999).

2   See P. Lawson, *The East India Company: A History* (London, Longman 1993) pp46–48; J.P. Losty, *Calcutta: City of Palaces* (London, Arnold 1990) pp11–18.

3   P.G.M. Dickson, *The Financial Revolution in England: A Study in the Development of Public Credit, 1688–1756* (London, Macmillan 1967) p57.

4   Lawson, *The East India Company: A History* pp55–56.

5   Lawson pp51–57; H.V. Bowen, *The Business of Empire: The East India Company and Imperial Britain, 1756–1833* (Cambridge, Cambridge University Press 2006) p30; P.J. Cain and A.G. Hopkins, *British Imperialism 1688–2000* (Edinburgh, Pearson 2001) p68.

6   Dickson, *The Financial Revolution in England* pp287–298.

7   Bowen, *The Business of Empire* p30.

8   C.A. Bayly, *Imperial Meridian: The British Empire and the World 1780–1830* (London, Longman 1989) chs 1–3.

9   C.A. Bayly, 'The First Age of Global Imperialism c1760–1839' in P. Burroughs and A.J. Stockwell (eds), *Managing the Business of Empire: Essays in Honour of David Fieldhouse* (London, Frank Cass 1998).

10   Bowen, *The Business of Empire* p35.

11   Ibid., pp70–71.

12   C.H. Philips, *The East India Company 1784–1834* pp67–68.

13   In fact, Company exports of British manufactures to India were quite substantial in the late eighteenth century. See H.V. Bowen, 'Sinews of Trade and Empire: The Supply of Commodity Exports to the East India Company in the Late Eighteenth Century' *Economic History Review* 55:3 (2002) pp466–486.

14   P.J. Marshall, *East Indian Fortunes: The British in Bengal in the Eighteenth Century* (Oxford, Clarendon Press 1976).

15   Ibid., pp112–113.

16   Ibid., pp153–154.

17   Bowen, *The Business of Empire* p13 and pp89–90.

18   H.V. Bowen, 'Privilege & Profit: Commanders of East Indiamen as Private Traders, Entrepreneurs and Smugglers, 1760–1813' *International Journal of Maritime History* 19:2 (2007) pp43–88.

19   For a sense of how agency house merchants interacted on a personal level with Indians and Company servants and their families, see A. Webster, *The Richest East India Merchant: The Life and Business of John Palmer of Calcutta 1767–1836* (Woodbridge, Boydell Press 2007) chs 3 and 4.

20   C.H. Philips, *The East India Company* (Manchester, Manchester University Press 1961) p5 and ch 9.

21   C.H. Philips, *The Correspondence of David Scott: Volume One* (London, Camden Third Series 1951) page xi

22   A. Tripathi, *Trade and Finance in the Bengal Presidency 1793–1833* (Calcutta, Oxford University Press 1979) p35.

23   Webster, *The Richest East India Merchant* pp24–25.

24   S.B. Singh, *European Agency Houses in Bengal, 1783–1833* (Calcutta, Firma Mukhopadhyay 1966) p10.

25 Ibid., pp10–12.

26 Tripathi, *Trade and Finance in the Bengal Presidency* pp21–22.

27 B. Chowdhury, *Growth of Commercial Agriculture in Bengal 1757–1900: Volume One* (Calcutta, Indian Studies, Past and Present 1964) p97.

28 Tripathi, *Trade and Finance in the Bengal Presidency* p11.

29 Webster, *The Richest East India Merchant* p139.

30 Ibid., p32.

31 M. Greenberg, *British Trade and the Opening of China 1800–1842* (Cambridge, Cambridge University Press 1951) p6.

32 For an insight into the growing consumption of tea and other commodities in the late eighteenth century, see J.R. Ward, 'The Industrial Revolution and British Imperialism 1750–1850' *Economic History Review* 47:1 (1994) pp44–65.

33 Greenberg, pp50–74.

34 The Loan Act of 1773. See Marshall, *East Indian Fortunes* p223.

35 Tripathi, *Trade and Finance in the Bengal Presidency* pp5–6.

36 Ibid., pp7–8.

37 Philips, ch2.

38 Philips, p71.

39 Philips, *The Correspondence of David Scott* page x; Philips, *The East India Company* p61.

40 Philips, *The Correspondence of David Scott* page x.

41 Tripathi, *Trade and Finance in the Bengal Presidency* p22.

42 Scott to William Pitt, 28 November 1789 in Philips, *The Correspondence of David Scott* p3.

43 Tripathi, *Trade and Finance in the Bengal Presidency* pp28–29.

44 Scott to Dundas, 13 March 1793, and extract of a letter from William Fairlie to David Scott, 2 June 1793, British Library (BL), Oriental and India Office Collections (OIOC), India Office: Charters and Treaties A/2/10.

45 Ibid.

46 Memorial on the clandestine trade, and the East India Company's observations thereon, BL, OIOC, India Office: Charters and Treaties A/2/10.

47 Philips, *The East India Company* pp81–83.

48 Bowen, *The Business of Empire* p89.

49 Philips, *The Correspondence of David Scott* page xiii.

50 Bowen, 'Sinews of Trade and Empire' p473.

51 Ibid., p467.

52 Memorial from Merchants of Exeter, 9 March 1793, BL, OIOC, India Office: Charters and Treaties A/2/11.

53 Dundas to Francis Baring, Chair of the East India Company, 23 March 1793, and minute of conversation with the Manchester delegation which took place in Downing Street on 20 March 1793, BL, OIOC, Home Misc 401 pp298–300.

54 Meeting of muslin and calico manufacturers in Manchester on 5 April 1793, India Office: Charters and Treaties A/2/11 p112.

55 Dundas to Baring, 23 March 1793, Minute of Conversation with Gregg and Frodsham, Manchester delegates, BL, OIOC, Home Misc 401 pp295–297.

56 Thomas Earle to the Privy Council Committee on Trade, 8 March 1793, BL, OIOC, India Office: Charters and Treaties A/2/11 pp110–111.

57 John Dunlop to Dundas, 19 March 1793, pp139–141, Home Misc 401 pp300–302.

58 Dundas to Baring, 23 March 1793, enclosing letter from Lord Falmouth and six others, BL, OIOC, Home Misc 401 pp287–289.

59 Tripathi, *Trade and Finance in the Bengal Presidency* p22.
60 John Cochrane, 'General Observations on Monopolists – the East India Company in Particular – Animadversion on their Reports' London, 14 April 1793, BL, OIOC, India Office: Charters and Treaties A/2/11 pp351–367; p351. For more on Cochrane see Tripathi, *Trade and Finance in the Bengal Presidency* p64.
61 Ibid., p352.
62 Ibid., p351.
63 Ibid., p353.
64 William Fairlie to David Scott, 31 August 1792, BL, OIOC, India Office: Charters and Treaties A/2/10, pp116–123.
65 Ibid., pp351–352.
66 Thomas Brown, Chair of the Committee of Merchant Drapers, buyers of Indian goods at the Indian Sales, to Henry Dundas, 6 April 1793, BL, OIOC, India Office: Charters and Treaties A/2/11 pp116–123.
67 Ibid., p123.
68 Ibid., p122.
69 Ibid., p122.
70 Minute of Conversation with Gregg and Frodsham, Manchester delegates, BL, OIOC, Home Misc 401 pp295–297; p295.
71 Dunlop to Dundas, 19 March 1793, p301.
72 Dundas to Baring, 16 February 1793, BL, OIOC, Home Misc 401 p248.
73 Tripathi, *Trade and Finance in the Bengal Presidency* p33; Philips, *The East India Company* pp78–79.
74 Tripathi, *Trade and Finance in the Bengal Presidency* p35.
75 Committee of London Merchants who act for clients in India to Dundas, March 1793, BL, OIOC, India Office: Charters and Treaties A/2/11 pp283–298.
76 Muilman & Co., Raikes & Co. and Boehm & Co. to Dundas, 2 April 1793, ibid. pp299–300.
77 Bowen, *The Business of Empire* p40.
78 Dunlop to Dundas, 19 March 1793, p301.

Three: War, Politics and India

1 A view particularly promoted by D.J. Moss, 'Birmingham and the Campaigns against the Orders in Council and the East India Company Charter, 1812–3' *Canadian Journal of History* 11 (1976) pp173–188; p173.
2 See N. Robins, *The Corporation that Changed the World: How the East India Company Shaped the Modern Multinational* (London, Pluto 2006) p146.
3 P. Lawson, *The East India Company: A History* (London, Longman 1993) p137.
4 Philips, *The East India Company* pp80–82.
5 Ibid., p86.
6 Ibid., p105.
7 Ibid., p106.
8 Tripathi, *Trade and Finance in the Bengal Presidency* p2. Based upon a nominal exchange rate of Rs10 to £1.
9 Philips, p124.
10 Bowen, *The Business of Empire* p36.

11 Fourth Report of the Select Committee on East Indian Affairs, *Parliamentary Papers* VI, 1812 p495.

12 Singh, *European Agency Houses in Bengal 1783–1833* pp17–18.

13 Ibid., p10.

14 Webster, *The Richest East India Merchant* p31.

15 Ibid., p25.

16 Ibid., p23.

17 Singh, pp45–46.

18 See in particular the Board of Trade (Commercial) Indexes 1794–1802 (Vols 20–28), West Bengal Archives, Calcutta, India.

19 Board of Trade (Commercial) Index 1796 (Vol. 22) pp77–78.

20 Ibid., pp73–77.

21 Board of Trade (Commercial) Index 1795 (Vol. 21) p131; and Index 1799 (Vol. 25) pp72–74.

22 Board of Trade (Commercial) Index 1797 (Vol. 23) p101.

23 Board of Trade (Commercial) Index 1801 (Vol. 27) p94.

24 Board of Trade (Commercial) Index 1798 (Vol. 24) p95.

25 Ibid., pp96–97.

26 Board of Trade (Commercial) Index 1801 (Vol. 27) p178.

27 Philips, *The East India Company* pp69–70; pp107–8; Tripathi, *Trade and Finance in the Bengal Presidency* pp 38–40 and pp57–60.

28 Tripathi, *Trade and Finance in the Bengal Presidency* p38.

29 Richard Johnson to Henry Dundas, 23 January 1794, BL, OIOC, Home Misc 435 pp113–116.

30 Tripathi, *Trade and Finance in the Bengal Presidency* p39.

31 Ibid., pp40–41.

32 Philips, *The East India Company* p91.

33 Ibid., pp85–86.

34 Ibid., pp97–100; Tripathi, *Trade and Finance in the Bengal Presidency* pp54–56.

35 Tripathi, *Trade and Finance in the Bengal Presidency* p50.

36 Philips, p106.

37 Based on Philips' figures; ibid., p105.

38 Ibid., p106.

39 BL, OIOC, Home Misc 494 p75.

40 John Cochrane to Henry Dundas, 3 March 1799, BL, OIOC, Home Misc 405 pp1–14; p1.

41 Ibid., p3.

42 Ibid., pp10–11.

43 Memorial to Dundas from the merchants of Exeter, 11 May 1799, BL, OIOC, Home Misc 405 p25.

44 Substance of Mr Prinsep's speech at the General Court of Proprietors, 5 July 1799, BL, OIOC, Home Misc 405 pp29–32.

45 Prinsep to Lushington, 1 October 1799, BL, OIOC, Home Misc 405 pp33–59.

46 Philips, *The East India Company* p107.

47 Ibid., pp107–8.

48 William Lennox to Henry Dundas, 9 April 1800, enclosing abstract of letter from Colvins and Bazett of Calcutta, 19 November 1799, BL, OIOC, Home Misc 405 pp627–631.

49   Philips, *The East India Company* pp108–9; Tripathi, *Trade and Finance in the Bengal Presidency* pp58–61.
50   Bowen, *The Business of Empire* pp122–123.
51   Ibid., p130; Tripathi, *Trade and Finance in the Bengal Presidency* p62.
52   Tripathi, *Trade and Finance in the Bengal Presidency* p.62.
53   A. Porter, *Religion Versus Empire? British Protestant Missionaries and Overseas Expansion, 1700–1914* (Manchester, Manchester University Press 2004) pp99–101.
54   Tripathi, *Trade and Finance in the Bengal Presidency* pp63–64; Philips, *The East India Company* pp109–110.
55   T. Henchman, *Observations of the Report of the Directors of the East India Company* (London 1801).
56   Letter read to the Court of Proprietors, 28 May 1801, BL, OIOC, Trade Papers, Eur Mss D 107 pp11–15.
57   Court of Directors to Proprietors, 1 June 1801, Trade Papers, Eur Mss D 107 p19.
58   'Memorial to the Board of Control from merchants who are agents for persons residing in the East Indies', 8 June 1801, BL, OIOC, Home Misc. 491 pp9–27.
59   Philips, *The East India Company* p114.
60   Ibid., p115; Tripathi, *Trade and Finance in the Bengal Presidency* p67.
61   Henry Archer to Patrick Hadan, 15 March 1803, BL, OIOC, Papers of Sir Charles Forbes, Eur Mss D100, No. 17 pp52–53.
62   Ibid., p53.
63   'Memorial of the Merchants, Agents and others Engaged in the Export Trade from Calcutta to the Port of London', 20 November 1807, BL, OIOC, Papers of Sir Charles Forbes, Eur Mss D 100, No. 33 pp85–87.
64   Philips, *The East India Company* p156.
65   Tripathi, *Trade and Finance in the Bengal Presidency* pp96–97.
66   Philips, *The East India Company* p181.
67   Tripathi, *Trade and Finance in the Bengal Presidency* p99.
68   For details on the Orders in Council see B.H. Tolley, 'The Liverpool Campaign against the Order in Council and the War of 1812' in J.R. Harris (ed), *Liverpool and Merseyside: Essays in the Economic and Social History of the Port and its Hinterland* (London, Cass 1969) pp98–146; especially pp99–100; D.J. Moss, 'Birmingham and the Campaigns against the Orders in Council and the East India Company Charter Act, 1812–13' *Canadian Journal of History* 11 (1976) pp173–188; especially pp174–175.
69   Tolley, p99.
70   Moss, pp175–176.
71   Tolley, p109.
72   See J.E. Cookson, 'Political Arithmetic and War in Britain, 1793–1815' *War and Society* 1:2 (1983) pp37–60; pp50–51; J.E. Cookson, 'British Society and the French Wars, 1793–1815' *Australian Journal of Politics and History* 31 (1985) pp192–203; also see A. Webster, 'The Political Economy of Trade Liberalization: The East India Company Charter Act of 1813' *Economic History Review* 43:3 (1990) pp404–419; p417.
73   Cookson, 'British Society and the French Wars' pp200–201; Webster, 'The Political Economy of Trade Liberalization' pp410–411.
74   Philips, *The East India Company* p181.
75   Brougham to Roscoe (from London), 3 December 1808, Liverpool Record Office, Central Library, Liverpool, Papers of William Roscoe, 920.ROS, letter no. 461.
76   Rathbone to Roscoe, 22 April 1807, Liverpool Record Office, Roscoe Papers, letter no. 3060.

77 Rathbone to Roscoe, 24 April 1808 (from Bristol), Liverpool Record Office, Roscoe Papers, letter no. 3066.

78 Brougham to Roscoe, 20 February 1810, Liverpool Record Office, Roscoe Papers, letter no. 463.

79 Moss, p176–178.

80 Ibid., p179.

81 Attwood to the organisers of the Glasgow campaign, 21 March 1812, Glasgow Archives, Mitchell Library, Papers of the Glasgow East India Association MS891001/3, letter no. 1.

82 Moss, p180.

83 Ibid., and *Parliamentary Debates* XXII pp89–337 for the various petitions on the Charter. See also Committee of the Whole House on East Indian Affairs, *Parliamentary Papers* VII, 1812–13.

84 Melville's observations of 21 March 1812 on 'hints' suggested by the Court of Directors, John Rylands Library, Manchester, Melville Papers, box 692 no. 2008; Melville to the Chair and Deputy Chair of the Court of Directors, 21 March 1821, BL, OIOC, India Office: Charters and Treaties A/2/14 pp83–86.

85 Philips, *The East India Company* p183.

86 Minute of a conversation between Buckinghamshire and Sir Hugh Inglis, 19 April 1812, BL, OIOC, India Office: Charters and Treaties A/2/14 p113.

87 Thomas Brown to the Chair of the East India Company, 21 April 1812, BL, OIOC, India Office: Charters and Treaties A/2/14 p133.

88 Resolutions of a meeting of the merchants, manufacturers, traders and others interested in the export trade to India and China, from the Port of London, 25 April 1812, BL, OIOC, India Office: Charters and Treaties A/2/14 pp138–142.

89 Brown, Chair of a meeting of buyers and others interested in the sale of East Indian piece goods to Spencer Perceval, 25 April 1812, Liverpool Papers Add Mss 38410 pp70–72, BL.

90 Philips, *The East India Company* pp182–183.

91 For example: Minutes of a conversation at an interview with Spencer Perceval and the Earl of Buckinghamshire, attended by a deputation from the outports, 9 May 1812, BL, Liverpool Papers, Add Mss 38410 pp81–83; Attwood to Lord Liverpool, 18 September 1812, ibid., pp87–91; Thomas Earle, Chairman of the Liverpool Committee to Lord Liverpool, 1 January 1813, ibid., pp184–185; Edinburgh Chamber of Commerce to Lord Liverpool, 14 January 1813, ibid., p186.

92 Petition from Glasgow merchants to the House of Commons, 19 March 1812, *Parliamentary Debates* Vol. XXII pp91–92.

93 Yukihisa Kumagai, 'The Lobbying Activities of Provincial Mercantile and Manufacturing Interests against the Renewal of the East India Company's Charter, 1812–13 and 1829–33' (PhD thesis, University of Glasgow 2008).

94 Ibid., pp78–81.

95 Ibid., p158.

96 Ibid., pp91–92; p101.

97 See my earlier position as outlined in A. Webster, 'The Political Economy of Trade Liberalization'.

98 Kumagai, pp92–93.

99 Rose to Melville, 3 April 1812, Bathurst Papers, BL Loan 57, Vol. 5 p449. The letter was subsequently passed on to Buckinghamshire, the new President of the Board of Control.

100 *Hansard* (Commons) XXVI, 16 June 1813, p686.
101 B.R. Mitchell and P. Deane, *Abstract of Historical Statistics* (Cambridge, Cambridge University Press 1962) p498.
102 Joint testimony of Henry Trail, Henry Fawcett, John Innes and R.C. Bazett, 10 April 1810, Fourth Report of the Select Committee on East Indian Affairs, *Parliamentary Papers* VI, 1812, p292; see also testimony of Thomas Garland Murray, East Indiaman Captain, 10 May 1813, Select Committee on East Indian Affairs, *Parliamentary Papers* VII, 1812–13, pp426–427.
103 Committee of the Whole House on East Indian Affairs, *Parliamentary Papers* VII, 1812–13; testimony of William Fairlie, 9 April 1813, p117; testimony of Colonel Thomas Munro, 13 April 1813, p136.
104 Testimony of John Vivian, Solicitor in Excise, Select Committee on East Indian Affairs, *Parliamentary Papers* VII, 1812–13, p219.
105 Ibid., p227.
106 Testimonies of Henry Trail, 15 May 1809, and Henry Fawcett, 15 May 1809, Fourth Report of the Select Committee on East Indian Affairs, *Parliamentary Papers* VI, 1812, pp208–209.
107 Testimony of William Hole, 20 May 1812, Select Committee on the Orders in Council, *Parliamentary Papers* III, 1812, p312.
108 Testimony of James Sedgwick, 3 May 1813, Select Committee on East Indian Affairs, *Parliamentary Papers* VII, 1812–13, p310.
109 Testimony of Thomas Munro, 14 April 1813, Committee of the Whole House on East Indian Affairs, *Parliamentary Papers* VII, 1812–13, p154.
110 Anonymous letter to Lord Bathurst, 26 April 1812, Bathurst Papers, BL Loan 57, Vol. 21, pp80–101.
111 Bathurst to Liverpool, 3 October 1812, Liverpool Papers, BL, Add Mss 38,250 p43.
112 Webster, 'The Political Economy of Trade Liberalization' p410.
113 Ibid., p415.
114 Petition from London merchants engaged in the private East India trade to the Board of Trade, 6 March 1813, National Archives, BT1/74 p291.
115 *Hansard* (Commons) XXV, 3 May 1813, pp1117–1120.
116 Staunton's paper, 'Considerations upon the China trade', Court of Directors, 19 March 1813, BL, OIOC, India Office: Charters and Treaties A/2/14 pp279–303.
117 Philips, *The East India Company* p186.
118 Bowen, *The Business of Empire* p253.

Four: Accommodating Free Trade

1 A. Webster, *The Richest East India Merchant: The Life and Business of John Palmer of Calcutta 1767–1836* (Woodbridge, Boydell Press 2007) p56.
2 Probably the best description of this system is still M. Greenberg, *British Trade and the Opening of China 1800–42* (Cambridge, Cambridge University Press 1951) pp8–13.
3 See statistics gathered from the Bengal Commercial Reports in A. Webster, 'British Export Interests in Bengal and Imperial Expansion into South-east Asia, 1780 to 1824: The Origins of the Straits Settlements' in B. Ingham and C. Simmons (eds), *Development Studies and Colonial Policy* (London, Cass 1987) pp138–174; p173.
4 Greenberg, p221.

5   Webster, *The Richest East India Merchant* p53.

6   R.G. Thorne, *The House of Commons 1790–1820 V: Members Q–Y* (5 Vols, London, Secker and Warburg 1986) p409.

7   Tripathi, *Trade and Finance in the Bengal Presidency* p55; p148.

8   Philips, *The East India Company* p193.

9   Tripathi, *Trade and Finance in the Bengal Presidency* p121.

10 Webster, *The Richest East India Merchant* p23.

11 See for example Palmer to W.E. Bird, 30 November 1808, Papers of John Palmer, Bodleian Library, Oxford, Mss Eng Lett c69 p22.

12 Petition to the Insolvent Court on behalf of A.F. Hamilton in the case of the bankruptcy of Palmer and Co., 30 July 1830. Uncatalogued Records of the Calcutta High Court, Calcutta, India.

13 Palmer to Nesbitt, 16 May 1813, Palmer Papers, Bodleian Library, Oxford, Mss Eng Lett c82 pp215–216.

14 Palmer to Lieutenant-Colonel Dear, 31 May 1813, Palmer Papers, Bodleian Library, Oxford, Mss Eng Lett c82 pp257–259; Palmer to Lieutenant Eckford, 23 June 1813, Mss Eng Lett c82 pp314–315.

15 Undated memorial from Lucius O'Brien to the Court of Directors, Lt Colonel of Bengal Light Cavalry (printed), BL, OIOC, Mss Eur F89/2/C pp1–2.

16 Webster, *The Richest East India Merchant* pp77–78.

17 Toone to Warren Hastings, 17 May 1816, Papers of Warren Hastings, BL, Add Mss 29190, p252.

18 Palmer to Toone, 2 September 1818, Bodleian Library, Oxford, Mss Eng Lett c87 p95.

19 Webster, *The Richest East India Merchant* p74.

20 Tripathi, *Trade and Finance in the Bengal Presidency* p120.

21 Palmer to Henry Trail, 31 March 1813, Bodleian Library, Oxford, Mss Eng Lett c82 pp129–130.

22 Palmer to Trail, 3 May 1814, Bodleian Library, Oxford, Mss Eng Lett c84, pp144–147.

23 Palmer to Henry Hobhouse, 1 December 1816, Bodleian Library, Oxford, Mss Eng Lett c85 p55.

24 'Shipbuilding in India: A Checklist of Ships' Names', BL, OIOC, India Office: Records 1995 p50.

25 Tripathi, *Trade and Finance in the Bengal Presidency* pp122–123.

26 K.N. Chaudhuri, 'Foreign Trade and Balance of Payments 1757–1947' in D. Kumar (ed), *The Cambridge History of Modern India Volume 2: 1757–2003* (Hyderabad, Orient Longman India 2005) pp804- 877; p828.

27 Notebook on the Trade of Bengal, Papers of John Adam, BL, OIOC, Eur Mss F/109/34 p7.

28 Ibid., p12

29 K.N. Chaudhuri, 'Foreign Trade and Balance of Payments 1757–1947' pp828–830.

30 Notebook on the Trade of Bengal p12.

31 Chaudhuri, 'Foreign Trade and Balance of Payments 1757–1947' pp828–830.

32 Notebook on the Trade of Bengal pp5–6.

33 J. Crawfurd, 'A Sketch of the Commercial Resources and Monetary and Mercantile System of British India with suggestions for their Improvement by Means of Banking Establishments' (1837) in K.N. Chaudhuri (ed), *The Economic Development of India under*

the East India Company (Cambridge, Cambridge University Press 1971) pp217–316; pp277–278.

34 Palmer to Captain James Thomas at the Jerusalem Coffee House, London, 3 July 1818, Bodleian Library, Oxford, Ms Eng Lett c87 p9.

35 Palmer to M. Forbes in Bombay, 15 August 1819, Bodleian Library, Oxford, Mss Eng Lett c88 pp146–147.

36 Palmer to Trail, 31 October 1819, Bodleian Library, Oxford, Mss Eng Lett c88, pp304–305.

37 Webster, *The Richest East India Merchant* p115.

38 Select Committee of the House of Commons on the means of improving and maintaining Foreign Trade – East Indies and China, *Parliamentary Papers*, 1821, Vol. VI, interview with Patrick Maclachlan, 9 April 1821, pp277–280.

39 Minutes of evidence, testimony of Kirkman Finlay, 16 May 1833, to the House of Commons Select Committee on Manufacturers, Commerce and Shipping, *Parliamentary Papers*, 1833, Vol VI, p44.

40 Ibid., interview with George Larpent, 6 June 1833, pp137–143.

41 Ibid., p139.

42 Ibid., p140.

43 Ibid., pp143–144.

44 Minutes of Evidence, Select Committee of the House of Lords on the East India Company *Parliamentary Papers* 1830, Vol. VI, c646, testimony of Joshua Bates, 10 June 1830, pp364–366.

45 Ibid., interview with Charles Everett, 11 June 1830, p390.

46 Ibid., p389.

47 Select Committee of the House of Lords on Foreign Trade: East India and China, *Parliamentary Papers* 1821, Vol VI, c476, interview with John Forbes Mitchell, 27 June 1821, p55.

48 Ibid., interview with George Lyall, 27 June 1821.

49 'The History and Present State of Commerce in Liverpool' *Fishers Colonial Magazine and Commercial Maritime Journal* Volume 2, May–August 1840, pp 80–90.

50 J.S. Gladstone, *History of Gillanders, Arbuthnot and Co. and Ogilvy Gillanders and Co.* (London 1910) p6.

51 Ibid., pp9–10.

52 Ibid., p8.

53 Ibid., pp14–15.

54 Ogilvy and Gillanders, Liverpool, to Messrs Charles S. Mason and Co., Staffordshire Potteries, 1 November 1836, Out Letter Book of Ogilvy Gillanders and Co. of Liverpool, Flintshire Record Office, Hawarden, Ogilvy and Gillanders Papers, GG2595; Ogilvy and Gillanders of Liverpool to John Craig, Glasgow, 7 November 1836, ibid.

55 Ogilvy & Gillanders to Mason & Co., 1 November 1836, ibid.

56 Ogilvy and Gillanders, Liverpool, to Messrs Fielden, Entwhistle and Co., London, 1 November 1836, ibid.

57 Ogilvy and Gillanders, Liverpool, to Maxwell and Newall, Bordeaux, 2 November 1836; to Messrs Barton and Guestier, Bordeaux, 2 November 1836; to Messrs Charles Latham and Co., Le Havre, 4 November 1836, ibid.

58 Minutes of Evidence, Select Committee of the House of Lords on the East India Company, *Parliamentary Papers* 1830, Vol. VI, no. 646, testimony of William Brown, 22 June 1830, pp432–435; p432.

59 Ibid.; p433.

60 Ibid.
61 Ibid.
62 Report of a Committee of the Liverpool East India Association appointed to take into consideration the Restrictions on the East India trade – Presented to the Association at a General Meeting, 9 May 1822, Liverpool Record Office H380.6EAS.
63 Ibid., pp3–4.
64 Ibid., pp17–18.
65 Report of the Public Meeting at Liverpool on Wednesday January 28 1829 for the purpose of taking into consideration the best means of removing the restrictions imposed upon commerce by the present Charter of the East India Company (London, W. Lewer 1829).
66 Ibid., p4.
67 Ibid., p24.
68 Bowen, *The Business of Empire* pp115–116.
69 Philips, *The East India Company* p243.
70 Ibid., p250.
71 Ibid., p275.
72 See for example: G.R. Knight, 'John Palmer and Plantation Development in Western Java in the Early Nineteenth Century' *Bijdragen* 131:2/3 (1975) pp309–337; N. Tarling, 'The Palmer Loans' *Bijdragen* 119:2 (1963) pp161–188.
73 Castlereagh to Fagel, 10 February 1819, National Archives (NA), FO 37/109.
74 Minute by Governor-General Hastings, November 1818, BL, OIOC, Dutch Records I/2/29.
75 A. Webster, 'British Export Interests in Bengal and Imperial Expansion into South East Asia, 1780 to 1824: The Origins of the Straits Settlements' in C. Simmons and B. Ingham (eds), *Development Studies and Colonial Policy* (London, Cass 1987) pp138–174.
76 Webster, *The Richest East India Merchant* p23.
77 N. Tarling, 'The Prince of Merchants and the Lion's City' in *Journal of the Malaysian Branch of the Royal Asiatic Society* 37:1 (1964) pp20–40.
78 Webster, *The Richest East India Merchant* pp101–102.
79 Select Committee of the House of Lords on Foreign Trade: East India and China, *Parliamentary Papers* 1821, Vol VI, c476 and Select Committee of the House of Commons on Foreign Trade: East India and China, *Parliamentary Papers* 1821, Vol VI, c746.
80 Testimony of Henry Blanshard, Commons Committee on Foreign Trade: East India and China 1821, p233.
81 Ibid., testimony of Patrick Maclachlan, 9 April 1821, p280.
82 Ibid., testimony of John Forbes Mitchell, 12 April 1821, p291.
83 Ibid., testimony of Robert Rickards, 7 May 1821, pp333–334.
84 Select Committee of the House of Lords on Foreign Trade: East India and China, *Parliamentary Papers* 1821, Vol VI, c476, testimony of William Fairlie, 16 March 1821, p205.
85 Ibid., testimony of Charles Grant, 6 July 1820, p121; testimony of John Gladstone, 14 March 1821, p198.
86 T. Courtenay, 'Observations upon the state of the negotiations between the British and the Netherlands' (March 1822), BL, OIOC, Dutch Records, I/2/31.
87 Webster, *Gentlemen Capitalists* pp96–100.
88 Palmer to J. Begbie, 25 April 1823, Bodleian Library, Oxford, Mss Eng Lett c.96 p169.

89 *Bengal Hurkaru* 29 April 1823. The whole edition was given over to the aims and activities of the new organisation.

90 Begbie and Larpent for the East India Trade Committee to Lord Bathurst, Secretary of State for the Colonies, 13 December 1823, BL, OIOC, Dutch Records I/2/31.

91 Begbie to J. Wilmot-Horton, Undersecretary for War and the Colonies, 29 January 1824, ibid.

92 Larpent to Courtenay, 18 December 1823, in H. Marks, *The First Contest for Singapore 1819–24* (The Hague, Nijhoff 1961) pp215–217.

93 W.T. Money to Canning, 30 December 1823, West Yorkshire Archives, Canning Papers, Harewood Mss 99a.

94 Webster, *The Richest East India Merchant* p95.

95 J.S. Gladstone, *History of Gillanders, Arbuthnot and Co. and Ogilvy, Gillanders and Co* (1910) p11, Flintshire Record Office, North Wales, Glynne-Gladstone Mss 2749.

Five: Crisis and Trade Liberalisation

1   J.S. Buckingham, 'The Past, Present and Future Commercial State of Calcutta' *Alexanders East India Magazine* 7:38 (January 1834) pp42–46.

2   John Crawfurd, 'A Sketch of the Commercial Resources and Monetary and Mercantile System of British India, with Suggestions for their Improvement by means of Banking Establishments' (1837) in K.N. Chaudhuri (ed), *The Economic Development of India under the East India Company 1814–58* (Cambridge, Cambridge University Press 1971) pp217–316.

3   Webster, *The Richest East India Merchant* pp114–115.

4   Ibid., pp118–119.

5   See V. Lieberman, 'Secular Trends in Burmese Economic History' *Modern Asian Studies* 25:1 (1991) pp1–31.

6   Thant Myint-U, *The Making of Modern Burma* (Cambridge, Cambridge University Press 2001) pp13–19.

7   G.P. Ramachandra, 'The Outbreak of the First Anglo-Burmese War' *Journal of the Malaysian Branch of the Royal Asiatic Society* 51 (1978) pp68–99.

8   D.M. Peers, 'War and Public Finance in Early Nineteenth Century British India: The First Burma War' in *The International History Review* 9:4 (1989) pp628–647; p639.

9   Ibid., p640.

10 Tripathi, *Trade and Finance in the Bengal Presidency* p162.

11 Peers, 'War and Public Finance' p642.

12 Tripathi, *Trade and Finance in the Bengal Presidency* p162.

13 Ibid., pp164–165.

14 S.B. Singh, *European Agency Houses in Bengal 1783 to 1833* (Calcutta, Firma K.L. Mukjopadhyay 1966) pp266–267.

15 B. Chowdhury, *Growth of Commercial Agriculture in Bengal 1757–1900 Volume 1* (Calcutta, Indian Studies, Past and Present 1964) pp88–89.

16 Testimony of George Larpent, 29 March 1832, Select Committee of the House of Commons on China and the Affairs of the East India Company 1831–32, Vol VI 735 (II) p166.

17 Webster, *The Richest East India Merchant* p60; pp148–150.

18 Tripathi, *Trade and Finance in the Bengal Presidency* pp161–162; Peers, 'War and Finance in India' p630.

19 B.B. Kling, *Partner in Empire: Dwarkanath Tagore and the Age of Enterprise in Eastern India* (Los Angeles, University of California 1976) pp55–56.

20 Chowdhury, pp91–93.

21 S. Bhattacharya, 'Eastern India' in D. Khumar and M. Desai, *The Cambridge Economic History of India c1750–c1970, Volume Two* (Cambridge, Cambridge University Press 1983) pp270–332; p294.

22 C.A. Bayly, *Rulers, Townsmen and Bazaars: North Indian Society in the Age of British Expansion 1770–1870* (Cambridge, Cambridge University Press 1983) pp263–277.

23 Singh, *European Agency Houses in Bengal* pp298–300.

24 D.M. Peers, *Between Mars and Mammon: Colonial Armies and the Garrison State in Early Nineteenth Century India* (London, I.B. Tauris 1995) p203; A.K. Bagchi, *The Evolution of the State Bank of India: The Roots 1806–1876* (Bombay, Oxford University Press 1987) p134.

25 Testimony of Sir George Larpent, 6 June 1833, Report of the Select Committee of the House of Commons on Manufactures, Commerce and Shipping 1833 *Parliamentary Papers* Vol. 6 (Minutes of Evidence) pp127–129.

26 Webster, *The Richest East India Merchant* p3.

27 Chowdhury, pp84–85; anonymous article in the *Calcutta Courier*, 'The Calcutta Agency Houses' reprinted in the *Bengal Hurkaru* on 20 January 1834.

28 Webster, *The Richest East India Merchant*.

29 Ibid., pp128–129.

30 Ibid., pp134–135.

31 Comment by George Lycke, report of a meeting of the creditors, 22 February 1832, *Alexanders East India Magazine* 4:24 (1832) p498–499.

32 Webster, *The Richest East India Merchant* p128.

33 Memoirs of William Prinsep, BL, IOC, Mss Eur D 1160/1 p319; see also A. Webster, 'An Early Global Business in a Colonial Context: The Strategies, Management and Failure of John Palmer and Co. of Calcutta c1800 to 1830' *Enterprise and Society* 6:1 (2005) pp98–113; p122.

34 Webster, *The Richest East India Merchant* p121.

35 Ibid., p125.

36 Tripathi, *Trade and Finance in the Bengal Presidency* p195.

37 Ibid., p196.

38 Testimony of Sir George Larpent to the House of Commons Select Committee on Manufactures, Commerce and Shipping, 6 June 1833 *Parliamentary Papers* VI, 1833, p134; Tripathi, *Trade and Finance in the Bengal Presidency* p196.

39 Webster, *The Richest East India Merchant* pp133–134.

40 B.B. Kling, *Partner in Empire* p57.

41 B.B. Kling, 'The Origin of the Managing Agency System in India' *Journal of Asian Studies* 26:1 (1966) pp37–47.

42 Ibid., p39.

43 Prinsep Memoirs, BL, OIOC, Eur Mss D/1160/2 p124.

44 Ibid., pp130–131; pp177–180.

45 Journal of Joshua Bates, Vol. 1 (23 October 1830 to 16 January 1834), Baring Archive, City of London, 8 September 1833, pp66–67.

46 Ibid., 15 September 1833, p67.

47 Prinsep Memoirs, BL, OIOC, Eur Mss D/1160/2 p182–183.

48 G. Tyson, *The Bengal Chamber of Commerce and Industry 1853–1953: A Centenary Survey* (Calcutta, The Statesman Ltd 1953) p12; pp181–182.

49 Webster, *The Richest East India Merchant* p132.
50 A.K. Bagchi, *The Evolution of the State Bank of India: The Roots 1806–1876* (Delhi, Oxford University Press 1987) pp149–152.
51 A.K. Bagchi, 'Transition from Indian to British Indian Systems of Money and Banking 1800–1850' *Modern Asian Studies* 19:3 (1985) pp501–519; p516.
52 Bowen, *The Business of Empire* pp255–256.
53 Ibid., pp258–259.
54 Ibid., p256.
55 Philips, *The East India Company* p287.
56 Minutes of the Glasgow East India Association, Mitchell Library, Glasgow, MS 891001/2 p1.
57 Yukihisa Kumagai, 'The Lobbying Activities of Provincial Mercantile and Manufacturing Interests against the Renewal of the East India Company's Charter, 1812–13 and 1829–33' (PhD thesis, University of Glasgow 2008).
58 Ibid., p115 and p181.
59 Ibid., pp120–122 and p202.
60 Ibid., p131.
61 Ibid., p132.
62 Ibid., p133.
63 Ibid., pp145–146.
64 R.W. Hidy, *The House of Baring in American Trade and Finance: English Merchant Banker at Work 1763–1861* (Cambridge, Mass, Harvard University Press 1949) p79.
65 Ibid., pp103–104.
66 Ibid., p128.
67 Minutes of the Glasgow East India Association, Mitchell Library, Glasgow, 22 February 1830, MS 891001/2 p26.
68 Select Committee on the State of Affairs of the East India Company, and Trade between Great Britain, East India and China, Minutes of Evidence, *Parliamentary Papers* 1830, Vol VI (644) pp218–233; pp329–332, pp497–500; Select Committee of the House of Lords on the East India Company, Minutes of Evidence, *Parliamentary Papers* 1830 (646), testimony of Joshua Bates, 10 June 1830, pp364–366.
69 Commons Select Committee 1830 (644), testimony of Joshua Bates, 15 March 1830, p228.
70 Ibid., Bates' testimony, 30 March 1830, p330.
71 Finlay to Paton from London, 15 March 1830, Mitchell Library, Glasgow, Glasgow East India Association, Incoming Correspondence MS 891001/4.
72 Ibid.
73 Joshua Bates to Alexander Baring, 17 May 1830, 'Sundry miscellaneous papers relating to the investigation of the Affairs of the East India Company', Baring Archive 209803.
74 Kumagai, p137.
75 Finlay to Paton, 3 March 1830, Mitchell Library, Glasgow, Glasgow East India Association papers, Incoming Correspondence MS 891001/4.
76 E. Said, *Orientalism* (London, Vintage 1978).
77 Sir L. Stephen & Sir S. Lee, *Dictionary of National Biography* Vol V (Oxford, Oxford University Press 1921–22) pp60–61.
78 Finlay to the Glasgow East India Association, 25 February 1830, Mitchell Library, Glasgow, Glasgow East India Association papers, Incoming Correspondence MS 891001/4.

79 Philips, *The East India Company* p289.
80 Quoted in Kumagai, p129.
81 Quoted in Bowen, *The Business of Empire* p297.
82 Philips, *The East India Company* p291.
83 Ibid.
84 Ibid., pp277–278.
85 Ibid., p294.
86 Ibid. p295.
87 Bowen, *The Business of Empire* p298.
88 Cain and Hopkins, *British Imperialism* p282.
89 Ibid., pp52–53.

Six: Re-ordering Anglo-Asian Commerce and Politics

1   K.N. Chaudhuri, 'India's Foreign Trade and the Cessation of the East India Company's Trading Activities' *Economic History Review* 19 (1966) pp345–363; p345.
2   Bowen, *The Business of Empire* p257.
3   A. Siddiqi (ed), *Trade and Finance in Colonial India 1750–1860* (Delhi, Oxford University Press 1995), Siddiqi's introduction pp17–27; see also A. Siddiqi, 'Money and Prices in the Earlier Stages of Empire: India and Britain 1760–1840' *Indian Economic and Social History Review* 18:3 and 4 (1981) pp231–262.
4   C.A. Bayly, *Rulers, Townsmen and Bazaars: North Indian Society in the Age of British Expansion 1770–1870* (Cambridge, Cambridge University Press 1988 edn) pp269–270.
5   Philips, *The East India Company* p243.
6   G. de H.H. Larpent, *On Protection to West-India Sugar* (London, J.M. Richardson 1823).
7   H. Marks, *The First Contest for Singapore 1819–24* (The Hague, Nijhoff 1959) pp215–217.
8   Testimony of Sir George Larpent, 6 June 1833, Report of the Select Committee of the House of Commons on Manufactures, Commerce and Shipping, 1833 *Parliamentary Papers* Vol. 6 (Minutes of Evidence) pp127–129.
9   Bagchi, *The Evolution of the State Bank of India* pp96–109; D. Tripathi, *The Oxford History of Indian Business* (New Delhi, Oxford University Press 2004) pp141–143.
10 Tripathi, *Oxford History of Indian Business* pp141–144
11 Plan of a Bank for India by Larpent, 1 November 1833, with J.H. Palmer's remarks thereon, University of London Library, Papers of Sir George Larpent, MS 172 (i).
12 Prospectus for a Bank for India, London, 12 May 1836, University of London Library, Larpent papers MS 172 (xix).
13 Plan of a Bank for India by Larpent, 1 November 1833; Tooke's views on the bank (undated, but almost certainly 1833) University of London Library, Larpent papers MS 172 (xi).
14 Tooke's views on the bank (undated, but almost certainly 1833) University of London Library, Larpent papers MS 172 (xi).
15 Horsley Palmer on the plan for a bank (undated) University of London Library, Larpent papers MS 172 (v).
16 A.J.S. Baster, *The Imperial Banks* (London, P.S. King & Sons 1929) p49, pp67–70.
17 G. Jones, *British Multinational Banking 1830–1990* (Oxford, Clarendon Press 1993) p14.
18 Baster, pp24–25.

19 Jones, *British Multinational Banking* p14.
20 Kumagai, 'The Lobbying Activities of Provincial Mercantile and Manufacturing Interests' pp139–140; Thomas Boothman, Secretary to the Manchester Chamber of Commerce, to the Glasgow East India Association (Glasgow EIA) 21 November 1835, Mitchell Library, Glasgow, Glasgow East India Association papers MS 891001/7 p27.
21 First Report of the Committee of the London East India and China Association, 3 January 1837, BL, OIOC.
22 Ibid.
23 Minutes of Glasgow EIA, AGM 31 March 1836, Mitchell Library, Glasgow, Glasgow East India Association papers, MS 891001/2 p128.
24 Cain and Hopkins, *British Imperialism* pp52–53.
25 Prospectus of a bank for India, London, 12 May 1836, University of London Library, Larpent papers MS 172 (xix).
26 Circular on the Bank of India sent to Thomas Baring, 20 July 1836, City of London, Baring Brothers Papers HCI.48B.
27 Jones, *British Multinational Banking* p14.
28 Baster, *The Imperial Banks* pp94–95.
29 Kling, *Partner in Empire* pp201–202.
30 R.M. Martin, 'Origins and Progress of the Bank of Asia' *Fisher's Colonial Magazine and Maritime Journal* Vol 7, Jan–April 1842, pp419–420; see especially appendix A: 'Minute of a conference with the India Board on 11 May 1840' p420.
31 F.H.H. King, *Survey our Empire (Robert Montgomery Martin 1801–1868: A Bio-Bibliography)* (Hong Kong, Centre of Asian Studies, University of Hong Kong 1979) p156, especially footnote 9.
32 Financial letter no. 7 from the East India Company Court of Directors to the Indian government, 20 July 1836, BL, OIOC, Financial Despatches to India, L/F/3/680.
33 *Review of a Pamphlet Entitled 'Reasons for the Establishment of a New Bank in India' by an Indian Merchant* (Glasgow 1836); J.R. McCulloch, *Reasons for the Establishment of a new Bank in India, with answers to the Objection Against it* (London 1836).
34 Report of the sub committee of the Glasgow East India Association on the proposed Bank of India, 25 July 1836, University of London Library, Larpent papers MS 172 (xx).
35 This is suggested by the fact that another Mr Speir was reported attending a meeting of the Bank of Bengal in Calcutta in February 1837, when Thomas Speir was certainly still in Glasgow. *Bengal Hurkaru* 22 February 1837.
36 J. Crawfurd, 'A Sketch of the Commercial Resources and Monetary and Mercantile System of British India, with Suggestions for their improvement, by means of banking establishments' (1837) in K.N. Chaudhuri, *The Economic Development of India under the East India Company 1814–58* (Cambridge, Cambridge University Press 1971) pp217–316.
37 A. Wardrop of the Glasgow EIA to Allen, 5 September 1836, Mitchell Library, Glasgow, Glasgow East India Association papers, Outgoing correspondence MS 891001/13 p252; and Wardrop to Allen, 7 October 1836, p254; *Asiatic Journal* Vol 21, Sept–December 1836, pp161–163; pp238–242.
38 'New Bank for India' in *Alexanders East India Magazine* October 1836, pp299–303; February 1837, pp103–106; March 1837, pp207–220.
39 East India and China Association of London to Wardrop, Mitchell Library, Glasgow, Glasgow East India Association papers, Incoming correspondence MS 891001/7 p73.
40 Kirkman Finlay MP to Wardrop, 10 October 1836, Mitchell Library, Glasgow,

Glasgow East India Association papers, Incoming correspondence MS 891001/7 p80; Glasgow EIA to the Lords of the Treasury, 25 November 1836, Outgoing correspondence MS 891001/14 pp3–4; Annual report of AGM, 30 March 1837,Glasgow East India Association papers.

41 Thomas Speir to Alexander Wardrop, 26 September 1836, Mitchell Library, Glasgow, Glasgow East India Association papers, Incoming correspondence MS 891001/7.

42 Lord Auckland to Sir J.C. Melvill, Chief Secretary to the East India Company, 26 August 1836, BL, OIOC, Melvill papers Eur Mss B/137, letter 7; H.T. Prinsep's paper on the proposed Bank of India, 16 August 1836, BL, OIOC, India Board's Collections F/4/1700 68490A.

43 'Paper by Mr J. Fullarton on the principle of banking in its application to the condition of things in India, and the means of deriving advantage from it on the conduct of the business of government to September 1836', BL, OIOC, in File on Banks and Banking in India L/F/5/68 pp128–135.

44 *Bengal Hurkaru* 24 February 1837.

45 *Bengal Hurkaru* 8 March 1837; *Bengal Hurkaru* 21 March 1837.

46 Stikeman to Wardrop, 11 January 1837, Mitchell Library, Glasgow, Glasgow East India Association papers, Incoming correspondence MS 891001/8 p1.

47 King, *Survey our Empire* pp154–155.

48 Ibid., pp160–162.

49 King, p173.

50 Minute of Charles Trevelyan, National Archives (NA), London, T1/4845 bundle 4.

51 Larpent to Gladstone, 14 June 1843, NA, T1/4845 bundle 4.

52 Select Committee of the House of Commons on East India Produce, *Parliamentary Papers* 1840, Vol 8; Larpent's testimony, 6 April 1840, p167.

53 First Annual Report of the London EICA, January 1837, pp6–7.

54 the London EICA annual report 1841 pp3–8.

55 Ibid., pp11–12.

56 I. Nish, 'British Mercantile Co-operation in the India-China Trade from the End of the East India Company's Trading Monopoly' *Journal of Southeast Asian History* 3:2 (1962) pp74–91; pp86–87.

57 Court of Directors on policy towards the agency houses, 20 July 1831, letter 340; and Court of Directors to the government of Bengal on the agency houses, 27 August 1834, in C.H. Philips (ed), *The Correspondence of Lord William Cavendish Bentinck Vols 1 & 2* (Oxford, Oxford University Press 1977) p660 and p1364.

58 G. Tyson, *The Bengal Chamber of Commerce and Industry 1853–1953* pp15–16.

59 R.J.F. Sulivan, *One Hundred Years of Bombay: History of the Bombay Chamber of Commerce 1836–1936* (Bombay, Times of India Press 1937) p14; R.J. Daruwala, *The Bombay Chamber Story – 150 years* (Bombay, Bombay Chamber of Commerce 1986) pp3–4.

60 Arbuthnot, Chairman of the Madras Chamber of Commerce, to Chief Secretary to the Madras Government, Fort St George, Madras, 11 October 1836, BL, OIOC, Boards Collections F/4/1719 no. 69300 pp3–6.

61 Extract from public letter from Fort St George, 31 December 1836, BL, OIOC, Boards Collections F/4/1719 no. 69309 pp1–2.

62 C.M. Turnbull, *A History of Singapore* (Oxford, Oxford University Press 1977) pp35–36.

63 Wong Lin Ken, 'The Trade of Singapore 1819–69' *Journal of the Malaysian Branch of the Royal Asiatic Society* 33:4 (1960) pp11–301; p182.

64 C. Buckley, *An Anecdotal History of Old Times in Singapore Vol 1* (Singapore, Fraser and Neave 1902) pp313–314.

65   The London EICA to the Glasgow East India Association, 25 August 1836, India Board to the Glasgow East India Association, 26 August 1836, Mitchell Library, Glasgow, Glasgow East India Association papers MS 891001/7 pp73–74.

66   Nish, 'British Mercantile Co-operation in the India-China Trade' pp86–88.

67   Letters to the London EICA from the Chambers of Commerce of Bengal (6 December 1836), Madras (20 December 1836), Bombay (25 September 1837) and Singapore (10 March 1837); London EICA annual report 1838 pp23–26.

68   A.Wardrop to J. Stikeman, 9 March 1839, Mitchell Library, Glasgow, Glasgow East India Association papers, Outgoing correspondence MS 891001/14 p71.

69   Wardrop to Stikeman, 5 November 1840, ibid., p133.

70   Wardrop to Stikeman, 18 May 1843, ibid., p204; Wardrop to Stikeman, 14 June 1842, ibid., p210.

71   D. Thorner, *Investment in Empire: British Railway and Steam Shipping Enterprise in India 1825–1849* (Philadelphia, University of Pennsylvania 1950) pp28–34.

72   Minute of the Assam Company Vol. 1 (12 February 1839 – 17 December 1845), Guildhall Library, London, papers of the Assam Co., MS 9924/1.

73   Minute of a conversation at the East India House on 14 February 1839 between Larpent and the Chair of the East India Company, ibid., pp8–9.

74   Report of AGM of the Assam Co., 7 May 1841, Guildhall Library, London, papers of the Assam Co. MS 27052/1 pp90–94.

75   Report to AGM of the Assam Co., 5 April 1843, Guildhall Library, London, papers of the Assam Co. MS 27052/1 p179; Report to AGM, 1 May 1846, MS 27052/2 p6.

76   Report to AGM of the Assam Co., 6 May 1842, Guildhall Library, London, papers of the Assam Co. MS 27052/1 p127; *Dictionary of National Biography*, http://www.oxforddnb.com/articles/17/17934-article.html?back.

77   H. Mukherjee, *The Early History of the East Indian Railway 1845–1879* (Calcutta, Firma KLM Private Ltd 1994) pp16–18.

78   See 'A letter to the Rt Hon Lord John Russell MP on the subject of Indian Railways by an East India Merchant' (London, Smith, Elder & Co.) pp4–5.

79   Ibid., pp5–6.

80   Ibid., pp6–8; Mukherjee, *The Early History of the East Indian Railway* p21.

81   'Deccan Transit' June 1844, BL, OIOC, Papers of John Chapman, Eur Mss E/234/9 pp14–25.

82   Ibid., p25.

83   Mr Ritchie to John Chapman, 13 September 1844, BL, OIOC, Papers of John Chapman, Eur Mss E/234/9 p75.

84   Chapman to the Manchester Chamber of Commerce, 24 February 1845, ibid., p118.

85   Mukherjee, *The Early History of the East Indian Railway* p21.

86   Ibid., p22.

87   'A letter to the Rt Hon Lord John Russell MP' pp45–46.

88   Ibid., pp23–24.

89   Ibid., p25.

90   J.A. Scott, Secretary to the Bombay Chamber of Commerce, to Chapman (in Bombay), 1 October 1846, BL, OIOC, Chapman papers, Eur Mss E/234/68 p5; Lord Wharncliffe to Chapman, 7 November 1846, ibid., p20.

91   W. Nicol, Chair of Liverpool East India Association, to Chapman, 15 November 1846, ibid., p47.

92   Boothman, Chair of Manchester Chamber of Commerce to Chapman, 17 June

1847, BL, OIOC, Chapman papers, Eur Mss E/234/69 p187; J. Walkinshaw of the Glasgow Chamber of Commerce to Chapman, 17 June 1947, ibid., p184; John Bright to Chapman, 7 September 1847, Eur Mss E/234/70 pp91–92.

93 Chapman to Mr Smith in Bombay, 7 August 1847, BL, OIOC, Chapman papers, Eur Mss E/234/70 p7.
94 Chapman to Leach, 9 August 1847, ibid., p9.
95 Hamilton to Chapman, 10 August 1847, ibid., pp11–12.
96 Chapman to Smith in Bombay, 23 August 1847.
97 Chapman to Smith in Bombay, 24 June 1847, BL, OIOC, Chapman papers, Eur Mss E/234/69.
98 Hamilton to Chapman, 15 August 1847, BL, OIOC, Chapman papers, Eur Mss E/234/70, pp28–29.
99 Chapman to Smith in Bombay, 6 September 1847, ibid., pp85–86; Hamilton to Chapman, 7 September 1847, ibid., pp97–98.
100 Hobhouse to John Bright, 9 September 1847, BL, OIOC, Broughton Papers, Eur Mss F/213/18 pp248–249.
101 K.N. Chaudhuri, 'Foreign Trade and Balance of Payments (1757–1947)' in D. Kumar (ed) *The Cambridge History of Modern India Volume 2: 1757–2003* (Hyderabad, India, Orient Longman 2005) pp804–877; p833.
102 A. Siddiqi (ed), *Trade and Finance in Colonial India* (Oxford, Oxford University Press 1995) Siddiqi's introduction pp1–55; p16.
103 Chaudhuri, 'Foreign Trade and Balance of Payments' p833; D. Rothermund, *An Economic History of India from Pre-Colonial Times to 1986* (London, Croom Helm 1988) p25.
104 K.N. Chaudhuri, 'India's Foreign Trade and the Cessation of the East India Company's Trading Activities' *Economic History Review* 19 (1966) pp345–363; p354.
105 Chaudhuri, 'Foreign Trade and Balance of Payments' p861.
106 Chaudhuri, 'Foreign Trade' p842; Rothermund p27.
107 Ibid.
108 A. Webster, 'Liverpool and the Asian Trade 1800–50: Some Insights into a Provincial Commercial Network' in S. Haggerty, A. Webster and N. White (eds) *The Empire in One City: Liverpool's Inconvenient Imperial Past* (Manchester, Manchester University Press 2008) pp35–54; p43.
109 Ibid., p40.
110 Ibid., p39.
111 G. Milne, *Trade and Traders in Mid-Victorian Liverpool: Mercantile Business and the Making of a World Port* (Liverpool, Liverpool University Press 2000) pp81–84.
112 A. Tripathi, 'Indo-British Trade between 1833 and 1847 and the Commercial Crisis of 1847–8' in Siddiqi, *Trade and Finance in Colonial India* pp265–289; p271.
113 Chaudhuri, 'Foreign Trade' p861.
114 C.A. Bayly, *Rulers, Townsmen and Bazaars: North Indian Society in the Age of British Expansion, 1770–1870* (Cambridge, Cambridge University Press 1983) pp263–302.
115 A. Siddiqi, 'Money and Prices in the Earlier Stages of Empire: India and Britain 1760–1840' *Indian Economic and Social History Review* 18:3 and 4 (1981) pp231–262; p249; Siddiqi, *Trade and Finance in Colonial India* pp17–22.
116 A. Tripathi, 'Indo-British Trade between 1833 and 1847' pp278–279.
117 Ibid., p278.
118 *Bankers Magazine* Vol 8 (March 1848), 'State of the Exchanges with India' pp153–156.
119 Tripathi, 'Indo-British Trade between 1833 and 1847' pp278–279.

120 Ibid., pp277–279.
121 Ibid., p279.
122 Proposal for the Establishment of a Joint Stock Bank at Bombay (1837), BL, OIOC, Boards Collections F/4/1561, 63986.
123 D. Tripathi, *Oxford History of Indian Business* p143.
124 Letter from the Bengal administration to the Court of Directors, 4 January 1837, BL, OIOC, Governor General's minute, Boards Collections F/4/1700; 'Paper by Mr J. Fullarton on the principle of banking in its application to the condition of things in India and the means of deriving advantage from it in the conduct of the business of the government – dated 1 September 1836', BL, OIOC, in L/F/5/68 pp128–135.
125 Fullarton's paper p133.
126 King, *Survey our Empire* p157.
127 King, *Survey our Empire* pp174–5; Larpent, Gregson and Stikeman representing the London EICA to Gladstone, Board of Trade, 14 June 1843, NA, T1/485 pp115–119; p119; Trevelyan's printed minute of 1843 on 'East India Bank', T1/4845.

Seven: Crisis, Resurgence and End

1 P. Mathias, *The First Industrial Nation: The Economic History of Britain 1700–1914* (London, Routledge 1983) p209.
2 D. Morier Evans, *The Commercial Crisis 1847–48; Being Facts & Figures Illustrative of the Events of that important Period, considered in relation to the three Epochs of the Railway Mania, the Food & Money Panic & the French Revolution* (London, Letts & Steer 1848) pp70–72.
3 Ibid., p73.
4 *Bankers Magazine* 8 (November 1848) pp662–663.
5 J. Crawfurd, 'A Sketch of the Commercial Resources and Monetary and Mercantile System of British India, with Suggestions for their Improvement by Means of Banking Establishments' in K.N. Chaudhuri (ed), *The Economic Development of India under the East India Company 1814–58* (Cambridge, Cambridge University Press 1971) pp284–287.
6 A.Tripathi, 'Indo-British Trade between 1833 and 1847 and the Commercial Crisis of 1847–8' in Siddiqi, *Trade and Finance in Colonial India* pp265–289; p281.
7 Memorial of the Glasgow East India Association, 19 May 1835 (signed by Kirkman Finlay and William Paton), 'Hypothecation of Goods', in Liverpool Record Office, 380 COM27/2, Annual Report of the Liverpool East India and China Association, 15 February 1849, pp13–32; pp31–32.
8 Tripathi, 'Indo-British Trade between 1833 and 1847' p288.
9 Testimony of Charles Turner, 15 February 1848, the Select Committee of the House of Commons on Commercial Distress 1847/8, Vol. 8, pp50–54.
10 Morier Evans, *The Commercial Crisis*, Appendix, p(i).
11 Ibid., pp(ix)–(x).
12 'List of Failures in Calcutta during the Past Year' *Bankers Magazine* 8 (1848) p662–663.
13 Ibid.
14 S.D. Chapman, 'The Agency Houses: British Mercantile Enterprise in the Far East c.1780–1920' *Textile History* 19:2 (1988) pp239–254; p242.
15 Hugh Hunter's testimony, 21 February 1848, Select Committee of the Commons on Sugar and Coffee Planting, Vol. 23 part 1(first report) p214.

16 Larpent's testimony, 26 February 1848, Select Committee of the Commons on Sugar and Coffee Planting, p41 (second report).

17 Ibid., Blyth's testimony, 23 February 1848, p260 (first report).

18 Morier Evans, *The Commercial Crisis* p72.

19 J. Hobhouse to Tucker, 6 October 1847, BL, OIOC, Broughton Papers, Eur Mss F213/18 p287.

20 Annual Report to the AGM of the Assam Co., 5 May 1848, Guildhall Library, Assam Co. Papers MS 27052/2 pp2–15.

21 Walkinshaw, Glasgow East India Association (Glasgow EIA), to Stikeman, London EICA, 23 September 1847, Mitchell Library, Glasgow, Glasgow East India Association papers, MS 891001/15 p64.

22 BL, OIOC, Annual Reports of the London East India China Association for 1842 (p26) and 1850 (p.19).

23 K.N. Chaudhuri, 'Foreign Trade and Balance of Payments (1757–1947)' in D. Kumar (ed) *The Cambridge History of Modern India Volume 2: 1757–2003* (Hyderabad, India, Orient Longman 2005) pp804–877; p833.

24 Ibid.

25 D. Rothermund, *An Economic History of India from Pre-Colonial Times to 1986* (London, Croom Helm 1988) pp28–9.

26 Chaudhuri, 'Foreign Trade and Balance of Payments' p860.

27 W.J. Macpherson, 'Investment in Indian Railways, 1845–1875' *Economic History Review* 8:2 (1955) pp177–186; p184.

28 H. Mukherjee, *The Early History of the East India Railway 1845–1879* (Calcutta, Firma KLM Private Ltd 1994) p29.

29 Rothermund, p35.

30 K.N. Chaudhuri, 'Foreign Trade and Balance of Payments' p849.

31 http://www.oxforddnb.com/view/article/29660?docPos=10

32 http://www.oxforddnb.com/view/article/29865?docPos=1

33 http://www.oxforddnb.com/view/article/17088

34 R.J. Moore, 'Imperialism and "Free Trade" Policy in India, 1853–4' *Economic History Review* 17:1 (1964) pp135–145; p139.

35 See for example R. Cobden, *How Wars are Got up in India: The Origin of the Burmese War* (London, W. & F.G. Cash 1953).

36 G.S. Chhabra, *Advanced Study in the History of Modern India* (New Delhi, Lotus Press 2007) pp220–222.

37 D. Tripathi, *The Oxford History of Indian Business* (New Delhi, Oxford University Press 2004) p144; S. Muirhead, *Crisis Banking in the East: The History of the Chartered Mercantile Bank of India, London and China, 1853–93* (Aldershot, Scolar Press 1996) pp6–7.

38 T. Kawamura, 'British Business and Empire in Asia: the Eastern Exchange Banks, 1851–63' in D. Bates and K. Kondo (eds), *Migration and Identity in British History. Proceedings of the fifth Anglo-Japanese Conference of Historians, 27–29 September 2006* (London, Institute of Historical Research 2006) pp193–207, p198; Cumming Bruce (India Board) to Hamilton (Treasury), 30 November 1852, National Archives (NA), T1/5769A.

39 James Wilson, Document on Indian Banking, 12 June 1853, BL, OIOC, Papers of Sir Charles Wood, Eur Mss F/78/16 pp1–20; pp14–15.

40 Kawamura, pp195–196; 'Printed Prospectus for the Chartered Bank of India, Australia and China, to be incorporated by Royal Charter', BL, OIOC, Wood Papers, Eur Mss F /78/16 p31.

41 Kawamura, p196.

42 Memorial to the Lords Commissioners of the Treasury from the provisional directors of the Bank of Asia, 16 May 1853, BL, OIOC, Wood Papers, Eur Mss F/78/16 p60; BL, OIOC, London East India and China Association Annual Report 1852, p11.

43 Melvill to C.S. Cumming Bruce MP at the India Board, 11 November 1852, NA, Treasury Papers, T1/5769A, no. 23421.

44 Cumming Bruce to G.A. Hamilton at the Treasury, 29 November 1952, NA, Treasury Papers, T1/5769A, no. 23421.

45 Letter from East India houses to the East India Company petitioning against new banks, 25 July 1853, BL, OIOC, Financial Papers of the East India Company, L/F/2/165.

46 Letter from the Manchester Chamber of Commerce and the Manchester Commercial Association to the East India Company, 25 July 1853, BL, OIOC, Financial Papers of the East India Company, L/F/2/165.

47 Liverpool EICA to Cardwell, President of the Board of Trade, 2 September 1853, and to the Court of Directors of the East India Company, 13 September 1853, BL, OIOC, Financial Papers of the East India Company, L/F/2/166.

48 Muirhead, *Crisis Banking in the East* p18.

49 Kawamura. p198; Muirhead. p.17.

50 James Wilson, 'Banking in India', 12 June 1853, BL, OIOC, Wood Papers. Eur Mss F78/16 pp1–20; pp8–9.

51 Ibid., p9.

52 Ibid., pp17–20.

53 A.M. Pollock, Secretary to the Chartered Bank of Asia to the Treasury, 15 February 1856, NA, T1/6009A, no. 2944.

54 Muirhead, pp54–62.

55 G.A. Hamilton and James Wilson of the Treasury, 22 August 1856, NA, T16009A, no. 13010.

56 Muirhead, pp64–67.

57 Leone Levi, *Chamber and Tribunals of Commerce, and a proposed General Chamber of Commerce in Liverpool* (London, Simpkin Marshall and Co. 1849) pp16–17; see also A. Webster, 'Liverpool & the Asian Trade, 1800–50: Some Insights into a Provincial Commercial Network' in S. Haggerty, A. Webster and N. White (eds), *The Empire in One City? Liverpool's Inconvenient Imperial Past* (Manchester, Manchester University Press 2008) pp35–54; p51.

58 Liverpool Record Office, Annual Report of the Liverpool EICA 1849, p16.

59 Liverpool Record Office, Annual Report of the Liverpool Chamber of Commerce 1853, 380COM/24/1, p93.

60 Liverpool Record Office, Annual Report of the Liverpool Chamber of Commerce 1858, pp320–321.

61 Ibid., p347.

62 C. Buckley, *An Anecdotal History of Old Times in Singapore Vol 2* (Singapore, Fraser and Neave 1902) p773.

63 C.M. Turnbull, *A History of Singapore* (Oxford, Oxford University Press 1977) pp35–36.

64 Wong Lin Ken, 'The Trade of Singapore 1819–69' *Journal of the Malaysian Branch of the Royal Asiatic Society* 33:4 (1960) pp11–301; p182.

65 C. Buckley, *An Anecdotal History of Old Times in Singapore Vol 1* (Singapore, Fraser and Neave 1902) pp313–314; London EICA to Glasgow EIA, 25 August 1836; India Board to Glasgow EIA, 26 August 1836, Mitchell Library, Glasgow, Glasgow East India Association papers, MS 891001/7 pp73–74.

66 Government of India to the Court of Directors, 7 February 1838, BL, OIOC, Board Collections, F/4/1903 (81155) pp3–5; Government of India to Court of Directors, 18 July 1838, ibid., p25.

67 London EICA to the Court of Directors, 23 May 1838 (enclosing Crawfurd's memorandum) BL, OIOC, Board Collections, F/4/1905 pp1–41; Government of India to Court of Directors, 20 April 1840, Board Collections, F/4/1903 (81155) pp137–152; p143–144.

68 *Currency Adapted to the Straits Settlements: and the Nature & Extent of the Commerce of Singapore with Remarks on Act XVII of 1855 (Published under the Direction of the Committee Appointed at a Public Meeting held at Singapore, August 11th 1855* (Singapore, G.M. Frederick 1855); BL, OIOC, 20th Annual Report of London EICA 1856, pp11–12.

69 Wong Lin Ken, 'The Trade of Singapore' p190.

70 J. Crawfurd, *Memorandum on the British Settlements in the Straits of Malacca, Penang, Singapore and Malacca* (London, C.W. Beynell 1858) p3.

71 Petition of the European inhabitants of Singapore, presented to the House of Commons in 1858, Correspondence relative to the proposed transfer of the Straits Settlements to the Colonial Office, *Parliamentary Papers* 259 (1862) pp585–588; p585.

72 Oriental Bank to George Arbuthnot at the Treasury, 16 August 1855, NA, T1/6009A no. 14696.

73 Treasury to the Chair and Deputy Chair of the Oriental Bank, 20 June 1859; Governor of the Straits Settlements to the Secretary to the Government in India, 5 August 1859, BL, OIOC, Financial Papers of the East India Company, L/F/3/252 OIOC.

74 Petition from Singapore merchants 30 July 1859, ibid.

75 G.A. Hamilton (Treasury) to J. Melvill (East India Company), 26 July 1860; Melvill to Hamilton, 22 August 1860, BL, OIOC, Financial Papers of the East India Company, L/F/2/242.

76 Kawamura, pp204–205.

77 C. Buckley, *An Anecdotal History of Old Times in Singapore Vol 2* p773.

78 Minutes of Meeting at Edward Boustead's Office, 31 January 1868, NA, Colonial Office Records for Malaya, CO/273/24 p189.

79 J.Y. Wong, *Deadly Dreams: Opium and the Arrow War (1856–1860) in China* (Cambridge, Cambridge University Press 2003) pp396–398.

80 W.J. Barber, *British Economic Thought and India 1600–1858: A Study in the History of Development Economics* (Oxford, Clarendon Press 1975) p214.

81 P. Harnetty, 'The Imperialism of Free Trade: Lancashire and the Indian Cotton Duties, 1859–1862' *Economic History Review* 18:2 (1965) pp333–349; p333.

82 BL, OIOC, Wood papers, 'The Financial Administration of India' pp1–54, Wilson to Wood, 10 July 1859, Wood papers, Eur Mss F/78/57–1.

83 Harnetty, 'The Imperialism of Free Trade'.

84 P.J. Cain and A.G. Hopkins, *British Imperialism 1688–2000* (Edinburgh, Pearson 2001) pp291–292.

85 Ibid., pp294–297.

86 Rory M. Miller and Robert G. Greenhill, 'Liverpool and South America, 1850–1930' in S. Haggerty, A. Webster and N. White (eds), *The Empire in One City? Liverpool's Inconvenient Imperial Past* (Manchester, Manchester University Press 2008) pp78–99; pp88–90.

87 Liverpool Record Office, Annual Report of the Liverpool Chamber of Commerce 1869, pp605–606.

88   Liverpool Record Office, Annual Report of the Liverpool Chamber of Commerce 1876, pp124–125.
89   Liverpool Record Office, Annual Report of the Liverpool Chamber of Commerce 1872, p803.
90   Liverpool Record Office, Annual Report of the Liverpool Chamber of Commerce 1883, pp622–623.
91   Liverpool Record Office, Annual Report of the Liverpool Chamber of Commerce 1871, p752.
92   See J. Davies, 'The Liverpool Chamber of Commerce and the Burma-China Railway' *Transactions of the Historic Society of Lancashire and Cheshire* 139 (1990) pp113–136.
93   A.Webster, 'Business and Empire: A Reassessment of the British Conquest of Burma in 1885' *Historical Journal* 43:4 (2000) pp1003–1025; pp1015–1020.

Eight: Conclusion

1   H. Bowen, *The Business of Empire: The East India Company and Imperial Britain 1756–1833* (Cambridge, Cambridge University Press 2006) pp19–28.
2   K.N. Chaudhuri, 'The East India Company in the 17th and 18th Centuries: a Pre-modern Multinational Organization' in L. Blussé and F. Gaastra (eds) *Companies and Trade* (Leiden, Leiden University Press 1981); N. Robins, *The Corporation that Changed the World: How the East India Company Shaped the Modern Multinational* (London, Pluto Press 2006).
3   H. Furber, *Rival Empires of Trade in the Orient, 1600–1800* (London, Oxford University Press 1976); C.H. Philips, *The East India Company 1784–1834* (Manchester, Manchester University Press 1961).
4   M. Daunton, '"Gentlemanly Capitalism" and British Industry 1820–1914' *Past & Present* 122 (1989) pp119–158.
5   Ibid., pp138–140.
6   Ibid., pp152–154.
7   E.H.H. Green, 'Gentlemanly Capitalism and British Economic Policy, 1880–1914: the Debate over Bimetallism and Protectionism' in R.E. Dumett (ed), *Gentlemanly Capitalism and British Imperialism* (London, Longman 1999) pp44–67; p66.
8   A.C. Howe, 'Free Trade and the City of London' *History* 77:251 (1992) pp391–410.
9   Ibid., p407.
10   Daunton, p149.
11   J. Darwin, 'Imperialism and the Victorians: the Dynamics of Territorial Expansion' *English Historical Review* (June 1997) pp614–642.

BIBLIOGRAPHY

Primary Sources: Documents

OFFICIAL RECORDS AND THE RECORDS OF
COMMERCIAL ASSOCIATIONS

British Library (BL) *Oriental and India Office Collections* (OIOC)
Annual Reports of the London East India and China Association
Banks and Banking in India (file)
Boards Collections
Charters and Treaties
Financial Despatches to India
Financial Papers of the East India Company
Home Miscellaneous Series
Dutch Records

National Archives (NA), *London*
Board of Trade records
Colonial Office records
Foreign Office records
Treasury records

Liverpool Record Office
Report of a Committee of the Liverpool East India Association appointed to take into consideration the Restrictions on the East India trade – Presented to the Association at a General Meeting 9 May 1822
Report of the Public Meeting at Liverpool on Wednesday January 28 1829 for the purpose of taking into consideration the best means of removing the restrictions imposed upon commerce by the present Charter of the East India Company
Annual Reports of the Liverpool East India and China Association
Annual Reports of the Liverpool Chamber of Commerce

Glasgow Record Office, Mitchell Library
Papers of the Glasgow East India Association

Calcutta, India
The Board of Trade records, West Bengal archives
Uncatalogued Records of the Calcutta High Court

PERSONAL PAPERS AND PAPERS OF INDIVIDUAL FIRMS

British Library (BL) *Oriental and India Office Collections* (OIOC)
Papers of Sir Charles Forbes   Eur Mss D100
Papers of John Adam   Eur Mss F109
Papers of Sir Charles Wood   Eur Mss F78
Memoirs of William Prinsep   Eur Mss D1160
Papers of Sir J.C. Melvill   Eur Mss B137
Papers of John Chapman   Eur Mss 234
Papers of Lord Broughton   Eur Mss 213

British Library (BL) *Manuscripts Collection*
Papers of Lord Liverpool   Add Mss 38410
Papers of Lord Bathurst   Loan 57
Papers of Warren Hastings   Add Mss 29169

University of London Library
Papers of Sir George Larpent

Baring Archive, City of London
Journal of Joshua Bates

Guildhall Library, City of London
Papers of the Assam Company

Liverpool Record Office
Papers of William Roscoe

Flintshire Record Office
Papers of Ogilvy and Gillanders

John Rylands Library, Manchester
Papers of Lord Melville

Bodleian Library, Oxford
Papers of John Palmer

West Yorkshire Archives
Papers of George Canning

Primary Sources: Published

NEWSPAPERS AND CONTEMPORARY JOURNALS

Alexanders East India Magazine
Bankers Magazine

Bengal Hurkaru
Fishers Colonial Magazine and Commercial Maritime Journal

PARLIAMENTARY PAPERS

Hansard (Commons) **XXVI**
Parliamentary Debates **XXII**
Committee of the Whole House on East Indian Affairs, Vol VII, 1812–12
Fourth Report of the Select Committee on East Indian Affairs, Vol VI, 1812
Select Committee on East Indian Affairs, Vol VII, 1812–13
Select Committee on the Orders in Council, Vol III, 1812
Select Committee of the House of Commons on the means of improving and maintaining Foreign Trade – East Indies and China, 1821, Vol VI
Select Committee of the House of Lords on Foreign Trade: East India and China, 1821, Vol VI
Select Committee of the House of Lords on the East India Company *Parliamentary Papers*, 1830, Vol VI
Select Committee of the House of Commons on China and the Affairs of the East India Company 1831–32, Vol VI
Select Committee of the House of Commons on Manufacturers, Commerce and Shipping 1833, Vol VI
Select Committee of the House of Commons on East India Produce, Vol VIII
Select Committee of the House of Commons on Commercial Distress 1847/8, Vol VIII
Select Committee of the Commons on Sugar and Coffee Planting, 1848, Vol XXIII

Secondary Sources

BOOKS

Bagchi, A.K. *The Evolution of the State Bank of India: The Roots 1806–1876* (Bombay, Oxford University Press 1987)
Barber, W.J. *British Economic Thought and India 1600–1858: A Study in the History of Development Economics* (Oxford, Clarendon Press 1975)
Baster, A.J.S. *The Imperial Banks* (London, P.S. King & Sons 1929)
Bayly, C.A. *Rulers, Townsmen and Bazaars: North Indian Society in the Age of British Expansion 1770–1870* (Cambridge, Cambridge University Press 1983)
Bayly, C.A. *Imperial Meridian: The British Empire and the World 1780–1830* (London, Longman 1989)
Bowen, H.V. *The Business of Empire: The East India Company and Imperial Britain, 1756–1833* (Cambridge, Cambridge University Press 2006)
Buckley, C. *An Anecdotal History of Old Times in Singapore Vol 1* (Singapore, Fraser and Neave 1902)
Cain, P.J. and Hopkins, A.G. *British Imperialism 1688–2000* (Edinburgh, Pearson 2001)
Chaudhuri, K.N. *The English East India Company: The Study of an Early Joint Stock Company, 1600–1640* (Reprint, London, Routledge 1999)
Chhabra, G.S. *Advanced Study in the History of Modern India* (New Delhi, Lotus Press 2007)

Chowdhury, B. *Growth of Commercial Agriculture in Bengal 1757–1900: Volume One* (Calcutta, Indian Studies, Past and Present 1964)

Cobden, R. *How Wars are Got up in India: The Origin of the Burmese War* (London, W. & F.G. Cash 1953)

Daruwala, R.J. *The Bombay Chamber Story – 150 Years* (Bombay, Bombay Chamber of Commerce 1986)

Dickson, P.G.M. *The Financial Revolution in England: A Study in the Development of Public Credit 1688–1756* (London, Macmillan 1967)

Furber, H. *Rival Empires of Trade in the Orient, 1600–1800* (London, Oxford University Press 1976)

Gladstone, J.S. *History of Gillanders, Arbuthnot and Co. and Ogilvy Gillanders and Co.* (London 1910)

Greenberg, M. *British Trade and the Opening of China 1800–1842* (Cambridge, Cambridge University Press 1951)

Hidy, R.W. *The House of Baring in American Trade and Finance: English Merchant Banker at Work 1763–1861* (Cambridge, Mass, Harvard University Press 1949)

Jones, G. *British Multinational Banking 1830–1990* (Oxford, Clarendon Press 1993)

King, F.H.H. *Survey our Empire (Robert Montgomery Martin 1801–1868: A Bio-Bibliography)* (Hong Kong, Centre of Asian Studies, University of Hong Kong 1979)

Kling, B.B. *Partner in Empire: Dwarkanath Tagore and the Age of Enterprise in India* (Los Angeles, University of California 1976)

Larpent, G. de H.H. *On Protection to West-India Sugar* (London, J.M. Richardson 1823)

Lawson, P. *The East India Company: A History* (London, Longman 1993)

Losty, J.P. *Calcutta: City of Palaces* (London, Arnold 1990)

Marks, H. *The First Contest for Singapore 1819–24* (The Hague, Nijhoff 1961)

Marshall, P.J. *East Indian Fortunes: The British in Bengal in the Eighteenth Century* (Oxford, Clarendon Press 1976)

Mathias, P. *The First Industrial Nation: The Economic History of Britain 1700–1914* (London, Routledge 1983)

Milne, G. *Trade and Traders in Mid-Victorian Liverpool: Mercantile Business and the Making of a World Port* (Liverpool, Liverpool University Press 2000)

Mitchell, B.R. and Deane, P. *Abstract of Historical Statistics* (Cambridge, Cambridge University Press 1962)

Morier Evans, D. *The Commercial Crisis 1847–1848* (London, Letts, Son and Steer 1849)

Mui, H. and Mui, L.H. *The Management of Monopoly. A Study of the East India Company's Conduct of its Tea Trade, 1784–1833* (Vancouver, University of British Columbia Press 1984)

Muirhead, S. *Crisis Banking in the East: The History of the Chartered Mercantile Bank of India, London and China, 1853–93* (Aldershot, Scolar Press 1996)

Mukherjee, H. *The Early History of the East Indian Railway 1845–1879* (Calcutta, Firma KLM Private Ltd 1994)

Peers, D.M. *Between Mars and Mammon: Colonial Armies and the Garrison State in Early Nineteenth Century India* (London, I.B. Tauris 1995)

Philips, C.H. *The Correspondence of David Scott: Volume One* (London, Camden Third Series 1951)

Philips, C.H. *The East India Company 1784–1834* (Manchester, Manchester University Press 1961)

Philips, C.H. (ed), *The Correspondence of Lord William Cavendish Bentinck Vols 1 and 2* (Oxford, Oxford University Press 1977)

Porter, A. *Religion Versus Empire? British Protestant Missionaries and Overseas Expansion, 1700–1914* (Manchester, Manchester University Press 2004)

Robins, N. *The Corporation that Changed the World: How the East India Company Shaped the Modern Multinational* (London, Pluto Press 2006)

Rothermund, D. *An Economic History of India from Pre-Colonial Times to 1986* (London, Croom Helm 1988)

Rubinstein, W.D. *Capitalism, Culture & Decline in Britain 1750–1990* (London, Routledge 1993)

Said, E. *Orientalism* (London, Vintage 1978)

Siddiqi, A. (ed), *Trade and Finance in Colonial India 1750–1860* (Delhi, Oxford University Press 1995)

Singh, S.B. *European Agency Houses in Bengal, 1783–1833* (Calcutta, Firma Mukhopadhyay 1966)

Stephen, Sir L. and Lee, Sir S. *Dictionary of National Biography* Vol V (Oxford, Oxford University Press 1921–22)

Sulivan, R.J.F. *One Hundred Years of Bombay: History of the Bombay Chamber of Commerce 1836–1936* (Bombay, Times of India Press 1937)

Thant Myint-U, *The Making of Modern Burma* (Cambridge, Cambridge University Press 2001)

Thorne, R.G. *The House of Commons 1790–1820 I: Members Q–Y* (London, Secker and Warburg 1986)

Thorner, D. *Investment in Empire: British Railway and Steam Shipping Enterprise in India 1825–1849* (Philadelphia, University of Pennsylvania 1950)

Tripathi, A. *Trade and Finance in the Bengal Presidency 1793–1833* (Calcutta, Oxford University Press 1979)

Tripathi, D. *The Oxford History of Indian Business* (New Delhi, Oxford University Press 2004)

Turnbull, C.M. *A History of Singapore* (Oxford, Oxford University Press 1977)

Tyson, G. *The Bengal Chamber of Commerce and Industry 1853–1953: A Centenary Survey* (Calcutta, The Statesman Ltd 1953)

Webster, A. *Gentleman Capitalists: British Imperialism in South East Asia 1770–1890* (London, I.B. Tauris 1998)

Webster, A. *The Richest East India Merchant: The Life and Business of John Palmer of Calcutta 1767–1836* (Woodbridge, Boydell Press 2007)

Wong, J.Y. *Deadly Dreams: Opium and the Arrow War (1856–1860) in China* (Cambridge, Cambridge University Press 2003)

ARTICLES AND PAMPHLETS

Anon., *Review of a Pamphlet Entitled 'Reasons for the Establishment of a New Bank in India' by an Indian Merchant* (Glasgow 1836)

Bagchi, A.K. 'Transition from Indian to British Indian Systems of Money and Banking 1800–1850' *Modern Asian Studies* 19:3 (1985) pp501–519

Bayly, C.A. 'The First Age of Global Imperialism c1760 – 1839' in P. Burroughs and A.J. Stockwell (eds), *Managing the Business of Empire: Essays in Honour of David Fieldhouse* (London, Frank Cass 1998)

Bhattacharya, S. 'Eastern India' in D. Khumar and M. Desai, *The Cambridge Economic History of India c1750–c1970, Volume Two* (Cambridge, Cambridge University Press 1983) pp270–332

Bowen, H.V. 'Sinews of Trade and Empire: The Supply of Commodity Exports to the

East India Company in the Late Eighteenth Century' *Economic History Review* 55:3 (2002) pp466–486

Bowen, H.V. 'Privilege & Profit: Commanders of East Indiamen as Private Traders, Entrepreneurs and Smugglers, 1760–1813' *International Journal of Maritime History* 19:2 (2007) pp43–88

Cain, P.J. and Hopkins, A.G. 'The Political Economy of British Expansion Overseas 1750 to 1914' *Economic History Review* 33:4 (1980) pp463–490

Cain, P.J. and Hopkins, A.G 'Gentlemanly Capitalism and British Expansion Overseas I: The Old Colonial System 1688–1850' *Economic History Review* 39:4 (1986) pp501–525

Chapman, S.D. 'The Agency Houses: British Mercantile Enterprise in the Far East c.1780–1920' *Textile History* 19:2 (1988) pp239–254

Chaudhuri, K.N. 'India's Foreign Trade and the Cessation of the East India Company's Trading Activities' *Economic History Review* 19 (1966) pp345–363

Chaudhuri, K.N. 'The East India Company in the 17th and 18th Centuries: A Pre-Modern Multinational Organization' in L. Blussé and F. Gaastra (eds), *Companies and Trade* (Leiden, Leiden University Press 1981)

Chaudhuri, K.N. 'Foreign Trade and Balance of Payments (1757–1947)' in D. Kumar (ed), *The Cambridge History of Modern India Volume 2: 1757–2003* (Hyderabad, India, Orient Longman 2005) pp804–877

Cookson, J.E. 'Political Arithmetic and War in Britain, 1793–1815' in *War and Society* 1:2 (1983) pp37–60

Cookson, J.E. 'British Society and the French Wars, 1793–1815' *Australian Journal of Politics and History* 31 (1985) pp192–203

Crawfurd, J. 'A Sketch of the Commercial Resources and Monetary and Mercantile System of British India with suggestions for their Improvement by Means of Banking Establishments' (1837) in K.N. Chaudhuri (ed), *The Economic Development of India under the East India Company* (Cambridge, Cambridge University Press 1971) pp217–316

Crawfurd, J. *Memorandum on the British Settlements in the Straits of Malacca, Penang, Singapore and Malacca* (London, C.W. Beynell 1858)

Darwin, J. 'Imperialism and the Victorians: The Dynamics of Territorial Expansion' *English Historical Review* (June 1997) pp614–642

Daunton, M. ' "Gentlemanly Capitalism" and British Industry 1820–1914' *Past & Present* 122 (1989) pp119–158

Davies, J. 'The Liverpool Chamber of Commerce and the Burma-China Railway' *Transactions of the Historic Society of Lancashire and Cheshire* 139 (1990) pp113–136

Green, E.H.H. 'Gentlemanly Capitalism and British Economic Policy, 1880–1914: The Debate over Bimetallism and Protectionism' in R.E. Dumett (ed), *Gentlemanly Capitalism and British Imperialism* (London, Longman 1999) pp44–67

Harnetty, P. 'The Imperialism of Free Trade: Lancashire and the Indian Cotton Duties, 1859–1862' *Economic History Review* 18:2 (1965) pp333–349

Howe, A.C. 'Free Trade and the City of London' *History* 77:251 (1992) pp391–410

Kawamura, T. 'British Business and Empire in Asia: The Eastern Exchange Banks, 1851–63' in D. Bates and K. Kondo (eds), *Migration and Identity in British History. Proceedings of the fifth Anglo-Japanese Conference of Historians, 27–29 September 2006* (London, Institute of Historical Research 2006) pp193–207

Kling, B.B. 'The Origin of the Managing Agency System in India' *Journal of Asian Studies* 26:1 (1966) pp37–47

Knight, G.R. 'John Palmer and Plantation Development in Western Java in the Early Nineteenth Century' *Bijdragen* 131:2/3 (1975) pp309–337

Levi, L. *Chamber and Tribunals of Commerce, and a proposed General Chamber of Commerce in Liverpool* (London, Simpkin Marshall and Co. 1849)

Lieberman, V. 'Secular Trends in Burmese Economic History' *Modern Asian Studies* 25:1 (1991) pp1–31

Macpherson, W.J. 'Investment in Indian Railways, 1845–1875' *Economic History Review* 8:2 (1955) pp177–186

McCulloch, J.R. *Reasons for the Establishment of a new Bank in India, with answers to the Objection Against it* (London 1836)

Miller, R.M. and Greenhill, R.G. 'Liverpool and South America, 1850–1930' in S. Haggerty, A. Webster and N. White (eds), *The Empire in One City? Liverpool's Inconvenient Imperial Past* (Manchester, Manchester University Press 2008) pp78–99

Moore, R.J. 'Imperialism and "Free Trade" Policy in India, 1853–4' *Economic History Review* 17:1 (1964) pp135–145

Moss, D.J. 'Birmingham and the Campaigns against the Orders in Council and the East India Company Charter, 1812–3' *Canadian Journal of History* 11 (1976) pp173–188

Nish, I. 'British Mercantile Co-operation in the Indo-China Trade from the End of the East India Company's Trading Monopoly' *Journal of Southeast Asian History* 3:2 (1962) pp74–91

Peers, D.M. 'War and Public Finance in Early Nineteenth Century British India: The First Burma War' *The International History Review* 9:4 (1989) pp628–647

Ramachandra, G.P. 'The Outbreak of the First Anglo-Burmese War' *Journal of the Malaysian Branch of the Royal Asiatic Society* 51 (1978) pp68–99

Siddiqi, A. 'Money and Prices in the Earlier Stages of Empire: India and Britain 1760–1840' *Indian Economic and Social History Review* 18:3 and 4 (1981) pp231–262

Tarling, N. 'The Palmer Loans' *Bijdragen* 119:2 (1963) pp161–188

Tarling, N. 'The Prince of Merchants and the Lion's City' in *Journal of the Malaysian Branch of the Royal Asiatic Society* 37:1 (1964) pp20–40

Tolley, B.H. 'The Liverpool Campaign against the Order in Council and the War of 1812' in J.R. Harris (ed), *Liverpool and Merseyside: Essays in the Economic and Social History of the Port and its Hinterland* (London, Cass 1969) pp98–146

Tripathi, A. 'Indo-British Trade between 1833 and 1847 and the Commercial Crisis of 1847–8' in A. Siddiqi *Trade and Finance in Colonial India* (Delhi, Oxford University Press 1995) pp265–289

Ward, J.R. 'The Industrial Revolution and British Imperialism 1750–1850' *Economic History Review* 47:1 (1994) pp44–65

Webster, A. 'British Export Interests in Bengal and Imperial Expansion into Southeast Asia, 1780 to 1824: The Origins of the Straits Settlements' in B. Ingham and C. Simmons (eds), *Development Studies and Colonial Policy* (London, Cass 1987) pp138–174

Webster, A. 'The Political Economy of Trade Liberalization: The East India Company Charter Act of 1813' *Economic History Review* 43:3 (1990) pp404–419

Webster, A. 'Business and Empire: A Reassessment of the British Conquest of Burma in 1885' *Historical Journal* 43:4 (2000) pp1003–1025

Webster, A. 'An Early Global Business in a Colonial Context: The Strategies, Management and Failure of John Palmer and Co. of Calcutta c1800 to 1830' *Enterprise and Society* 6:1 (2005) pp98–113

Webster, A. 'Liverpool and the Asian Trade 1800–50: Some Insights into a Provincial Commercial Network' in S. Haggerty, A.Webster and N. White (eds), *The Empire in One City: Liverpool's Inconvenient Imperial Past* (Manchester, Manchester University Press 2008)

Wong Lin Ken, 'The Trade of Singapore 1819–69' *Journal of the Malaysian Branch of the Royal Asiatic Society* 33:4 (1960) pp11–301

PhD THESES

Kumagai, Y., 'The Lobbying Activities of Provincial Mercantile and Manufacturing Interests against the Renewal of the East India Company's Charter, 1812–13 and 1829–33' (PhD thesis, University of Glasgow 2008)

INDEX